Randall J. Brewer

CALLED TO BE SAINTS
HOW TO BECOME WHAT YOU WERE CALLED TO BE

RANDALL J. BREWER

PUBLISHED by PARABLES
Earthly Stories with a Heavenly Meaning

Randall J. Brewer

Called To Be Saints
Randall J. Brewer

Published By Parables
January, 2020

All Rights Reserved. No part of this book may be reproduced or utilized in any form or by any means, electronic or mechanical, including photocopying, recording, or by any information storage and retrieval system, without permission in writing from the author.

ISBN 978-1-951497-25-5
Printed in the United States of America

Readers should be aware that Internet Web sites offered as citations and/or sources for further information may have been changed or disappeared between the time this was written and the time it is read.

CALLED TO BE SAINTS
HOW TO BECOME WHAT YOU WERE CALLED TO BE

RANDALL J. BREWER

PUBLISHED by PARABLES
Earthly Stories with a Heavenly Meaning

Randall J. Brewer

To Anne. My one and only

Called To Be Saints

-INTRODUCTION-

I see it everywhere I go, Christians willfully and habitually sinning with no thought of what will happen to them tomorrow. They eat, drink, and be merry with no regard for Gal. 6:7 which says, "Do not be deceived, God is not mocked; for whatever a man sows, that he will also reap." The end is near and Jesus is coming back for a glorious church, not one marred by willful disobedience and sin.

Recently I was shocked and appalled when I heard a news story out of Egypt. A Muslim cab driver picked up a Christian man and dropped him off at a Muslim brothel. The cab driver was greatly angered that this Christian man would commit blasphemy by doing this so he went and put together an angry mob of fellow Muslims. They stormed the brothel and pulled the Christian man outside where they stabbed him 16 times, poured acid on him, and set him on fire. They then went and ransacked all the Christian businesses that were in the area.

My, oh my! What is going on here? 1 Peter 4:17 gives us the answer, "For the time has come for judgment to begin at the house of God." My friend, sin is a serious matter but far too many believers sin at will with no regard that they will be held accountable for their words and actions. So why do they dive into the abyss of sin? Years ago a fallen television evangelist gave us a startling revelation as to why some believers act the way they do.

This preacher was known all over the world but a sexual encounter with a woman in his organization caused him to fall from grace. On top of that, a financial scandal sent him to jail for many years. Upon his release he was asked in an interview, "Why did you do these things? Didn't you love God?" His answer should burn in all our hearts. He said, "Yes, I loved God. I still love God. My problem was I didn't fear God."

Sin is rampant in the Christian camp because people do not fear God. Simply put, people are not afraid to sin. Our God is patient and all merciful and because people are not struck down instantly like Ananias and Sapphira people think they can go on sinning and get away with it. Sad to say, these people are in for a rude awakening. The wages of sin is death and we must be diligent to tell believers everywhere that the day is coming when all of us will be held accountable for our words and actions.

In the parable of the ten virgins Jesus taught us to always be prepared for the coming of the Bridegroom. The five unwise virgins were not prepared and were thus locked out of the bridal chamber. One way we prepare for the catching away of the church is to face head-on the issue of sin. I have written this book as a means of dealing with this subject and I pray that like a loud trumpet blast God will use me to open the eyes of those who are spiritually blind to the consequences of willful and habitual sinful actions. May this message shake them to the core of their innermost being because, for sure, it is a fearful thing to fall into the hands of the living God (Heb. 10:31).

-1-
"A SOLID FOUNDATION"

The good news of the gospel message is penetrating into the uttermost regions of the earth yet many are not responding to what they've heard. There is a danger that comes with hearing but not doing for with it comes deception that will lead people astray. James 1:22 says, "But be doers of the word, and not hearers only, deceiving yourselves." This is not demonic deception, this is deception people bring on themselves. Christians love to hear a good sermon but it's another thing to put action to what you've heard. God told Ezekiel that people would come to him to receive a word from the Lord and Ezek. 33:31,32 tells what happened, "So they come to you as people do, they sit before you as My people, and they hear your words, but they do not do them; for with their mouth they show much love, but their hearts pursue their own gain. Indeed, you are to them as a very lovely song of one who has a pleasant voice and can play well on an instrument; for they hear your words, but they do not do them." This same thing is happening in the church today.

People hear a lot of good things but are not even doing half of what they know to do. James compares those who are hearers only with a man who looks in a mirror and sees great detail about who he is and what he's like. Vs. 24 says "he observes himself, goes away, and immediately forgets what kind of man he was." To be a doer of the Word, you've got to remember what you've heard. You can't forget on

Monday what you heard at church on Sunday because if you forget it, you're not going to do it. Much effort and diligence will be needed for you to remember the good things God says to you. Have a pen and notebook close by so you can write down those specific things that apply to your own personal life. If you don't write it down, for sure you will soon forget what was said. You need to value the things God says to you to the point that you will do everything you can to remember what was said. James 1:25 (NLT) says, "But if you look carefully into the perfect law that sets you free, and if you do what it says, and don't forget what you heard, then God will bless you for doing it."

Those who are empowered to prosper and given the ability to overcome are those who don't forget what they've heard and become doers of the Word of God. The problem is people want to be entertained more than they want to learn. They go to church wanting to be made happy to the point where they can stand up and clap and shout. It doesn't matter what was taught as long as they were entertained. These people are going to church for the wrong reason and are the very ones who deceive themselves. Yes, they're happy, they're excited and they feel good, but an hour later they cannot remember one thing the preacher taught that day. If they forget what was said, they won't do what was said. These people need to realize that what happens in the church service is not what's important. What is important is what happens once the church service is over. Will they do on Monday what they were told to do on Sunday? Their intentions may be good but the Word says you will be judged by what you do, not by what your intentions are.

What is in your heart is revealed by what you do. If you intended to do something but never did it, then something else was more important to you. The Lord will hold you accountable for what you know and whether or not you acted on it. If you don't walk in the light you now have, you won't be blessed and you won't be given more light. People deceive themselves when they think knowing something is the same as doing it. There are people who pride themselves in knowing the Bible frontwards and backwards yet they're not doing what the Word tells them to do. These people are deceived and are not getting the results the Bible says they can have. This is why they have the same problems today that they had thirty years ago. It's not what you know that counts, it's what you do. The doers are the ones who get their bills paid and their bodies restored to good health. Jesus said in Matt. 7:20,21, "Therefore by their fruits you will know them. Not everyone who says to Me, 'Lord, Lord,' shall enter the kingdom of heaven, but he who does the will of My Father in heaven."

Jesus asked in Luke 6:46, "But why do you call Me, 'Lord, Lord,' and do not do the things which I say?" If you're not doing what Jesus told you to do, then He is not your Lord. He may be your Savior but He's not your Lord unless you're doing what He says. If you're doing your own thing and running your life the way you want to run it, then you are your lord, not Jesus. He continued in vs. 47,48, "Whoever comes to Me, and hears My sayings and does them, I will show you whom he is like: He is like a man building a house, who dug deep and laid the foundation on the rock. And when the flood arose, the stream beat vehemently against that house, and could not shake it for it was founded on the rock." You dig deep by remembering what God said and by putting it into practice. This allows you to place solid pillars deep into the bedrock of the earth. "But he who heard and did nothing is like a man who built a house on the earth without a foundation, against which the stream beat vehemently; and immediately it fell. And the ruin of that house was great."

There is something wrong when a person builds a house without a foundation under it. What's wrong is that the person is deceived into thinking that everything is going to be all right. They go to church every Sunday and there is a Bible sitting on the end table in their living room and a picture of Jesus is hanging on the wall. They go to a lot of seminars and revival meetings and their closet is filled with all sorts of Christian material. They think they're sitting on a solid foundation but in reality it's sinking sand because they were hearers only and not a doer of the Word. To be a doer of the Word you have to take what you heard and apply it to your personal life. If you hear you're not supposed to gossip then check up on yourself and see if you're talking bad about other people. If you are a doer of the Word then you'll stop saying the negative things that have been coming out of your mouth. You'll do what God tells you to do and this is how a solid foundation is built under your house. When the wind stops blowing your house will still be standing.

The storms of life come to everybody but no storm lasts forever. You'll have no fear when they do come because for the past six months your pastor has been teaching about love and you've been out putting into practice what you've heard. You've been a doer of the Word and a solid foundation is under you. You didn't just hear about prayer, you went home and prayed. You didn't just hear about giving, you dug deep in your pocket book and you gave. You didn't just hear about faith, you actually walked in it. You are a doer of the Word and not a hearer only and, when the storm clouds roll away and the birds sing, your house will be standing firm and strong. You won't catch that flu bug that's going around and at work you won't be laid off during a slowdown but will be given a promotion instead. This only happens when you're a doer of the Word. If you're a hearer only then you better get ready for a long wait in the unemployment line. People who hear the Word but don't do it is "like a dumb carpenter who built a house but skipped the foundation" (Luke 6:49 MSG).

Called To Be Saints

God is very gracious and He doesn't hold you accountable for what you don't know. He makes allowances for your lack of knowledge in a certain area. He does, however, hold you accountable for what you do know. He knows what you know because He's the One who showed it to you in the first place. Don't play ignorant and say you didn't know something when in truth you did know it. The problem is you didn't do what you knew to do. You were a hearer only and not a doer of the Word and, when the swollen river came crashing in, your house collapsed like a house of cards. In the parable of the talents the third servant knew he was supposed to take his one talent and multiply it, thus making a profit for his master. He knew he was supposed to do this but instead went and buried his talent and did nothing. This angered the master and this wicked and lazy servant was cast into utter darkness where there was weeping and gnashing of teeth (Matt. 25:14-30). This servant knew what the master expected of him and was judged because he didn't do it.

James 4:17 says, "Therefore, to him who knows to do good and does not do it, to him it is sin." When you know to do something, it is sin not to do it. Light comes when you know what to do and sin is a violation of that light.

God holds you accountable for what you see and know because the light of the Word has shown you what to do. God knows what you know and He expects you to do it. When problems come because of disobedience many people call all their friends asking for prayer, but prayer is not what they need. They need to do what they know they're supposed to do. They may act confused and say they don't know what to do, and these are the very ones who have deceived themselves. They can't fool God but they can fall into the trap of fooling themselves. This is when the enemy comes in to steal, kill, and destroy. The solution to all this is to repent and become a doer of the Word. Life is too short and too precious to go around all the time acting like you're confused and not getting your problems solved. Get off of that telephone and become a doer of the Word of God.

Eph. 5:8-10 (MSG) says, "You groped your way through that murk once, but no longer. You're out in the open now. The bright light of Christ makes your way plain. So no more stumbling around. Get on with it! The good, the right, the true - these are the actions appropriate for daylight hours. Figure out what will please Christ, and then do it." Light is a major theme throughout the entire Bible. 1 John 1:5 says, "God is light, and in Him is no darkness at all." The Word brings light which causes you to see and to know and, when you're walking with God, the light gets brighter and brighter every day. This is what God holds you accountable for, that what you see and know. People see a whole lot more than what they're admitting to, pretending that they don't know. This is why they struggle in life year after year. They know the truth yet won't do what they know they're supposed to do. They then turn around and blame God for the mess their life is in. They're walking in darkness and will not receive any more light.

When you are a doer of the Word, you're walking in the light you have. Too many people are dishonest about what they see and how much they know, and this is why their life is in the condition it's in now. They're not victorious because they're not a doer of the Word. They hear it, they enjoy it, but they won't do it. 1 John 1:6 says, "If we say that we have fellowship with Him, and walk in darkness, we lie and do not practice the truth." The Message Bible says, "If we claim that we experience a shared life with Him and continue to stumble around in the dark, we're obviously lying through our teeth - we're not living what we claim." People cry and say they're doing the best they can. The Bible says these people are liars because they're not doing the best they can. They are being disobedient and not walking in the light they have. They're making a game out of life and are on the losing end.

They are walking in deception and this they did to themselves. They don't know it yet but they are on their way to a rude awakening.

There is no excuse for not doing what you know to do. You need to walk in the light you have and start doing what God has shown you to do. Stop making excuses and stop pretending you don't know. Jesus is coming soon, time is short, so you best get started right now. Don't put it off any longer for those who wait until tomorrow usually die today. Lay procrastination aside and walk the walk of a doer of the Word of God. Ps. 89:15 says, "Blessed are the people who know the joyful sound! They walk, O Lord, in the light of Your countenance." When light comes to you, it will rejoice your heart. It will cause your heart to jump and shout. Prov. 13:9 says, "The light of the righteous rejoices, but the lamp of the wicked will be put out." The worst thing you can do is let reasonings and the opinions and beliefs of other people cause you to forget and lose sight of that which the Lord has enlightened you with. Don't allow anything or anybody to cause your light to go out.

You can talk a good talk but you need to walk a better walk. In the Christian camp there are phony talkers and then there are faith walkers. Those who talk the most are usually the ones who do the least. Years pass and all they have to show for it is that they talked a lot. They did little or nothing for the kingdom of God. They talked the talk but didn't walk the walk and because of that they deceived themselves into thinking that everything was all right in their lives. What these people need to do is stop talking so much and start walking in the light they have. It may be a little light but, if they'll walk in it, more and more light will come. This is what builds a solid foundation under your house. It's what causes your house to stand strong when the winds blow and the waves hit. You may not know and understand the entire Bible, but you can walk in the light you do have. There is no excuse for not doing so. Ps. 118:27 says, "God is the Lord, and He has given us light." When you read and meditate on the Word of God there will always be light for you to walk in.

When light comes, with it comes joy. It rejoices your heart to see the light and joy is an indicator that light has come. It causes you to want more light and, once you have it, God expects you to walk in it. He shines light on your path so you'll know what to do and where to go. Ps. 119:105 says, "Your word is a lamp to my feet, and a light to my path." You're not supposed to just stand there and talk about it. No, you need to put one foot in front of the other and walk in the light He has given you. Not only does God want you to see the light, He wants you to walk in it as well. As you do, the mysteries of life will become more clear to you and your life will get better and better. You will go from glory to glory. No more will you be confused and upset because you are walking in the light of God's Word. You're putting action to your faith and your needs are being met. God is using you to touch the lives of other people and the world is beginning to become a better place. God is light and His light is shining on you.

Prov. 15:30 says, "The light of the eyes rejoices the heart, and a good report makes the bones healthy." A good report is a joyful sound and it makes your bones fat and healthy and strong. When the light comes in, the heart rejoices every time. You can know the Bible inside out but if it doesn't bring joy to your heart, then you're not believing what you know is there. Knowing it is not the same as believing it. You can see the light but then you have to walk in the light you see. Prov. 15:13 says, "A merry heart makes a cheerful countenance." If you get enough of the light inside you, it will register on your face. You can't walk in the light and walk around sad all the time. A sign of immaturity is when a person walks around always talking about how they feel. A mature believer does not do that. It hinders you and will prevent you from walking in the light. Feelings come and go, they're up and down, they're fickle and never stable. This is why you need to walk by faith and not by sight (2 Cor. 5:7).

Don't ask yourself how you feel, tell yourself how you feel. You're forgiven, you're cleansed, you are the righteousness of God in Christ Jesus. It matters not how you feel because greater is He who is in you than he who is in the world. If that doesn't cause you to stand up and shout, nothing will. Stop yielding to how you feel for this is how the devil is defeating millions of people all over the world. You need to grow up, talk right, and walk in the light you have. Be a doer of the Word and not a hearer only. Act on the Word you know and, when you do, more light will come. God will show you what to do, and when He does, you need to be willing to obey Him and walk in the new light that has come. Mark 10:17-22 tells how the rich young ruler had some light for he obeyed the ten commandments from his youth. Jesus then gave him more light. He called him into the ministry and told him to sell everything he had and come follow Him. The young man rejected this light and walked away grieved for he had great possessions.

There are a lot of confused and bewildered Christians in the world and it's their own fault because they refuse to walk in the light they received. They saw the light but chose to ignore it and not do what they were supposed to do. This is a dangerous thing for it leads to deception and darkness and will cause people to be even more confused and frustrated. Hosea 4:6 says, "My people are destroyed for lack of knowledge." Some would say that ignorance is the problem here and that is partially true. The question that needs to be asked is why are people ignorant and why don't they know what's going on? The answer is found in the same verse. "Because you have rejected knowledge, I also will reject you from being priest for Me." The people are ignorant because they rejected knowledge. God is faithful to provide every person with the opportunity to see the light. Some receive it, many don't. They refuse to walk in the light and then turn around and blame God for all their problems. One day the truth will come out for Rom. 3:4 says, "Let God be true and every man a liar."

People see and know a lot more that what they will admit. They have perfected the art of playing ignorant. They try to con people but it backfires and they end up conning themselves. This is how they get self-deceived. They say they don't know something when in truth God showed it to them years ago. 1 John 1:8,9 says, "If we say we have no sin, we deceive ourselves, and the truth is not in us. If we confess our sins, He is faithful and just to forgive us our sins and cleanse us from all unrighteousness." People don't understand what's being said here. Sin is a violation of light and to confess your sins you have to admit that you saw the light but willingly refused to walk in it. You can't act ignorant and be forgiven. This is why it is so important to be honest about what you know and what you don't know. Don't act like you know everything but at the same time don't play dumb and act like you don't know anything at all. Walk in the light you do have and in time God will give you more light. The path of the righteous gets brighter and brighter.

When you confess your sins you are admitting that you could have and should have done better. You acknowledge that light came but for one reason or another you didn't walk in it. Be honest with God and don't use ignorance as an excuse to cover up your sin. For sure, your sin will find you out. Adam and Eve tried to cover their sin and it didn't work. But if you will humble yourself and be honest about what you did, God will give you mercy and forgive you of your mistake. Prov. 28:13 says, "He who covers his sins will not prosper, but whoever confesses and forsakes them will have mercy." The Message Bible says, "You can't whitewash your sins and get by with it; you find mercy by admitting and leaving them." Being honest and admitting your sin is dealing with reality but those self-righteous people who play ignorant will not admit the truth of their ways and will not be forgiven and will not be cleansed. They'll walk in darkness all the days of their life and will be an open target for the attacks of the enemy.

Many people want to hear a word from the Lord and, when He does speak to them, like the rich young ruler they reject what He says. They walk in darkness because that's all there is when there's no light. They heard what God said but didn't act on it. There is a danger when you don't act immediately on the word God gives you for this gives the devil time to talk you out of it. God speaks to everybody but the devil will try to fill your mind with excuses as to why you shouldn't walk in the light that has come. God is faithful and He is endeavoring to lead you into His perfect plan for your life. The reason people are sad, confused, and depressed is because they don't walk in the steps God tells them to take. It is a dangerous thing to not walk in the light you have. When God speaks to you, do what He says right away. Don't put it off for the enemy is forever ready to steal the Word from you. In the parable of the sower Jesus said, "And it happened, as he sowed, that some seed fell by the wayside; and the birds of the air came and devoured it" (Mark 4:4).

When light comes, faith is there. A solid foundation is under you so get excited and continue to put action to your faith. Do what you know you're supposed to do and do it immediately. Don't give deception time to come in. Eph. 4:27 says "nor give place to the devil." Procrastination does this for if you don't respond right away you run the risk of forgetting what God told you to do. Don't allow the fowls of the air to come in and snatch away the light of the Word that was given to you. Don't just sit there, do something. Do what God told you to do. Do it and do it now! If you don't then your joy will leave and darkness will come. Don't let this happen. Get excited and stay excited. There is life in the Word and with this life comes joy and excitement. It is hard to sit still and do nothing when you're jumping up and down with joy. When you walk in the light you will be blessed and those around you will be blessed as well. The light shines and it spreads out to other people. When you're a doer of the Word there will be a continual outpouring of light.

If the Bible doesn't change your life, then you're not a doer of the Word. Healing comes and miracles happen when you walk in the light and do what you know you're supposed to do. There are people who have gone to church all their life but that doesn't mean they're a doer of the Word of God. The only people who get results are those who act on what they know. Hosea 6:3 says, "Let us know, let us pursue the knowledge of the Lord." The Message Bible says, "We're ready to study God, eager for God knowledge. As sure as dawn breaks, so sure is His daily arrival. He comes as rain comes, as spring rain refreshing the ground." When revelation comes you must be disciplined where you will check up on yourself and see how a particular verse applies to your life. You must do something with the Word you heard, with the light that has been revealed to you. Start doing what you should be doing and stop doing what you shouldn't be doing. If your life doesn't get changed then you either didn't hear the Word of God or you're not a doer of the Word. If it's the Word of God then something is supposed to change.

Walking in the light is a progressive walk. You get some light, you walk in it, then you get more light. Prov. 4:18 says, "But the path of the just is like the shining sun, that shines ever brighter unto the perfect day." It's like walking down a road where street lights are placed at certain intervals. The farther down the road you go, the brighter each light becomes. If you stand still and don't go forward, you will only have the light that you're currently standing in which is dimmer than the lights down the road. To get more light you can't stand still and do nothing. You must walk in the light you now have and keep walking until you get to the next street light. This light is brighter than the one before and the next light is brighter still. To get to each light you must continually be a doer of the Word and walk in the light you currently have. The Amplified Bible says, "The path of the just is like the light of dawn." This is like a glow more than a bright light, but as time passes the sun gets higher and higher and brighter and brighter until it reaches its full glory.

God will give you a little light and He expects you to walk in it. Rom. 4:12 says you are to "walk in the steps of the faith which our father Abraham had while still uncircumcised." You don't take flying leaps of faith, you take steps of faith. Abraham received a word from the Lord and Heb. 11:8 says he left home "not knowing where he was going." He wasn't told the end of the story and the only light he had was he knew he was supposed to step out. Gen. 12:4 says, "So Abraham departed as the Lord had spoken to him." He took a step of faith and walked in the light he had been given. God requires faith from everybody and if He told you everything then it wouldn't require any faith. There are some things you just have to trust God for. You don't need light for the future until you get there. What God will do is He'll give you light for the step you're supposed to take today. God is the author of the phrase, "One step at a time." The faith you use to take that first step pleases God and tells Him that you are ready to take the next step. It's a progressive walk, it's how you grow. You walk in the light by taking one step at a time.

God is leading you to a special place and He'll give you a glimpse of light so you can take a step of faith. Too many people require a lot of light before they're willing to move but God doesn't work that way. He won't give you more light until you take that first step. 1 Sam. 16 tells how God sent Samuel to Jesse's house for one of his sons was to be the next king. God gave the prophet a glimpse of light to walk in. He didn't tell him which son it would be, only that he was supposed to go to Jesse's house. Vs. 4 says, "So Samuel did what the Lord said." He walked in the light he had been given. He obeyed God and once he got to Jesse's house more light was given. Then and only then was it revealed who the next king would be. If God tells you to do something, just do it even if you don't know what the next step will be. This is where faith comes in. This is when you show God that you really do trust Him. You must step out to find out, so step out in faith and believe that God will show you what to do when the time is right. His hand is upon you and by faith you can know that He will direct your steps according to His perfect will for your life.

-2-

"WALKING IN THE LIGHT"

There is a misconception in the body of Christ where many people believe that if they will read their Bible enough it will solve all their problems. This is not true for it is only the doer of the Word who gets results. It's when you act on what you know that you will get the results you desire. When you are a doer of the Word, you are walking in the light you have. God says not to judge other people because you don't know what's been revealed to them down in their heart. You can, however, judge yourself as to whether or not you are walking in the light as He is in the light (1 John 1:7). It is a sin to not do what you know you're supposed to do. You need to value and esteem the light you've been given to the point where you will use it and walk in it. More light will be given when you walk in the light you have. Jesus said in Matt. 13:12, "For whoever has, to him more will be given, and he will have abundance; but whoever does not have, even what he has will be taken away from him." In other words, use it or lose it.

Luke 16:10 says, "He who is faithful in what is least is faithful also in much; and he who is unjust in what is least is unjust also in much." In the parable of the talents, the master told the faithful servant, "Well done, good and faithful servant; you were faithful over a few things, I will make you ruler over many things. Enter into the joy of your lord" (Matt. 25:21). You don't get more light by begging and pleading for it, you get more light by walking in the light you already have. You must be faithful with what you've been given. It is no fairy tale to say that Jesus is coming soon and, when He does come, each person will have to stand before Him and give an account of what they did with the light they had received from Him. It won't matter how successful you were in business or how much money you have in the bank. What will matter is whether or not you did what the Master told you to do with what He gave you. Were you a doer of the Word and were you faithful to walk in the light? Every person will one day be asked that question. What will your response be?

You must be faithful in what is least in order to qualify for more. People who don't advance in the kingdom of God have not been faithful with what they've been given. They're hearers only and not doers of the Word. In the kingdom of God the most minor of jobs is more important than the most illustrious job in the world. Pushing a broom at church is more meaningful than being the CEO of a multi-million dollar corporation. It matters more only if you are faithful in what you are doing. The word "faithful" means 'trustworthy, reliable, to be worthy of trust.' Can you be relied upon to do what you know you're supposed to do? Will you walk in the light you have and do it with all your heart and soul? God is expecting faithfulness and commitment from His people. He expects you to take up your cross and follow Him, to be faithful even unto death. He did it for you and it is only right that He would expect you to do it for Him. You can trust Him every day and every night. Walk in the light that you have and show Him that He can trust you as well.

You can't be lazy and faithful at the same time, and you can't act like you don't know what to do. God gives light to everybody which means there is always something you should be doing in and for the kingdom of God. There is no excuse for not doing so. Another definition of "faithful" means 'to be true, to be firm, to be permanent.' If you bury your talent like the unfaithful servant did and do nothing, then you are a "punk" in the kingdom of God. One definition of "punk" is 'rotten lumber' and you can't build the Lord's house with rotten wood. You can't build something with material that is unstable and unreliable. You can't build a church with people who you don't know will show up or not. The Lord's house is built with people who are reliable and active and are busy doing what they know they're supposed to do. Good help is hard to find and this is why many are called but few are chosen (Matt. 20:16). Not everybody is walking in the light and worth trusting. Love is given freely but trust must be earned.

Prov. 25:19 says, "Confidence in an unfaithful man in time of trouble is like a bad tooth and a foot out of joint." The Message Bible says, "Trusting a double-crosser when you're in trouble is like biting down on an abscessed tooth." Serious things happen when you are unreliable and don't walk in the light. It hurts you and it hurts those you are associated with. It is a sad thing when pastors have to micro-manage those who work for them. This means the people are unreliable and can't be counted on to do the work they said they were going to do. Those who walk in the light, however, are the best workers in all the world. They work according to the high standard that was set before them. They go the extra mile and don't complain when more is expected of them. They rejoice because they've been given the opportunity to work in the kingdom of God. They're doers and not hearers only and before long promotion will come. These are the ones to whom God will say, "Well done, good and faithful servant."

If you want more, then be faithful with what you have. Be faithful and do something with it. Act on it, use it, put it into practice. If you do everything you can with what you've got, God will see your faithfulness and give you more to work with. Doers of the Word have their eyes and ears open and are eager to receive more light. Hearers only do not and

Jesus describes these people in Matt. 13:14,15 when He quoted the prophet Isaiah, "Hearing you will hear and shall not understand, and seeing you will see and not perceive; For the heart of this people has grown dull. Their ears are hard of hearing, and their eyes they have closed, lest they should see with their eyes and hear with their ears, lest they should understand with their heart and turn, so that I should heal them." The Message Bible says, "The people are blockheads!" The problem is not that God is unwilling to give them more light, the problem is that they closed their eyes to the things of God. When that happens, darkness prevails.

Doers of the Word are called "good and faithful," hearers only are "punks and blockheads." Hearers only are not ignorant for many of them know the Bible inside out. The problem is they "stick their finger in their ears so they won't have to listen; they screw their eyes shut so they won't have to look" (MSG). This causes hardness of the heart and self-deception. Light is available but these people refuse to see it. Not only are their eyes closed, the Amplified Bible says they are "tightly" closed. Anybody can close their eyes but it takes effort to close your eyes tightly. No wonder they're called "blockheads." Doers, however, have their eyes and ears wide open. Jesus continued in vs. 16,17, "But blessed are your eyes for they see, and your ears for they hear; for assuredly, I say to you, that many prophets and righteous men desired to see what you see, and did not see it, and to hear what you hear, and did not hear it." God gives more light only to those who will value it and do something with it. You can close your eyes at any time but, if you don't, the path you are on will get brighter and brighter.

Light is just not for seeing, it's for walking in. You can see the light but don't stop there. You must walk in the light you've been given. You see in order that you can walk. Yield to the light of God's Word and say what it tells you to say and do what it tells you to do. This is the key to living a good, victorious life. Many, however, are not living this way. Paul said in 2 Tim. 4:3,4, "For the time will come when they will not endure sound doctrine, but according to their own desires, because they have itching ears, they will heap up for themselves teachers; and they will turn their ears away from the truth, and be turned aside to fables." If people don't hear the truth, then what else is there to hear? These fables are in reality the lies of the evil one. Having "itching ears" means they'll only listen to what they selfishly want to hear, and to make it happen they find false teachers who will tell them what they want to hear and not what they need to hear. They want to hear that God will accept them in their sinful state rather than the truth that they need to bow down and repent of their sinful ways.

The truth is, people close their eyes on purpose "having a form of godliness but denying its power. And from such people turn away!" (2 Tim. 3:5). The NLT says, "They will act religious, but they will reject the power that could make them godly. Stay away from people like that!" The power that makes you godly comes when you're a doer of the Word. Those who don't walk in the light the Message Bible says, "They'll make a show of religion, but behind the scenes they're animals. Stay clear of the people." Vs..7 says they're "always learning and never able to come to the knowledge of the truth." Their eyes are closed to the truth yet they're always inquiring and gathering new information. This causes them to think they're smarter than they actually are and this is where self-deception comes in. They are not acknowledging the truth and are punks, blockheads, and animals. They have a form of godliness but no power whereas if they walked in the light they would be strong and mighty.

Light has God's approval and produces everything that is good and right and true. Everybody should be walking in the light but most people don't. There are only two reasons why people aren't doers of the Word: ignorance or rebellion. Do they know what to do or do they not know what to do? Ignorance needs instruction but rebellion needs discipline. People who are rebellious do not need more instruction for they know what they're supposed to do. They just choose not to do it. Corrective action needs to be taken and that holds true for everybody, adults and children alike. Workers on the job, politicians in office, players on a sports team, and members in the local church all need to be confronted when they openly rebel and don't do what they know to do. Eph. 5:11-13 says, "And have no fellowship with the unfruitful works of darkness, but rather expose them. For it is shameful even to speak of those things which are done by them in secret. But all things that are exposed are made manifest by the light, for whatever makes manifest is light."

It pays to obey and it will cost you if you don't. A lot of people may never know the wonderful opportunities that passed them by because they were in rebellion and didn't do what they knew they should have done. What's more, these same people who walk in darkness will put on a show and act a certain way to get you to think they really are walking in the light. The Bible calls these people "hypocrites" (Matt. 6:5) for they follow the example of the devil who "transforms himself into an angel of light" (2 Cor. 11:14). A hypocrite is like an actor who pretends he's a certain way and tries to get you to believe that it is true. The devil is a master actor and his followers act the same way he does. These are the ones who want to be pitied when bad things happen to them when it was their fault it happened in the first place. They claim ignorance when in truth they rejected the knowledge when it was first presented to them. God is holding these people accountable because the light was made available to them whether they received it or not. They knew what to do and in rebellion chose not to do it.

Another problem with hearers only, those who talk the talk, is they often criticize and judge the ones who walk the walk. By doing so, they take their attention off of themselves, the one place their focus should be centered. Jesus warned against this type of behavior when He said in Matt. 7:1,2, "Judge not, that you be not judged. For with what measure you use, it will be measured back to you." The NLT says "you will be treated as you treat others. The standard you use in judging is the standard by which you will be judged." Hearers only will always have an opinion of what others should do and how they should act and, what's more, they will not hesitate to let you know what they think. All they do is talk, talk, talk all the while they're doing nothing to better themselves which would make them an asset to the body of Christ. They'd rather criticize another person than do what's necessary to help that individual be transformed into the image of Christ. They tear down rather than build up.

Those who criticize others defend their actions by saying they're not judging anybody, they're only "speaking the truth in love." They say they have the gift of discernment where they can detect what's wrong with a person hundreds of miles away. It makes one wonder why they don't use that gift on themselves. These people are self-deceived for Eph. 4:29 says, "Let no corrupt communication proceed out of your mouth, but what is good for necessary edification, that it may impart grace to the hearers." What they fail to see is that the people they're talking bad about are not the ones who are going to be judged. The ones who get judged are the very ones who do the judging. They will be judged according to what they say others should do. Those who judge are only hurting themselves and they need to stop immediately. Jesus continued, "And why do you look at the speck in your brother's eye, but do not consider the plank in your own eye?" (Matt. 7:3). He then told these people what to do in vs. 5, "Hypocrite! First remove the plank from your own eye, and then you will see clearly to remove the speck from your brother's eye."

James 5:9 says, "Do not grumble against one another, brethren, lest you be condemned. Behold, the Judge is standing at the door!" The Message Bible says, "Friends, don't complain about each other. A far greater complaint could be lodged against you, you know. The Judge is standing just around the corner." There is a Judge and it's not you. Don't judge anybody but pay them the debt of love that you owe them. James 4:11,12 says, "Do not speak evil of one another, brethren. He who speaks evil of a brother and judges his brother, speaks evil of the law and judges the law. But if you judge the law, you are not a doer of the law but a judge. There is one Lawgiver, who is able to save and to destroy. Who are you to judge another?" When you judge another person, it only shows that you're not doing what you say they should be doing. This is why judgment will come back on those who judge. Those who criticize others are not doers of the Word. They walk in darkness rather than walk in the light. Hypocrites say to others, "Don't do what I do, do what I say." They tell others what to do but don't do it themselves.

Rom. 2:13 (NLT) says, "For merely listening to the law doesn't make us right with God. It is obeying the law that makes us right in His sight." Doers do not judge because they know what it takes to get the job done. Doers talk differently and they act differently. They've been in tough situations and know what steps to take that will lead them to victory. Anybody can be an armchair quarterback but it's a different story to be out on the field playing in the game. Doers play in the game, hearers only sit in the chair and judge. People need to grasp how diabolically wrong judging is. Rom. 2:1-3 says, "Therefore you are inexcusable, O man, whoever you are who judge, for in whatever you judge another you condemn yourself; for you who judge practice the same things. But we know that the judgment of God is according to truth against those who practice such things. And do you think this, O man, you also judge those practicing such things, and doing the same, that you will escape the judgment of God?"

The Message Bible says, "You didn't think, did you, that just by pointing your finger at others you would distract God from seeing all your misdoings and from coming down on you hard? Or did you think that because He's such a nice God, He'd let you off the hook? Better think this one through from the beginning. God is kind but He's not soft" (vs. 3,4). It should be a sobering thought to know that you will be judged by what you say others should do. The master told the wicked servant in Luke 19:22, "Out of your own mouth I will judge you." Jesus said in Matt. 12:37, "For by your words you will be justified, and by your words you will be condemned." You need to watch what you say. If you say another person should be doing something, then that means you've seen the light in that certain area. This is what God will hold you accountable for. Are you doing what you say other people should be doing? You better be because this is the very thing for which you will be judged. People who judge don't know what they're getting themselves into.

Life is too difficult to handle in your mortal condition and this is why you need to walk in the light as He is in the light. You need to be a doer of the Word and not a hearer only. Phil. 4:9 says, "The things which you learned and received and heard and saw in me, these do, and the God of peace will be with you." The Message Bible says, "Put into practice what you learned from me, what you heard and saw and realized. Do that, and God, who makes everything work together, will work you into His most excellent harmonies." These people saw some things in their association with Paul and these are the very things he said they should be doing. In other words, what you see is what you should do. When you see the light, you should do the light. There is no substitute for being a doer of the Word. You may receive a little revelation by what you hear and what you see other people do. Full revelation, however, only comes when you become a doer of the Word and walk in the light you have. Knowledge is good, action is better.

Paul talks about people who are "always learning and never able to come to the knowledge of the truth" (2 Tim. 3:7). There is revelation these people are not receiving. They're trying to see and understand but no matter how much they learn they still aren't getting what's available to them. You can read a hundred books about parachuting out of an airplane, but until you actually do it full revelation won't come. This is why you need to do more than just read your Bible or listen to a sermon at church. No, full revelation only comes when you put into practice that which you've seen and heard. You can't go to enough seminars and read enough Christian material to get full light. That only happens when you become a doer of the Word. You must put the rubber to the road and do what the Word is telling you to do. If you don't do that then you are deceiving yourself and will not receive the full benefits that a victorious Christian life would allow. It takes faith to step out and James 2:17 says "Faith by itself, if it does not have works, is dead."

Doing what you know to do is a full-time job. You should be so busy being a doer of the Word that you won't have time to judge and criticize other people for what they're doing or not doing. John 3:21 says, "But he who does the truth comes to the light, that his deeds may be clearly seen, that they have been done in God." The NLT says, "But those who do what is right come to the light so others can see that they are doing what God wants." This is progressive. You see the light and then you put into practice what you've seen. Before long more light will come and you'll see more things that you've never seen before. What you'll see will be brighter and more clear to you than it was before. You must then step forward and walk in the new light you've been given. The temptation will be there to get lazy and stop walking in the light you have. If you do that, no more light will come.

This is why it is so important to keep the Word ever before you and stay busy doing what you know to do. This you must do day in and day out. It truly is a full-time job.

People who walk in darkness do so because there is light they're not walking in. If they were walking with God as they should be then darkness would not be there. They think and say they're walking in light but the darkness is proof that they're not. These are the ones who deceive themselves into thinking all is well when devastation is just around the corner. 1 John 2:20 (NLT) says, "But you are not like that, for the Holy One has given you His Spirit, and all of you know the truth." You have an unction from the Holy One and you know you've passed from death to life. To walk in the light means to know what you're looking at. It brings revelation and understanding and the path you're on gets brighter and brighter with each step you take. You will know what to do for the Lord will show you what to do. The person who gets the most out of life, the one who gets the most grace and favor and opportunities, is the person who does the most with what he has. Because he has walked in the light, he will be given more light.

You don't stand still when you're walking in the light. Jesus said in John 8:12, "I am the light of the world. He who follows Me shall not walk in darkness, but have the light of life." God is moving for you can't follow somebody who is standing still. The plan of God is not stagnant and stationary. It is progressive and always on the move. Before you were even born God had a plan for your life and now that you are here you must endeavor every day to walk on the path He has set for your life. It is a path of progressive light and you must keep walking on it because you can't steer a parked car. The faster a vehicle moves, whether it be a car or an airplane, the easier it is to steer. You will hear from God more easily and direction will come when you are consistently walking in the light you have. You can study a lot and read many books, which is good in and of itself, but you won't be able to get all the light you need through a classroom experience. You need to put the books down, get up, and start walking in the light you have.

The time has come to put the pedal to the metal. It's time to get up and start being a doer of the Word. If you ask God for more light then He will first consider if you've been walking in the light He's already given you. Know with certainty that God does not forget the things He has told you to do. If you didn't obey Him in the past then there is no use for you to beg Him for more light. To get more light you must first walk in the light He's already given you. This is what qualifies you for more light. And then, when more light is given, don't walk away if at first you don't understand what God is saying to you. People received light from Jesus by listening to what He said and then one day He decided to give them more light. He said, "Most assuredly, I say to you, unless you eat the flesh of the Son of Man and drink His blood, you have no life in you" (John 6:53). Many of His disciples thought this was a hard saying and they could not understand it. For that reason vs. 66 says, "From that time many of His disciples went back and walked with Him no more."

These people got offended at Jesus because they didn't understand the light He had given them. It wasn't explained to them so they left and didn't come back. People get offended when they stop believing and trusting in a person they should believe and trust. If you have faith in somebody, if you trust them, you don't run away at the first thing you don't understand. Faith is not based on what you understand, it's a choice based on your trust in the person doing the speaking. There are many things about God and His kingdom you don't understand but you can believe it anyway. It may be hard to understand how a person can be dead one day and alive the next, yet believing this happened to Jesus is what makes you a Christian. It may be hard to understand how a person could be born of a virgin but you believe it happened to Jesus. The bottom line is you can believe something in your heart even if you don't understand it in your head, so don't run away if at first you don't understand the new light God is giving you.

Understanding will come if you'll keep going forward and continue to walk in the light. Your path will get brighter and brighter and in time revelation will come and you'll know more than you do today. Those who don't go forward are rebellious unbelievers. They're punks and blockheads. All you need to get started is the light you currently have. You won't need more light until you get to where you're going. Once you get there, more light will be given. You then repeat the same process over and over again. You walk from faith to faith and go from glory to glory. This is the walk of the righteous believer. These are the ones who get their needs met and do great exploits in the kingdom of God. If you trust somebody you'll keep going forward no matter what, even if the understanding isn't there. In faith you believe that understanding will come farther down the road, but you've got to get there first. This is why you have to put one foot in front of the other and keep walking in the light you have. Those are steps of faith and is what pleases God.

God knows the end from the beginning but that doesn't mean He'll tell you what the ending will be. What He will do is tell you what the next step is you are to take. The rich young ruler had a great future ahead of him and to get him going in the right direction Jesus told him the first thing he had to do. "Go your way, sell whatever you have and give to the poor, and you will have treasure in heaven; and come, take up your cross, and follow Me" (Mark 10:21). This was the start of an exciting adventure, a chance to walk side by side with Jesus and to be used by Him in a mighty way. All he had to do was trust Jesus and take that first step. Did he do it? Vs. 22 says, "But he was sad at this word, and went away grieved, for he had great possessions." Everybody who has ever followed Jesus, without exception, has had to turn loose of what was comfortable to them. They had to walk away from what was familiar and step from the known into the unknown. The rich young ruler did not take this first step and was forever grieved. It makes you wonder where he's at today.

God is not the author of confusion but still your faith will be tested and tried. Will you believe God and do what He tells you to do even if at first you don't understand it? Things may look well and good on the outside but the truth comes out when a person comes face-to-face with something they don't understand. Will they run away never to return or will they stay and see what God has planned for their life? This is when it's revealed what a person is made of on the inside. Were they serious when they said they would follow Jesus no matter what? Those who walked away didn't believe in Jesus because if they had they would have stayed. If you believe in somebody you stay even when you don't understand what's going on. God told Abraham to leave his kinfolks and set out on a journey. Heb.11:8 says, "And he went out, not knowing where he was going." Abraham didn't understand everything but he obeyed anyway. He didn't sit and do nothing until understanding came. No, he packed his bags and walked in the light he had been given. You must do the same.

-3-
"THE THOUGHTS OF GOD"

God has a plan and a purpose for everybody yet the majority of people don't know what that plan is and, if the truth be told, they don't want to know. It takes time and effort to find out God's perfect will for your life and most people don't want to pay the price for that to happen. They'd rather go off and do their own thing with no regard to what the Lord would have them do with their life. These are the ones who go through life broken and defeated no matter how successful they may appear to be on the outside. There is a place in everybody's heart reserved for the will of God and all the money in the world cannot fill that void. True meaning in life only comes when you find out why you are here and what you're supposed to do with your life. The world around you has a way of always dragging you down to its level of immaturity. Don't become so well-adjusted to your culture that you fit into it without even thinking. Instead, fix your attention on God. Find out what He wants from you and quickly respond to it.

If you've totally surrendered your heart to Jesus then you can come to a place where you will be able to discern and clearly know the will of God for your life. Paul says in Rom.12:1,2, "I beseech you therefore, brethren, by the mercies of God, that you present your bodies a living sacrifice, holy, acceptable to God, which is your reasonable service. And do not be conformed to this world, but be transformed by the renewing of your mind, that you may prove what is that good and acceptable and perfect will of God." God is telling you to not copy the behavior and customs of the world for there is a danger of being conformed to its evil ways if you don't make an effort not to be. Instead, you need to let God transform you into a new person by changing the way you think. Then you will learn to know God's will for you, which is good and pleasing and perfect. There are many believers bewildered by what the will of God might be for their lives and this ought not to be. The Lord is not hiding His will from anybody but you must make the effort to find out what it is.

It is not hard to know the will of God. Those who don't know have a problem and it's right between their ears. If everybody thought right then God wouldn't tell people they had to get their mind renewed. The bottom line is you've got to change the way you think. The word "renewed" means 'renovate' which implies that you have to get rid of the old and replace it with the new. There needs to be some demolition in your mind of things that were planted there by this world. You should not think like everybody else on this planet for if you do then you're acting like those who are unsaved. By changing the way you think you will be transformed into a better person. You'll learn to know God's will for your life and will be able to go out and make a positive difference in the world you live in. You'll leave your mark on this generation and it all begins with changing the way you think. Most people would rather do anything than that but it is the key to finding and knowing the will of God for your life. If you don't renew your mind then you'll never know what the will of the Lord is.

All around you there will be pressure to not rock the boat and be like everybody else. Continually you will be pressured to conform to the ways of the world. It's the total opposite of being transformed into the image of Christ and it's up to you to decide what you're going to let form you. Are you going to meditate on the things of the world or on the precepts of God? It matters what you think about for it determines the outcome of your life. In the cool of the evening God shared His thoughts with Adam and Eve and all was well. It was amazing, it was glorious, it was beautiful beyond description. Then the day came when the devil introduced to them other thoughts that were contrary to the thoughts of God. The serpent said surely they would not die if they ate of the forbidden fruit when God said they would. They pondered these thoughts, they received them, and finally they acted on them. They were conformed to the origin of these thoughts and stopped being like God and started to be like the devil. Whatever thought you receive is what you will become like.

A thought is an imagination that forms reality into the life of a person. Gen. 2:7 says God formed man out of the dust of the ground, but first he was formed in the mind of God. A thought is a spiritual force that can take something out of the spiritual realm and manifest it in the physical realm. It's the same thing as a vase being formed on a potter's wheel. It was formed in the potter's mind before he put his hands on the wet clay. Thoughts are not insignificant and it was wrong thoughts that brought about the fall of mankind. Generations passed and the condition of man continually grew worse and worse. The entire world was filled with ungodly, devilish thoughts. Gen. 6:5 says, "Then the Lord saw that the wickedness of man was great in the earth, and that every intent of the thoughts of his heart was only evil continually." People are deceived when they think it's okay to think a bad thought as long as they don't act on it. That is a lie from the devil. Wrong thoughts always leads to wrong actions and they brought the world to the point where it was destroyed by the great flood.

Every thought comes from somewhere and they are endeavoring to shape something in your life. There are thoughts that will cause you to perspire and make your heart beat faster, and there are other thoughts that will slow you down and put you in a peaceful slumber. Thoughts are powerful and they affect the way you live your life. Some thoughts make you sad and some thoughts make you smile. There are good thoughts and there are bad thoughts and they all have the power to form and shape what happens in your life. The way you are today is the result of what you thought about in the past. Prov. 23:7 says, "For as he thinks in his heart, so is he." Do not allow yourself to be conformed into this world. You are in the world but you are not of the world. Don't let the world turn you into itself for you are destined to not be like everybody else. You are thinking good thoughts and inside you are being transformed into the image of Christ. Old things have passed away, behold, all things become new.

A transformation is a metamorphosis, like the changing of a caterpillar into a butterfly. It's a complete change, from top to bottom, from the inside out. This change didn't happen when you got born again. Your spirit changed, not your mind. You become a new creature in Christ Jesus but your mind still thought the way it did before you got saved. This is why you have to renew your mind and change the way you think. God changes your heart but it's your responsibility to change your mind and get it renewed. You are what you think so you need to open your Bible and begin to think about what God tells you to think about. Pay attention to the thoughts God gives you. An indicator that the thought came from God is that it will excite you. It will cause your heart to leap for joy. God took Abraham outside and said the number of his descendants would be like the stars in the sky. This excited Abraham so much so that Gen. 15:5 says, "And he believed in the Lord, and He accounted it to him for righteousness." Abraham embraced that thought and was fully persuaded that God would perform His word.

The thoughts of God are exhilarating, they'll make you jump and shout. Ps. 92:5 says, "O Lord, how great are Your works! Your thoughts are very deep." The expansion of the universe is vast and deep and this is what God told Abraham to look at. The amazing thing is that God created you with the ability to think far and wide, to imagine His thoughts and all the things He has planned for you. Jer. 29:11 says, "For I know the thoughts that I think toward you, says the Lord, thoughts of peace and not of evil, to give you a future and a hope." Paul prayed that you "may be able to comprehend with all the saints what is the width and length and depth, and height - to know the love of Christ which passes knowledge; that you may be filled with all the fullness of God" (Eph. 3:18,19). Like Abraham, you were created with the ability to embrace these thoughts. They're huge, they're wide, they're deep. The vastness of the universe is but a fraction of the things God wants you to think about. He is bigger than the universe and so are His thoughts.

Let the thoughts of God transform you. It's a wonderful thing to not be limited to just what the human mind can think or imagine. His thoughts are very deep and very vast, and the more you ponder them the more you will see into them. Those who don't think His thoughts live a very shallow life. Ps. 139:17,18 says, "How precious also are Your thoughts to me, O God! How great is the sum of them! If I should count them, they would be more in number than the sand; When I awake, I am still with You." God wants you to think His thoughts for, when you do, you will never fear, worry, or be in despair. One thought from Him can show you how to have victory in your current situation. The thoughts of God are spiritual and have enough power to solve all your problems and set you on a higher level of living. They'll transform you into a new and better person. In a crisis people think they need this or that. No, what they need is a thought from God and a willingness to do what He tells them to do.

When your mind is renewed, when you replace your thoughts with His thoughts, you will know the good and perfect will of God. You will think it and by His grace you will do it. 1 Tim. 5:15 says, "Meditate on these things; give yourself entirely to them, that your progress may be evident to all." When you put action to the godly thoughts you think about, good things will happen to you and will be seen by everybody. When you immerse yourself in everything Jesus said and did, you will become like Him. You become what you think about, whether it be good or bad, and this is why you always need to think God's thoughts. 2 Cor. 3:18 says, "But we all, with unveiled face, beholding as in a mirror the glory of the Lord, are being transformed into the same image from glory to glory, just as by the Spirit of the Lord." The Message Bible says, "And so we are transfigured much like the Messiah, our lives gradually becoming brighter and brighter and more beautiful as God enters our lives and we become like Him."

Daily desire and strive to know the thoughts of God and train yourself to think on them day and night for as a man thinks, so is he. Ps. 1:1,2 says, "Blessed is the man who walks not in the counsel of the ungodly, nor stands in the path of sinners, nor sits in the seat of the scornful; But his delight is in the law of the Lord, and in His law he meditates day and night." When you learn a person's thoughts, you will learn their ways and this is how you can learn and know the will of God. When something good happens you can know it's from God because you know that's how He thinks. You know how He thinks because you've been thinking His thoughts. No longer are you clueless as to how God does things for you know His thoughts and you know His ways. This will enable you to reject the idea that a natural disaster was "an act of God" because you know He is not the one who comes to steal, kill, and destroy. You know that Jesus came to give His people life and life more abundantly (John 10:10).

Your mind is renewed when you think God's thoughts. Too many people in the church world don't even attempt to do this for they reason that God's thoughts are higher than their thoughts. They quote Is. 55:8,9 to defend this belief but they didn't read the entire passage. If they did they would have seen in vs. 7 that God was talking to the wicked. He was saying the thoughts of a good God are higher than the thoughts of a wicked person. He never said a born-again believer could not know His thoughts. Man-made religion is one of the most destructive things in all the world. People take a verse, or half a verse, and make it say something it never said and use that as a basis for not believing God. For example, 1 Cor. 2:9 says, "But as it is written: 'Eye has not seen, nor ear heard, nor have entered into the heart of man the things which God has prepared for those who love Him." They quote this verse and say you can't know the thoughts of God. What they didn't do is read the following verse. "But God has revealed them to us through His Spirit. For the Spirit searches all things, yes, the deep things of God" (vs. 10).

You can think the thoughts of God and boldly go where no religion has gone before. You can know His thoughts and you can understand His ways right now in this life. You don't have to wait to get to heaven to know God's thoughts. You need to know how He thinks now so you'll know how to deal with the challenges of everyday life today. You won't be able to have a good marriage or raise your children properly if you don't know the thoughts of God. You won't find the right job and you'll never fulfill your destiny if you don't think the way God thinks. There are some thoughts you don't need to hear and some thoughts you don't need to be around. Walk away from people who vocally express the thoughts of the devil, those who speak negatively all the time and say foul words continually. Stop gossiping on the phone for hours at a time saying and listening to bad things about other people. Stop listening to all the junk and begin to meditate on and ponder the thoughts of God.

You are involved in the transformation process for you are responsible for the things you think about. Don't copy and imitate the customs and standards of the world but let God transform you into a new person by changing the way you think. Being established and grounded in the perfect will of God is connected to the renewal of your mind. Daily your mind and the thoughts you think needs to be made "holy and clean, washed by the cleansing of God's word" (Eph. 5:26 NLT). When you read your Bible every day your spirit and your mind are both cleansed. You're washed, you're renewed, you're refreshed. You wake up every morning excited about what God has planned for you today. You are different from the rest of the world. Your cup is always full and overflowing whereas the cup of the world is empty and forever lacking. Do not be conformed to the ways of the world but be transformed by the renewing of your mind. You will be pressured to think and talk like everybody else. Don't let that happen. Be renewed by thinking the thoughts of God.

You are a child of God and you're supposed to be different from those who are in the world. Never apologize for being the way you are. Don't hide what you believe and how you think. Yes, cultures vary but the Word of God remains the same forever. You are the Lord's ambassador and it's your responsibility to show the world how to live in this evil day. This doesn't mean you have to pressure people wherever you go. All you have to do is let your light shine by being the person God transformed you into. Just be who you are. Don't stop talking about Jesus just because an unbeliever walks into the room. Raise your head high and let your light shine. They're the ones who need to change, not you. They need to let God transform them by changing the way they think. They need to do what you did. They need to get born again and then take on the responsibility to change the way they think. They need to get their minds renewed and begin to think the thoughts of God.

To be transformed you need to be on a continual diet of God's Word, getting His thoughts into you. Reject your old way of thinking and embrace God's way of thinking. If you will do that you will be changed into another person. You will become Christlike because you're thinking like Him. This will not happen until you first do something with your mind. It's your mind and it's your responsibility to do something with it. God will not change your mind for you. If He did then you'd be nothing more than a mindless robot. God wants sons and daughters who will follow Him willingly and do what He tells them to do and think what He tells them to think. You are not a puppet on a string but a child of the living God. You have a free will with which to choose how you will live your life. You can be conformed to this evil world or you can be transformed by renewing your mind. The choice is yours. Just know that God will not move until you move first. Transformation comes only after you begin to think the thoughts of God.

God will not make you do something you don't want to do. That's what demonic possession is all about. No, you must submit your will to Him willingly because you want to, not because you're forced to. God and nobody else can control your mind and make you think about something you don't want to think about. You have total freedom to choose what you want to think and say and this is what puts you in the same class as God. You are made in His image and this freedom to choose is a big part of what makes you that way. You can think anything you choose to think, and you can believe it and act on it. This is how God operates. Understand that every thought comes from somewhere and it's your responsibility to discern where each and every thought comes from. To do that you must immerse yourself in the Word of God for this is where you find the thoughts of God. If the thought does not line up with the Bible then cast it out and never think about it again. But if it does line up, embrace it and think about it all day long.

This world is trying to shape you and mold you into itself and you should not allow this to happen. You are not like the people of the world and are not supposed to be. They are, however, supposed to be like you. Every believer needs to be transformed and it doesn't come from prayer or the laying on of hands. It happens when you change the way you think. David said in Ps. 139:1,2 (MSG), "God, investigate my life; get all the facts firsthand. I'm an open book to you; even from a distance, you know what I'm thinking." God sees and understands your thoughts from afar off. He knows where they come from and where they're going. Thoughts are important, otherwise God wouldn't bother knowing what your thoughts are. One of the first steps to getting your mind renewed is you've got to embrace the fact that thoughts are important and are a significant part of your life as a born again believer. What's more, you can't leave the Word out of the process for in it are the very thoughts you are to renew your mind with.

The Bible is the expression of God's thoughts which are awesome and too wonderful for mere words. Still, they are expressed in the Word to various degrees through words. When you read and hear the Word, the thought that came up in God will come into you and will cause you to think God's thoughts. Daily you should hunger to know what God thinks about certain things because there is power in His thoughts to transform you into a new person. If you will do this consistently you will be a different person a year from now than who you are today. This is why His thoughts should be more precious to you than all the money in the world. Check up on yourself and ask God to reveal to you when and where you are not thinking His thoughts. Ps. 139:23,24 (MSG) says, "Investigate my life, O God, find out everything about me; Cross-examine and test me, get a clear picture of what I'm about; See for yourself whether I've done anything wrong - then guide me on the road to eternal life."

Strive to remove from your life everything that is not of God. The world is filled with twisted theologies about God that are not true. Just because something is said in a church with glass-stained windows does not mean it came from God. Time is short and you don't have time to deal with all these teachings that are not true. Ask God to purge you of all non-truths so you can fill your mind with only His thoughts. When you do this your mind will be renewed and you will be changed. God is real and He is mindful of the things you are thinking about. Don't disappoint Him by thinking the way the world thinks. No, think His thoughts. Focus on the things that are important to Him. If God's not in it, then neither should you be. Walk in close fellowship with Him so that His thoughts become your thoughts and His ways become your ways. You shall know the truth and the truth shall set you free from all the falseness that is in the world. It will transform you into a new person.

A thought paints the universe around you and determines the environment you'll live in. The word "thought" means 'to weave; to fabricate' and the word "imagine" means 'to mold into a form; to squeeze into a shape.' A thought is a spiritual substance and it shapes the world you live in. When you think God's thoughts you will be formed into the image of Jesus. Is. 64:8 says, "But now, O Lord, You are our Father; We are the clay, and You are the potter; And all we are the work of Your hand." Before long you'll act like Jesus, think like Him, talk like Him, and respond to the challenges of life like Him. This is your calling, your destiny. This is where you're headed and by the grace of God you'll get there. 1 John 3:2 says, "Beloved, now we are children of God; and it has not yet been revealed what we shall be, but we know that when He is revealed, we shall be like Him, for we shall see Him as He is." Always be who the Lord made you to be and don't let the world squeeze you into its wicked ways.

The difference between being spiritual and being worldly is what you think about. Rom. 8:5 (NLT) says, "Those who are dominated by the sinful nature think about sinful things, but those who are controlled by the Holy Spirit think about things that please the Spirit." It matters what you think about for Paul continues in vs. 6, "For to be carnally minded is death, but to be spiritually minded is life and peace." Some thoughts are deadlier than the venom of a rattlesnake and they can come to you at any time of the day or night. Even the most holy child of God will have thoughts come to them that are ugly and repulsive. The thoughts will come but you don't have to receive them. You do have a choice as to what you think on. You don't have to think about anything you don't want to and don't let anybody tell you differently. Those who say they can't help what they think about is lying to you and to themselves. An old saying says, "You can't stop a bird from flying over your head but you can stop him from building a nest in your hair."

Your thinking must change because, if the truth be told, there is too much ungodly, worldly thinking in most Christian's minds. Your mind is your mind and you can choose what you think about. As a child of God there are things you shouldn't think about and things you should. Paul says in Phil. 4:8 (NLT), "Fix your thoughts on what is true, and honorable, and right, and pure, and lovely, and admirable. Think about things that are excellent and worthy of praise." The Message Bible says, "Summing it all up, friends, I'd say you'll do best by filling your minds and meditating on things true, noble, reputable, authentic, compelling, gracious - the best, not the worst; the beautiful, not the ugly; things to praise, not things to curse." If you will think on these things day and night, if you'll meditate on them and speak them out of your mouth continually, you will be changed. You will be transformed into the image of Christ and you'll literally have His mind (1 Cor. 2:16).

One way to tell if you are thinking the right thoughts is that peace will be there. Is. 48:22 says, "'There is no peace,' says the Lord, 'for the wicked,'" There can't be any peace in a bad thought but a good thought will minister peace to you. If you have no peace then immediately stop thinking what you're thinking about. Cast those thoughts aside and begin to meditate on the thoughts of God. When you do, peace will come. Is. 26:3 says, "You will keep him in perfect peace, whose mind is stayed on You, because he trusts in You." In Hebrew it says you will have "peace, peace." It doubles the emphasis that when you meditate on the thoughts of God you'll have peace that passes all understanding. You'll be mellow, content, and at rest. If you are angry and frustrated all the time then you are thinking on the wrong things. You need to repent and begin to think on things that are lovely, pure, and of a good report. If you will follow after peace then you will be protected from the wiles of the devil and the bad thoughts he sends your way.

What will bring you more peace, believing that God will supply all your needs or worrying that you won't have enough money to pay your bills at the end of the month? If you worry about getting sick when the flu season rolls around then you are thinking on the wrong things. There is no peace when thoughts of poverty and sickness cloud your mind. Isaiah goes on to say in Is. 26:4, "Trust in the Lord forever, for in YAH, the Lord, is everlasting strength." The Message Bible says, "Depend on God and keep at it because in the Lord God you have a sure thing." When you trust in the Lord and fix your thoughts on Him, peace will come and this gives your faith the freedom to operate. You've got too much to be thankful for to worry about your needs not getting met. God is good and when you think His thoughts and learn His ways you can have the peace and confidence that He'll take good care of you. Eph. 3:20 says, "Now to Him who is able to do exceedingly, abundantly above all that we ask or think, according to the power that works in us."

When a bad thought comes, cast it down and set your mind on Him. Nobody ever said this was an easy thing to do but if you'll do it, God will keep you in peace, peace. Josh. 1:8

says, "This Book of the Law shall not depart from your mouth, but you shall meditate in it day and night, that you may observe to do according to all that is written in it. For then you will make your way prosperous, and then you will have good success." God will protect those who meditate on His thoughts and whose mind cannot be changed. God never changes and neither should your mind when your thoughts are stayed on Him and the redemptive realities that are found in the Word. Thoughts affect you and this is how you can tell if the thought is good or bad. If it makes you miserable then it's a bad thought. A good thought that originates in the mind of God will bring with it peace and joy. This concept is not that difficult to understand. Just ask yourself how you feel and act accordingly.

-4-

"IN HIS IMAGE"

There is a God in heaven and a god of this world system and both are trying to get you to think like they do. The one who is successful determines the outcome of your life. You are not an innocent bystander in this life or death tug-of-war for you and you alone are the one who determines who the winner will be. Your mind is your mind and nobody can make you think what you don't want to think about. Yes, you will be pressured to be conformed to the way the world thinks. Everybody else is thinking the wrong way, why don't you do it too? Come on, do it. No, you are different. You are a child of the living God and you've been made in His image. To you Paul writes in Rom. 12:2, "And do not be conformed to this world, but be transformed by the renewing of your mind." This is something you should take very seriously because every day you will be tempted and pressured to think the way the world thinks. The good news is that if God told you not to be conformed, then you have the power to not be conformed. God will not tell you to do something you cannot do.

Every decision you make and every action you take begins with a thought in your mind. Your most dominate thought is what determines the direction your life goes in. You believe what you continually focus on and this is why you must train yourself to always meditate on the thoughts of God. What happens on the outside always begins on the inside. If you sow a thought, you'll reap an action. Your thoughts are the pathway to your destiny and this is why your mind is the number one target of the enemy. It has been estimated that up to sixty thousand thoughts come to you each and every day and, if your mind is not renewed, four out of five of them will be toxic and negative. You must take control of what you think about. You need to meditate on the Word of God and hear yourself speak it out of your mouth. What you consistently hear is what your mind will grab onto and if it's hearing the Word of God it will be renewed. You will be transformed and your life will go in the direction it's supposed to go.

Yes, negative thoughts will come but you don't have to entertain them. Be selective about what you think about. Be aggressive and go on the offensive. Don't spend all your time resisting and rebuking bad thoughts. No, spend your time thinking of things that are pure and lovely and of a good report. Speak the Word out loud and then meditate on what you just heard yourself say. When a good thought comes in, the bad thought must leave. Think about what the Word says and how you're made in the image of God. Think of how special you are that the Heavenly Father would send His only begotten Son to die for you. Change comes when you're desperate for change. Pull yourself up by the boot straps and no longer allow the enemy to control what you think about. Remember, you are what you think and only you can determine what you think about. You will not change until you're fed up and tired of where you're currently at. You must draw a line in the sand, tell the devil that enough is enough, and begin to think on what God tells you to think about.

God's Word is like a mirror and it reflects the way God sees you. He doesn't make junk so stop hating who you are and stop wishing you were someone else. You are a one-of-a-kind original and are made in His image. Your life will change when you get in the Word of God and see yourself how God sees you. He sees you as someone who is valuable and important. You are gifted and an asset to the kingdom of God. You're the head and not the tail, above and not beneath. When you see yourself as God sees you, life will be different. Know that Satan is always going to question your identity. He said to Jesus, "If you are the Son of God, turn these stones into bread" (Matt. 4:3). Don't listen to him and don't entertain those thoughts. You've got the mind of Christ, you're a child of God, and you're made in His image. There is no greater revelation than that. When your mind is renewed, you can live with confidence that your destiny will be fulfilled and all your dreams will come true.

God made you in His image and He placed inside of you unlimited potential that will allow you to be successful and excel in life. He has a specific plan for your life and future and only you can fulfill that exact plan. People who have a poor self-image spend too much time focused on themselves that they never step up to the next level of fulfilling their destiny. God made you the way you are for a reason. You were tailor-made for your assignment so cling to your uniqueness, don't run away from it. You were created on purpose for a purpose. The world is waiting for you to step forward and be the person God created you to be. What you may think is a weakness in your life may in truth be your most dominate strength with which you can do what you've been called to do. Always remember that God made you the way you are. Ps. 139:13,14 says, "For You have formed my inward parts; You have covered me in my mother's womb. I will praise You, for I am fearfully and wonderfully made; Marvelous are Your works, and that my soul knows very well."

The NLT says, "Thank You for making me so wonderfully complex! Your workmanship is marvelous - how well I know it." Do not allow the world to squeeze you into who it wants you to be. No, be the person God had in mind before this world was even created. If God wants you to be one way, and this is how He made you, then never allow others to convince you to be otherwise. Be who you are. Be the person God created you to be. Embrace it and never forget how special you are. You are truly unique and this word means "only one of a kind, exceptional, distinctive, matchless, irreplaceable, and rare." That's you! You are one of a kind. There is nobody quite like you on this entire planet and that is how God purposed it should be. He doesn't want you to be any person other than the one He chose you to be. This is what renewing your mind is all about. It's about you seeing yourself in the Word and applying His principles to your everyday life that will help you become even more like Him.

You are God's most prized possession. He made you just so He could give Himself to you. He is a loving, forgiving God and when you allow Him to make you into a new creation you will live a wonderful, victorious life. No matter what your past has been like, you can have a fresh start in life by making Jesus the Lord of your life and by getting your mind renewed. Is. 43:18 (MSG) says, "Forget about what's happened; don't keep going over old history. Be alert, be present. I'm about to do something brand new. It's bursting out! Don't you see it? There it is!" If God remembers your sins no more, then neither should you. The person who does remember them is the devil and this is why you need to continually be meditating on what God says about you in the Bible. Cast down those evil thoughts and imaginations and renew your mind by thinking on the thoughts of God. It is your responsibility to take authority over those negative thoughts and obstacles that the enemy attacks you with, and you do it with the Word of God. Meditate on it and speak it out your mouth.

Don't entertain negative thoughts for one moment. God thinks you're special so don't let the devil tell you differently.

Called To Be Saints

Ps. 8:5 says you've been crowned with glory and honor. God made you in His image and has pronounced His blessing on you. He's given you His favor and His love and this allows you to wake up each morning with your head held high knowing that God is on your side. You're an heir of God and you've got royal blood flowing through your veins. If God be for you, who can be against you? God loves you so much that He's already arranged for you to come out on top in every area of your life if you'll just renew your mind and be obedient to His Word. The devil wants you to feel inferior, condemned, beat down, and unworthy and he'll try to make you feel that way every day of your life. This is why you need to read and meditate on the Bible every day. If you do, Jesus said in John 8:22, "And you shall know the truth, and the truth shall make you free."

God's Word will transform you for it has the power to change the direction of your life. It will cause your mind to be renewed and will make you superior to your circumstances. Ps. 112:7,8 says, "He will not be afraid of evil tidings; His heart is steadfast, trusting in the Lord. His heart is established; He will not be afraid." If you want to know where you're going to be five years from now, pay attention to what you're thinking about and what you're saying today. If you want to take your life to a whole new level then meditate on the thoughts of God and begin speaking them out of your mouth. If you're bold enough to say it, God is bold enough to bring it to pass (Ps. 91:2,3). Speak as if you know what you say is going to happen. Every time you speak something out of your mouth, you believe it in a stronger way. This is how you take charge of your life. You think it, then you speak it. Your life follows your thoughts. Whatever you focus on, you will attract. What you think about, you bring about.

By thinking God's thoughts, you will be transformed and radically changed from the person you are today. Paul wrote these instructions to the saints in Rome, people who were already saved and born again. He was telling them that even though their spirit-man got changed, their mind and their way of thinking needed to be changed as well. Every believer has the same mind the day after they got saved as they did the day before they gave their life to Christ. This is why you need to get your mind renewed so you'll start thinking like God thinks. The difference is you've now got the power to resist temptation and make the right decisions as to what you'll think about. Greater is He who is in you than he who is in the world. Once saved, you need to immediately begin renewing your mind so you'll think right. It truly is a matter of life and death. What you think about will determine if you'll walk in victory or defeat. As a man thinks, so does he become, so never take for granted the power of a thought. It will make you or break you.

You need to be transformed. Ask God to help you see what He sees, to think like He thinks, and to do what He does. Ask Him to help you see your bills paid, your body healed, and your relationships restored. 2 Cor. 3:17 says, "Now the Lord is the Spirit; and where the Spirit of the Lord is, there is liberty." When God shows you these things there will be freedom and liberty, not grief and despair. You can be in a very bad situation, but if your mind is renewed you can have joy and peace no matter what's going on around you. You must become strong in the godly thoughts you allow into your mind. You must believe that you are more than a conqueror and with the Lord's help and guidance you will live a victorious life and fulfill your destiny. This is how you think when your mind is renewed. You think victory, not defeat; prosperity, not poverty; health, not sickness. People who worry are looking at and thinking about the wrong things. Their thoughts are on the god of this world and not on the great God of the universe. Remember, you become what you think about.

If your mind is renewed, you will be transformed into another person. This is not hype but a divine truth from heaven above. 2 Cor. 3:18 says, "But we all, with unveiled face, beholding as in a mirror the glory of the Lord, are being transformed into the same image from glory to glory, just by the Spirit of the Lord." The Message Bible says, "And so we are transfigured much like the Messiah, our lives gradually becoming brighter and more beautiful as God enters our lives and we become like Him." Transformation doesn't happen instantly. The time a caterpillar spends in a cocoon varies from ten days to seven years or more depending on the species. Transformation is progressive and it happens as you behold and think about the right things. When you meditate on the thoughts of God you will be changed into His image and will go from glory to glory. Paul prayed in Eph. 4:18 (MSG) that God would "make you intelligent and discerning in knowing Him personally, your eyes focused and clear, so that you can see exactly what it is He is calling you to do."

Paul prayed that the eyes of your understanding would be enlightened so that you would know who you are in Christ and begin to think His thoughts. Each new revelation you get and every Godly thought you think about will take you to a higher level of glory. Your mind is being renewed and you are being transformed into a new person. This is what God had in mind when He said in Gen. 1:26, "Let Us make man in Our image, according to Our likeness." You get transformed so you can reflect the nature of God. Vs. 27 says, "So God created man in His own image; in the image of God He created him, male and female He created them." A thought means nothing unless it creates an image in your mind. You don't think in letters of the alphabet, you think in images. It produces a picture in your mind, and your life will gravitate toward the image it sees. This is why it is so important to only think the thoughts of God. It will put a divine image in your mind of who you are in Christ.

You can catch a small glimpse of how wonderful God's imagination is by considering the vastness of the universe and beholding all the beautiful places here on this planet. What's even more awesome is that when you meditate on the thoughts of God, the image in Him becomes the image in you. The Bible says you were created in His image. This means that God looked inside Himself and saw what you were supposed to be like. The amazing thing is that when you renew your mind you will see what God sees and will be transformed into the person He created you to be. You have the ability to conceive in your mind the image of you that God sees in His imagination. You then choose words that depict that image and the faith that comes as a result of that will transform you into a new person. This is how God created the universe back in the beginning of time and this is how you should be operating in one degree or another. If there is something about you that you don't like then renew your mind and see yourself how God sees you.

You become what you behold. When you see what God sees, you will become a new person. This is why it's so important to read your Bible every day and meditate on the thoughts of God continually. You need to let Him enlighten the eyes of your understanding and help you see yourself through His eyes. You are the apple of His eye and it's because of you that He made this planet and all its glory in the first place. You are His beloved child and He's made you cleansed and white as snow by the blood of the Lamb. You have already been predestined to be transformed into His image. He's not moved by your shortcomings but sees you ruling and reigning with Him. If He sees you that way then you need to renew your mind and see yourself that way also. God made you in His image and this is how you need to see yourself no matter how many times you've slipped and fallen. Never limit yourself as to how far you can go in life. You've been transformed, you've got the mind of Christ, and you can go as far as you want to go.

As you grow older you may not be able to do with your body what you did when you were sixteen years old. Your mind, however, should be better. As each year goes by you should grow in your capacity to think Godly thoughts. Your mind is sharp and more alert and there is no limit to what you can learn and understand. Never fear that one day you may lose your mind and memory for it's the fear that will cause it to happen. Confess daily that you have the mind of Christ and that you'll never lose your mind. As you advance in years you'll grow in your capacity to be used by God in His kingdom because you'll be thinking greater thoughts which have within itself the power to bring to pass whatever it is you're thinking. You're not getting older, you're getting better. You have embraced the Word of God and you think the thoughts of God morning, noon, and night. You have a strong mind and you are at peace. You have no fear or worries because God said He would take care of you and this is what you've been meditating on. He has delivered you from all your problems before and you know He'll do it again.

Ps. 94:19 says, "In the multitude of my anxieties within me, Your comforts delight my soul." The Message Bible says, "When I was upset and beside myself, You calmed me down and cheered me up." The psalmist was thinking bad thoughts and it got him down. He then thought Godly thoughts and it made him happy. This really is a simple concept to understand. Your life will go in the direction of your most dominate thought. Bad thoughts will defeat you, good thoughts will lead you to victory. It matters what you think about. The power is there to deliver you from every obstacle but you've got to choose to think it first. Your mind is your mind and you can choose what you think about. If the devil can't get you to think the wrong thing, he can't defeat you. There are good things to think about and bad things to think about. Jesus said in Luke 12:22 to not worry about what you should eat or wear, and in vs. 24 He said to consider the ravens. He told you what to think about and what not to think about. Your mind is renewed when you make the right choice. It's that simple.

God expects you to meditate on the things He tells you to think about. If you don't know what they are, then read you Bible because it's a book filled with the thoughts of God. When God says to consider the ravens and the lilies of the field, do it. If an unexpected bill comes in the mail then go outside and look at the birds flying in the air. Consider how the Lord provided for them and then meditate on how He'll meet your needs also. If you haven't spent much time lately thinking about birds and flowers then maybe you better start doing so. After all, God told you to do it. Do what He says and your mind will be renewed. If you'll look at those birds long enough, before long you won't worry about where your next meal will come from or what you'll wear when the cold winter season rolls around. Jesus is telling you what to think about and what not to think about. The problem is that most Christians ignore what Jesus is saying and go off and meditate on the wrong things. They then wonder why their life is in the condition it is in.

Ravens don't worry so why should you? Lilies don't struggle so why should the trials of life wear you down? Do what Jesus said and be raven-minded and lily-minded. Think on the things He told you to think about. If you'll do that, faith will come and you'll enter into His rest. Is. 26:3 says, "You will keep him in perfect peace whose mind is stayed on You." When you think about God all the time and meditate on His thoughts, you will then be able to discern and establish in your own awareness the perfect will of God. This is one of the most important things you'll ever do in your life yet you will find people everywhere who are confused about the will of God for their life. They struggle not knowing what to do because they refuse to think on the right things. Their minds are not renewed and they wander through life like a vagabond not knowing if they're coming or going. But when your mind is renewed, when you think on the right things, clarity will come and you'll be able to identify what you're supposed to do and where you're supposed to go.

Never allow yourself to think on the wrong things. Peter was thinking about Jesus when he got out of the boat and started to walk on the water. He then yielded to thoughts about the wind and the waves and this is what caused him to sink. He thought about the wrong things. The Lord told Peter to come out to Him on the water and this should have been the only thing on his mind. The problem is he considered something else. His mind went in the wrong direction and, if not for the intervention of Jesus, he would have drowned in the sea. If Jesus tells you to do something then know that you have the power and the ability to do it. Do not consider anything else. If you do then you'll sink in the muck and mire of everyday life. James 1:6,7 says "he who doubts is like a wave of the sea driven and tossed by the wind. For let not that man suppose that he will receive anything from the Lord." He who doubts is a person who thinks on the wrong things. A person with two minds will always hesitate and be unstable and unreliable in all his ways.

A person whose mind is renewed knows what to do and does it. He is confident and walks with stability and assurance. He doesn't waste his life away trying to figure out what he's supposed to do. The will of God has been revealed to him because all day long he meditates on the thoughts of God. It is not spiritual to spend hours and hours making the smallest of decisions. If people struggle with the small things, how will they handle the big decisions that will determine the direction their life will take? How will they know who to marry and what job offer to accept if they take two hours deciding what shoes to wear? This is how those who are unsaved think and act. Their minds are not renewed and they get frustrated deciding if they want chicken for supper or pot roast. Their minds are never made up and, when it's necessary to make an important decision, they run around in circles not knowing what to do. They are unstable in all their ways and can't make a decision if their life depended on it.

Peter was stressed out because he considered the wind and the waves. He was not raven-minded nor was he lily-minded. He thought about the wrong thing and almost paid for it with his life. When the Lord tells you what to think, all other options should not be considered. Do not allow your mind to be corrupted from the simplicity that is in Christ. To live a good Christian life and fulfill your destiny, all you have to do is think what God tells you to think, do what He tells you to do, and say what He tells you to say. It doesn't get any more complicated than that. Adam and Eve should not have considered what the serpent asked them to do. If it's not an option, don't consider it and don't get involved with it. Rom. 4:19 says Abraham did not consider his old body or the deadness of Sarah's womb when God told him he would be the father of many nations. It wasn't an option to do so. Because of that, vs. 20 says, "He did not waver at the promise of God through unbelief, but was strengthened in faith, giving glory to God."

You need to change and it takes the transforming power of God to change you from the person you've been all your life. People say you can't teach an old dog new tricks but you're not an old dog. You are a new creation in Christ Jesus. Old things are passed away, behold, all things become new. You can radically change even after many years of being a certain way. All you have to do is renew your mind by thinking about what God tells you to think about. God told Abraham to think about the stars and he did. He considered nothing else and this caused him to be fully convinced that what God had promised He was also able to perform (Rom. 4:21). You, too, can change if you will sit at the feet of Jesus and ponder everything you hear Him say. Consider nothing else and watch what happens. Abraham became a new man and after Sarah passed away he went on and fathered many more children with his new wife. Apparently you can teach an old dog new tricks.

Randall J. Brewer

-5-

"BABES IN CHRIST"

It matters what you think about. Rom. 8:5 says, "For those who live according to the flesh set their minds on the things of the flesh, but those who live according to the Spirit, the things of the Spirit." The mind is the arena where it is determined whether you are carnal or spiritual and it's based on what you let yourself think about all the time. Vs. 6 says, "For to be carnally minded is death, but to be spiritually minded is life and peace." Spiritual people walk in peace and this is a sign that they are thinking on the right things. You are a spirit being and it's in your spirit where God resides. It's where your strength comes from. People who meditate on the wrong things and give in to the cravings of the flesh are those who are weak in the spirit. Spiritual people don't say they're going to do something and not do it. They are not victims to their flesh and don't let fleshly desires run their life. 1 Cor. 2:14 says, "But the natural man does not receive the things of the Spirit of God, for they are foolishness to him; nor can he know them, because they are spiritually discerned."

People who make fun of the things of God are only showing how foolish and carnal they are. They don't know God and don't recognize the things of God. Yes, they may be saved but their mind is not yet renewed. Paul is saying that the more spiritual you are, the more you will discern and see what is of God and what's not. You will see God moving when others do not. You know His thoughts and you know His ways because you have the mind of Christ (1 Cor. 2:16). People who are carnal cannot receive the deep things of God. They are "babes in Christ" (1 Cor. 3:1) and are behaving like those who are unsaved in the world. Paul is using babies in the natural to show what it's like to be carnal and not spiritual. When a baby doesn't get its way they'll howl and screech with no regard to how they're affecting others. They don't even think about that. All they think about is what they want. If they're hungry, they want to eat right now, not an hour from now. You don't have to be a two year old to be this way. There are millions of adult believers who are acting the same way.

When you are spiritually minded you are sensitive to the Holy Spirit and are aware of what's going on around you. This has to happen if you are going to be used by God in any great capacity. Babes in Christ think about themselves and are never called upon to do the great works of God here on the earth. Paul describes the characteristics of a carnal believer in 1 Cor. 3:3, "For where there are envy, strife, and divisions among you, are you not carnal and behaving like mere men?" A telltale sign of a carnal believer is that they are in strife wherever they go. They complain about this and they complain about that. It's too hot in the summer and too cold in the winter. The car in front of them is going too slow and the car that passed them is going too fast. If you don't believe like they do they'll argue with you about it night and day. Walk away from people like that. It takes two to tangle and if you get in strife with them then you also are acting carnal. Be bigger than that. Walk away with your head held high and experience the peace that passes all understanding.

When a person gets born again they don't automatically begin to think like God. This is why you have to read your Bible and get your mind renewed. The nature of your flesh also did not change the moment you committed your life to Christ. It also has to be dealt with every single day of your life. The body wants what the body wants and you will have the same fleshly desires that you had before you got saved. The difference between then and now is that you are now a new creature in Christ and inside of you resides the power to resist those evil desires that are trying to pull you into a life of carnality. Babes in Christ refuse to grow up in Christ and are controlled by their flesh. Whatever their flesh wants, their flesh gets. You need to understand that God will not control your flesh for you. This is something you must do daily. It matters not how spiritual you are, the flesh will always be there so you can't let your guard down for a single moment. Many have fallen because they didn't resist the devil and gave in to what their flesh wanted them to do.

Most people don't want to talk about their fleshly desires or admit they have them. Still, they are there if they admit it or not. The flesh is one subject the Bible does not run away from. It talks about the flesh and it talks about it in great detail. God is real and real Christianity deals with real life. Consider what Paul wrote in 1 Cor. 5:1,2 (MSG), "I also received a report of scandalous sex within your church family, a kind that wouldn't be tolerated even outside the church: One of your men is sleeping with his step-mother. And you're so above it all that it doesn't even faze you! Shouldn't this break your hearts? Shouldn't it bring you to your knees in tears? Shouldn't this person and his conduct be confronted and dealt with?" There is a lot said in the Bible about fornication and believers should not be afraid to deal with this problem. It is there so why not deal with it? Many people in the church today are in bad shape because they don't want to deal with sexuality and fleshly desires. They falsely believe if they ignore it long enough it will go away.

Sexual sin needs to be dealt with immediately because if it isn't it can spread and affect others. It was in the context of a man sleeping with his father's wife that Paul wrote, "Do you not know that a little leaven leavens the whole lump? Therefore purge out the old leaven, that you may be a new lump, since you truly are unleavened" (1 Cor. 5:6,7). The Message Bible says, "You pass it off as a small thing, but it's anything but that." The Bible says you are in the world but not of the world. You can't let what the world says about sexuality dictate how you think and act. The world says, "If it feels good, do it." They have no limits or boundaries on what they can or cannot do. The world talks about sex openly but many believers run and hide in a closet when the subject is brought up. This should not be because real Christians should want to know what God says about it so they will have a foundation on which to base their behavior. You need to understand His will and His ways and practice it as best as you know how.

Those who are spiritual control their bodies, babes in Christ do not. 1 Thess. 4:3-5 (NLT) says, "God's will is for you to be holy, so stay away from all sexual sin. Then each of you will control his own body and live in holiness and honor - not in lustful passion like the pagans who do not know God and His ways." This passage of scripture was written to believers because it is a subject that must be dealt with. The Message Bible says, "God wants you to live a pure life. Keep yourselves from sexual promiscuity. Learn to appreciate and give dignity to your body, not abusing it, as is so common among those who know nothing of God." Fornication is a big word and it covers everything that has to do with improper sexual activities. Full and partial nudity is everywhere, from the movies you watch to the want ads in the daily newspaper. It is the devil's plan to desensitize people to the sinfulness of sexual sin by gradually exposing them to that which is wrong. This will make them less likely to feel shock or distress at what they're looking at because they've been overexposed to these sexual images.

The truth of the matter is that people desire what they look at. A man cannot look at a sexual image of another woman and have a desire to be with his wife. This is not true no matter what the man says. He is lusting after another woman and is only using his wife as a substitute for the person he's imagining in his mind. That is ungodly, carnal, and is an insult to the woman he is married to. This man is a traitor because he has violated a sacred trust between himself and his wife. Jesus said in Matt. 5:28, "But I say to you that whoever looks at a woman to lust for her has already committed adultery with her in his heart." Everybody has these desires and they must be controlled. There is a spiritual law where if you feed a desire, it will grow and get stronger. Sexual sin today has grown to evil proportions making Sodom and Gomorrah small in comparison to what is happening today. This is why people have to get their minds renewed. They have to start thinking the right things that are based on the Word of God.

Thoughts will come and if you think about them long enough you will act on them. This works for thoughts good and bad. If a bad thought comes then cut it off immediately. Don't entertain it for one second. You can't spice up your marriage by fantasizing about other people. Christian counselors who are babes in Christ are actually telling people to do this. It is a gross sin to do this so never do it. God has strong feelings about nudity. When Adam and Eve sinned it was God who made clothes for them out of animal skins. He wanted their nakedness to be covered up. David saw the nakedness of Bathsheba and this led to adultery and murder. It is wrong and despicable to view the nakedness of a person you're not married to either with your eyes or your imagination. Nothing good ever comes of it and this is why you have to control your own body and live in holiness and honor. Babes in Christ cannot do this because it takes spiritual strength to control your body no matter what your thoughts and feelings may be.

There are some lines you don't cross over and sexual sin is one of them. Most people haven't a clue as to how valuable their body is. Your body is precious and you have to treat it right. When you commit a sexual sin with your body you are treating it like it is worthless. The Bible speaks of severe judgment to those who commit such atrocities because these acts destroy people's lives. They break up homes and destroys the lives of children and bring fatal sexual diseases. God is a just God and in His justice He has to deal with this sinful behavior. 1 Cor. 6:9,10 says, "Do you not know that the unrighteous will not inherit the kingdom of God? Do not be deceived. Neither fornicators, nor homosexuals, nor sodomites, nor thieves, nor covetous, nor drunkards, nor revilers, nor extortioners will inherit the kingdom of God." In the Bible idolatry and adultery are often connected because idolatry is spiritual adultery. It's being intimate with a false god just like adultery is being intimate with someone other than your spouse. Only God has the right to have intimacy with you, as does your spouse.

To commit a sexual sin is the same thing on a natural level as it is to worship a false god. It's the same thing physically that is happening spiritually. Worship in the spiritual realm parallels sex in the realm of marriage. When you worship God you are open with Him and honest. You bare your soul before Him and worship Him from your heart. In the marriage bed you have a similar intimacy where you bare yourself and open your heart to the person you're married to. Never should you worship a false god or bare yourself to a stranger. Babes in Christ and sinners alike are blinded to this parallel. They cast off restraint and run wild with their lives not knowing the painful consequences of such behavior. Gal. 6:7,8 says, "Do not be deceived, God is not mocked, for whatever a man sows, that he will also reap. For he who sows to his flesh will of the flesh reap corruption, but he who sows to the Spirit will of the Spirit reap everlasting life." The

Message Bible says, "No one makes a fool of God. What a person plants, he will harvest."

In spite of its recent popularity, the Bible says that homosexuality is not an acceptable, alternate lifestyle. The government, media, and secular programming will tell you that you are small minded and prejudice unless you give your approval to this type of behavior. People who live this way say they were born a homosexual and they have no say in their sexual orientation. They say they're a man in a woman's body or vice versa. That is a lie. Homosexuality is a choice, not a predestination. It happens when a person yields to wrong desires. The eyes of man are never satisfied and if you can't satisfy the lust of the flesh you will come to a place where you'll do things you never imagined you would do in times past. When you yield to the flesh there is no end to the destruction that can come on you. The wages of sin is death and this is a truth you can't run away from. Desires do not define who you are but you will be held accountable for what you do with those desires. Strong believers cast them down but babes in Christ dwell on them and eventually put actions to their thoughts.

The world is getting darker and darker. What was once considered deplorable is now the norm in today's society. Crowds cheer when a celebrity stands up and announces they're having a relationship with a person of the same sex. They would not clap if they knew what will soon happen. Rom. 1:26,27 says, "For this reason God gave them up to vile passions. For even their women exchanged the natural use for what is against nature. Likewise also the men, leaving the natural use of the woman, burned in their lust for one another, men with men committing what is shameful, and receiving in themselves the penalty of their error which was due." The Message Bible says, "And then they paid for it, oh, how they paid for it - emptied of God, godless and loveless wretches." God is saying that homosexuality is wrong and there is a horrific price to pay if you are that way.

Sexual diseases that lead to an early death don't come on husbands and wives who have a proper sexual relationship. No, they come on those who have sex in an unnatural way and step outside the guidelines put in place by the Master Himself.

A person who is carnal is a person who can't control their desires. Not all desires are bad but they must be controlled. Your flesh has a desire to sleep and eat but if not controlled much damage can be done. Babes in Christ are those who have seen the light but refuse to walk in it. They know sexual sin is wrong but choose to submit to the lusts of their flesh rather than the Word of God. Their hearts are hardened and they follow the world's standards in this area. They may not realize it yet but they are setting themselves up for ultimate destruction if they do not repent. The Bible says they will be destroyed suddenly and without remedy. There is a price to pay for carnality and don't let anybody tell you differently. It pays to be spiritual and it will cost you if you're not. God is merciful when it comes to ignorance but once you've seen the light you will be held accountable for what you do with it. Carnality must be dealt with. You must repent from what you've done and change the way you're living. You must turn away from the standards set up by the world and follow the precepts of God as outlined in the world.

Sin is sin and to overcome carnality you must call it that. If you don't, you'll never be free and you'll never receive the strength and help to overcome it. You can't play games with this. Homosexuality is sin. Adultery is sin. Sexual fantasies are sin. Call it for what it is. If you don't then your flesh will try to convince you that sexual sin is proper and acceptable. It's not and you must call it as such. Your feelings and your desires are not the issue here. The question to be answered is whether or not Jesus is your Lord and is His Word the standard by which you live your life? That is what's at stake here. If the Bible says what you're doing is sin, then stand up and call it that. Confess that you've done wrong and God will be faithful and just to forgive you of that sin. You then have to ask God to help you "to be strengthened with might through His Spirit in the inner man" (Eph. 3:16). When your spirit is strong you can stand up and overcome the sinful nature of the flesh.

The Message Bible says, "My response is to get down on my knees before the Father, the magnificent Father who parcels out all heaven and earth. I ask Him to strengthen you by His Spirit - not a brute strength but a glorious inner strength - that Christ will live in you as you open the door and invite Him in." Babes in Christ are weak spiritually and this is the reason they cave in to sin. The more they sin, the weaker they become and after a while they have no control over what they're doing. To overcome sin you've got to renew your mind and be strengthened in your inner man. You can be so strong in the spirit that you'll starve the lusts of the flesh making it weaker and weaker. The next time an evil temptation comes your way you'll be able to cast it aside with no problem whatsoever. You are strong in the Lord and the devil and your flesh have no power over you. Rom. 13:14 says, "But put on the Lord Jesus Christ, and make no provision for the flesh, to fulfill its lusts." The NLT says, "Instead, clothe yourself with the presence of the Lord Jesus Christ. And don't let yourself think about ways to indulge your evil desires."

There is a principle in life that whatever you feed will in turn grow. If you feed your body, it will grow. If you feed your dog, it will grow. The same principle holds true with your spirit and your flesh. People who are tormented with sexual desire have fed it continually. They watch things they shouldn't watch and look at things they shouldn't look at. All of these wrong things they are doing is feeding that sexual desire and, the more they feed it, the stronger it becomes. The lusts of the flesh are never fulfilled and will torment you day and night unless you starve it and make it weaker. Stop watching those movies that enhance wrongful sexual desires. Put down those books that make you want to sleep with somebody you're not married to. Walk away from those co-workers who are saying things you shouldn't be listening to. Cut off those things that feed your flesh. If you will cut off the supply and the provision the flesh will get weaker and weaker. Give no place to the enemy. Resist him and he will flee.

Feelings are real and it doesn't mean you're not spiritual if you have them. Yes, they are there but the person who walks in the Spirit will control them. Instead of slapping a person who insulted you, you will instead go off and pray for them. You will be nice to an enemy when they don't deserve your kindness. Those who are spiritual control their fleshly feelings, babes in Christ do not. Feelings have a reputation of being uncontrollable. A man with a bad temper is going to get angry all the time and there's nothing he can do about it. People reason that's just the way he is so why try to get him to change. These are all lies of the devil. You can control your feelings and those fleshly desires that come your way. 1 Cor. 9:27 says, "But I discipline my body and bring it into subjection, lest, when I have preached to others, I myself should become disqualified." The NLT says, "I discipline my body like an athlete, training it to do what it should." Not controlling your body will disqualify you from enjoying many of the most prominent blessings in life.

Jesus said in Matt. 26:41, "Watch and pray, lest you enter into temptation. The spirit indeed is willing, but the flesh is weak." People yield to the wrong things through the weakness of their flesh. Your spirit, on the other hand, is born of God and is inclined and predisposed to do the right thing and it's through your spirit that you control your flesh. Paul said he brought his body under subjection and you must do the same. As a born again believer you have power that sinners do not have. Rom. 8:2 says, "For the law of the

Spirit of life in Christ Jesus has made me free from the law of sin and death." You can control your flesh and you can say no to sin. You can control sin for there is no such thing as a temptation you can't deal with. 1 Cor. 10:13 says, "No temptation has overtaken you except such as is common to man; but God is faithful, who will not allow you to be tempted beyond what you are able, but with the temptation will also make the way of escape, that you may be able to bear it." If you encounter a temptation, the Bible says you can overcome it.

People do what they can get away with and it is a lie when they say they can't help but succumb to the temptation. They could have resisted but chose not to. Babes in Christ do this often and are walking on dangerous ground. They've learned about forgiveness but through the weakness of the flesh they reason they can sin today and be forgiven tomorrow. Why control the flesh if God will forgive them anyway? They don't understand that God is not mocked and these people are in for a rude awakening. You can't play with fire and not be burned. There are, however, things you can do to control your flesh and it all begins with making the Word of God the final authority in your life. Nothing else will give you the solid foundation on which to stand. If the Word says it's wrong, it's wrong. You now have a decision to make. Will you obey the Word or will you turn and sin anyway? The Bible says to let not the sun go down on your wrath (Eph. 4:26) but babes in Christ go to bed angry saying they'll deal with the problem in the morning. They knew what to do but chose not to do it.

Too many Christians keep giving in to the flesh. They feel bad afterward but the next day they do the same thing all over again. This happens because of spiritual weakness and this is why you have to read your Bible every day and commit yourself to doing what it says. You can't believe just anything you want to believe and do anything you want to do. You must train and discipline yourself to see what the Word says about a certain matter before you do anything about it. Make the Bible the final authority in your life. If it says don't commit adultery, then don't commit adultery. If it says don't lust after somebody you're not married to, don't do it. If it says to control your appetite then stop eating all those jelly donuts and stop buying candy bars every time you go to the store. It's all about control. Will you control your flesh or will your flesh control you? Who you are and what you become in life is determined by you and you alone and it all begins with how you respond to the everyday feelings and desires of life.

Controlling your feelings is a lot easier said than done. To do this will take a lifetime of determination, endurance, and oftentimes intense struggle and hardship. Emotions are real and relevant in your life and you can't ignore them no matter how hard you try. After all, Jesus himself was a very emotional man. He wept, He got angry, at times He got very frustrated and, in the Garden of Gethsemane, He struggled so fiercely with His emotions that His sweat became as drops of blood. No, you cannot ignore your feelings and, in truth, you're not supposed to. The Bible does not teach you to ignore your feelings but rather to control them. It was Jesus who at times displayed His emotions so openly who said in Luke 21:19, "In your patience, possess your souls." He said that because He knew if you don't take control of your emotions, for sure they will take control of you. Self-control is a fruit of the Spirit (Gal. 5:22,23) and Jesus is saying that one's life should be lived with the trademark of self-control and the diligence and obedience that goes with it.

Living a life of self-control should be a top priority for every believer. The word is a translation of the Greek word 'egkrateia' and is derived from 'kratos' which means "strength and power." The fruit of self-control brings with it the same strength and power that raised Jesus from the dead (Eph. 1:19,20). A believer should have so much control over his emotions that his feelings become his slave. Since a slave has no legal rights of his own and is bound by law to his master, all emotions that are brought into subjection must be obedient to their owner. Do not ask yourself how you feel, tell yourself how you feel. When you take control of your emotions, you take control of your life. According to Paul, the result of not having self-control is to become a "castaway" (1 Cor. 9:27) and in Greek the word is defined as "unapproved, rejected, worthless." Because of a lack of self-control, babes in Christ have become worthless castaways and have dropped out of the race for the incorruptible crown reserved for those who take the Word seriously and are willing to do what it says.

Everything pertaining to your life that you don't control will, in time, control you. If you don't control your spending, it will control you. If you don't control your eating, it will control you. If you don't control what you say and what you look at, both will control you. It takes faith to please God and the more carnal you are, the less faith you will have. There is no such thing as being strong in faith and being weak in spirit. Babes in Christ who do not control their flesh do not walk in faith and are thus not pleasing God. The more they yield to their flesh, the more they forfeit their faith. It undermines their confidence and brings with it guilt and condemnation. They don't hear from God as they should and this allows the enemy to come in and wreak havoc in their lives. Destruction and much confusion will be all around them because they were carnally minded and didn't control their flesh. They lost their ministry, their marriage, and even their will to live all because they let control them that which they didn't control.

Why do people keep giving in to their flesh? They know it's wrong and they've been hurt by it so many times. Still, they give in to it over and over again. Why is this so? Ezek. 16:28,29 (MSG) says, "You went on to fornicate with the Assyrians. Your appetite was insatiable. But still you weren't satisfied. You took on the Babylonians, a country of businessmen, and still you weren't satisfied." The problem is that you can never satisfy the lust of the flesh. The more you feed it, the more it will grow. What the flesh craves today, it will crave twice as much tomorrow. The longer this goes on, the longer you give in to these fleshly feelings and cravings, the harder it will be to take control over it. This is why you have to start right now. Put your foot down and say "No!" to the things the flesh wants you to do. You can do this if your heart is set on doing it. Don't wait until tomorrow because tomorrow never gets here. Start today. Start right now. No temptation is too irresistible that you can't overcome it if you will just draw a line in the sand and say "No more!"

-6-
"OVERCOMING TEMPTATION"

Christianity is a life of freedom and you can be more free today than you were last month and last year. This happens when you put into practice the truths you learn in God's Word. The good news is that you have a Savior who knows what it's like to live in a world filled with darkness. He knows what you're going through because He's been there and is not out of touch with the harsh realities of day-to-day living. Heb. 4:15 (NLT) says, "This High Priest of ours understands our weaknesses, for He faced all of the same testings we do, yet He did not sin." The NIV says He was "tempted in every way, just as we are." Have you even been tempted to lie and steal? So was Jesus. Have you even been tempted to give in to the lusts of the flesh? So was Jesus. Have you ever been tempted to punch somebody in the face and to spit in his eye? So was Jesus. He knows what it's like to be you and, because of that, vs. 16 says, "Let us therefore come boldly to the throne of grace to help in time of need."

When temptations come, Jesus is the one to turn to. Heb. 2:18 (NLT) says, "Since He himself has gone through suffering and testing, He is able to help us when we are being tested." Jesus knows what it's like to be tested for, if He didn't, He wouldn't be able to relate to what you're going through. It is not a sin to be tempted because Jesus was tempted and He never sinned. Never feel condemned when you're tempted to do something you're not supposed to do.

This doesn't mean there's something wrong with you, it only means you're a member of the human race. Temptation comes to everybody but not everybody handles temptation the same way. Many give in to it, some don't. Babes in Christ submit to temptation but those who are spiritual run to Jesus whose motto about temptation is "been there, done that." He knows what you're going through and the NIV says in Heb. 2:18, "Because He himself suffered when he was tempted, He is able to help those who are being tempted." When temptation comes, there is no better person to run to than Jesus.

It would not be right for Jesus to hold you to such a high standard of living if He didn't go through the same things you're going through. He really does know what it's like to be tempted to lust after a pretty woman. Been there, done that. People might find that hard to believe because of who He is but He walked the earth as a human just like you. He had the same appetites you have and the same physical impulses you experience each and every day. He got angry and was tempted to let it get out of control. He was tempted to do what He wanted to do instead of submitting to the will of the Father. He was tempted in things that most people will never be tempted in, yet through it all, not once did He give in to the temptation and not once did He sin. The gospel message is that if Jesus can overcome temptation, then you can also if you will renew your mind and believe that it is possible. If you will turn to Him, you will find that He is more than willing and is wonderfully able to help you when temptation comes your way.

The problem many people have is they don't want to deal with temptation because they're afraid to admit they're being tempted. They run away from it because for centuries the church has taught people that there is something terribly wrong with a person if they're tempted to do something that is evil and despicable. In their wayward minds there is a shame associated with being tempted. Jesus never felt ashamed because temptation is not a sin. You have not been tempted with something Jesus was never tempted with and, if He never felt ashamed, neither do you have to feel that way. There is no sin and shame in being tempted, so don't let the dark clouds of guilt hang over your head when you are. There is nothing wrong with you if a certain thought comes to your mind. Just don't dwell on it if it's not a Godly thought. It's the giving in to temptation where there's a problem. Cast the thought aside and begin to meditate on things that are lovely, pure, and of a good report.

People in today's world have a perverted belief of what freedom is all about. They think freedom gives them the right to do anything they want no matter what God or anybody else says about it. If they want to marry a person of the same sex, they feel they have the freedom to do so. Many people don't go to church and make a full commitment to the Lord because they want to be free to live however they want. The enemy is telling people that if they get saved they'll be in bondage and won't be able to fulfill the lusts of their flesh. This is twisted thinking because the Bible says if you live this way you are in bondage and a slave to sin. True freedom comes when you come out of living a life of willful, habitual sin. Rom. 6:5-7 (NLT) says, "Since we have been united with Him in His death, we will also be raised to life as He was. We know that our old sinful selves were crucified with Christ so that sin might lose its power in our lives. We are no longer slaves to sin. For where we died with Christ we were set free from the power of sin."

There is no freedom in being a drug addict or a homosexual or having a mistress when you are married. This is bondage of the worst kind because people who do such things are not convicted that what they're doing is wrong. Their conscience has grown cold and their hearts they no longer listen to. They are slaves to sin. Deep down they may want to escape from this deplorable lifestyle but the world in which they live does not have the answer for them. Like quicksand, the only thing the world wants to do is pull them deeper and deeper into the abyss of sin. The only answer for them is Christ and Him alone. He was tempted with everything they are and overcame every one of them. In Christ you can go boldly to the throne of God and find grace to help in time of need (Heb. 4:16). Because He's been there and gone through the exact same temptation, He is able to help you overcome those evil desires and thoughts that you are tempted with. He is on your side and when you got born again your sin nature died with Christ and you were set free from the power of sin.

When you get born again you have the power inside of you to never again yield to temptation. No longer do you have to satisfy the wrong appetites or those desires that you know are wrong. No longer do you have to serve your body or a mind that is not renewed. You are free in Jesus and no longer have to serve sin. Sin is not your master for Paul writes in Rom. 6:10,11 (NLT), "When He died, He died once to break the power of sin. But now that He lives, He lives for the glory of God. So you also should consider yourselves to be dead to the power of sin and alive to God through Christ Jesus." The Message Bible says, "Sin speaks a dead language that means nothing to you; God speaks your mother tongue, and you hang on every word. You are dead to sin and alive to God. That's what Jesus did." It is a lie when babes in Christ say they couldn't help themselves and this is why they did what they did. There is no temptation that can overwhelm you and cause you to sin unless you yield to it. The power to resist temptation was there, they just didn't tap into it.

Rom. 6:12-14 (NLT) says, "Do not let sin control the way you live, do not give in to sinful desires. Do not let any part of your body become an instrument of evil to serve sin. Instead, give yourselves completely to God, for you were dead, but now you have new life. So use your whole body as an instrument to do what is right for the glory of God. Sin is no longer your master, for you no longer live under the requirements of the law. Instead, you live under the freedom of God's grace." Do not yield to sin and let it dominate your life. Yes, temptations will come but don't feel condemned about it. Recognize where it came from and refuse to give in to it. You are not a puppet on a string. The devil cannot make you do something you don't want to do. Just because the temptation is there does not mean you are a bad person. Jesus was tempted and He is not a bad person and neither are you. You are a child of the living God and the more your mind is renewed with the Word of God, the easier it will be to resist the temptations when they do come.

People fall into sin because they refuse to admit they have a problem. They run away from admitting they're being tempted in a certain area and because of that they give in to fleshly desires and fall into sin. They don't realize that being tempted puts them in good company because Jesus was also tempted with the same thing. Another reason people fall into sin is because their flesh suffers when resistance is made. It's a whole lot easier on the flesh to give in to temptation than it is to resist it even though the consequences will be much worse. In the Garden of Gethsemane, Jesus fought off temptation "when He had offered up prayers and supplications, with vehement cries and tears to Him who was able to save Him from death, and was heard because of His godly fear, though He was a Son, yet He learned obedience by the things which He suffered" (Heb. 5:7,8). The Message Bible says, "Jesus cried out in pain and wept in sorrow as He offered up priestly prayers to God." Nobody ever said resisting temptation was easy, but it's well worth the pain and effort to do it.

Before Jesus went off to pray, He told His disciples, "Pray that you will not give in to temptation" (Luke 22:40 NLT). He then went off and did what He told them to do. Vs. 44 says,

"He prayed more fervently, and He was in such agony of spirit that His sweat fell to the ground like great drops of blood." This may not paint a pretty picture for you until you realize what happened as a result of Jesus resisting this temptation. He is now seated at the right hand of the Heavenly Father and has become the source of eternal salvation for all those who obey Him. Yes, temptation is real and it's not always pleasant to deal with. A part of you wants to give in to it and another part of you doesn't. James 1:14 (NLT) says, "Temptation comes from our own desires, which entice us and drag us away." It's not always the devil who is tempting you; sometimes it's your own fleshy self. The Message Bible says, "The temptation to give in to evil comes from us and only us. We have no one to blame but the leering, seducing flare-up of our own lust."

A part of you wants to give in to the temptation but if it doesn't then the devil has nothing to work with. Heb. 11:25 says Moses chose "to suffer affliction with the people of God than to enjoy the passing pleasures of sin." Sin is fun for a season and this is why people are tempted to do it. Fleshly pleasures and the promise of having a good time is the bait on the hook that the devil uses to draw people into his deadly snare. Be aware of this because temptation comes to everybody. Most people don't consider the consequences of their actions. They're focusing on the pleasures of having an extra-marital affair and don't consider the sexual disease they might obtain or the breakup of their home and marriage. There is always a price to pay for sin. Nobody ever gets away with anything for sooner or later it will catch up to them. Those who do get caught will always say that what they did was not worth the consequences they paid for doing it. The problem is now it's too late to do anything about it. The officer delivering divorce papers to them is now knocking on their front door.

Jesus was tempted just like you and, because He didn't yield to it, He is able to help you rise up and not give in also. The Holy Spirit will help you even when a part of you is screaming because you want to do it. The Greater One is inside of you and you will be able to overcome the temptation. Like Jesus, you can pray and be strong and when pushed beyond measure you can rise up and say what He did when He was tempted, "Not My will, but Your will be done." Jesus suffered mightily in the Garden of Gethsemane and if you are to overcome like He did then you will need endurance. You don't resist temptation one time and that's the end of it. No, the same temptation will come back and you must resist it over and over again. Some people resist for a season and eventually give in to it and lose the battle. Not Jesus. He had endurance because His love for the Father was stronger than the temptation. He wanted to please Him more than anything He personally wanted to do. He submitted His will to the will of the Father.

When tempted, James 4:6,7 tells you what you must do, "But He gives more grace. Therefore He says: 'God resists the proud, but gives grace to the humble.' Therefore submit to God. Resist the devil and he will flee from you." The BBE Bible says, "For this cause be ruled by God; but make war on the Evil One and he will be put to flight before you." The NJB says, "Give in to God" and the Wuest translation tells you to "Be subject with implicit obedience to God at once and once for all. Stand immovable against the onset of the devil and he will flee from you." James is issuing an urgent call to his readers to repent from their ungodly behavior described in the preceding passages. He says in vs. 8, "Draw near to God and He will draw near to you. Cleanse your hands, you sinners; and purify your hearts, you double-minded." Like a commanding general James issues a series of military-like commands which call for incisive action. The command to submit is a basic requirement which must precede obedience to the subsequent commands.

Proud people by definition are elevated above others and do not submit and surely won't obey any of the other commands. Only the humble receive the grace of God and to be a partaker of this grace you must choose daily to submit and surrender your will and your desires to that good and acceptable and perfect will of God (Rom. 12:2b). Only the lowly person, the humble man or woman, will willingly surrender his or her rights to God. Humility is among the qualities that you simply can not pursue directly. Along with traits such as self-control, patience, endurance, peace, and joy, humility is a by-product of living God's way and seeking and submitting to His will. When you give God His place over you and you take your place under Him, now the devil has to take his place under your feet. Don't start quoting James 4:7 beginning with "Resist the devil." James is saying that unless you are submitted to God first you will not have the power to resist the devil.

The world is full of sloppy Christians and undisciplined believers. Many Christians are too passive. Passivity is allowing the enemy to destroy people and this is why all believers must rise up and be strong. You must submit to God and resist the devil. The devil will flee from you because you have a place of authority over him but this won't happen until you first give God His place of authority over you. Don't give place to the devil for if you are yielding to the enemy he does not have to yield to you. Total submission to the will of God is a Christian duty of prime excellence. Don't rebel against submission, embrace it with all your heart and soul. Rebellion opens the door for calamity to come into your life and the fear of submitting will keep you from enjoying all Godly blessings. You can be healed today and have the sickness return tomorrow if you rebel and don't submit. Submission and obedience make the blessings stay in your life.

People run from the very thing they should run to. Don't run from submission, run to it. Jesus submitted to the will of the Father and said in Matt. 11:29, "Take My yoke upon you and learn from me, for I am gentle and lowly in heart, and you will find rest for your souls." Submission is unconditional surrender and is not an easy thing to do. It involves suffering and if people say submission is easy for them they haven't got a clue what true submission is. Jesus was in total submission to the Father yet He suffered in the Garden of Gethsemane when He was tempted. Temptation is the avenue through which the devil attempts to get you to not submit to the will of God. You suffer when you have to put your flesh down. In the Garden of Gethsemane Jesus cried out in pain and wept in sorrow as He prayed three times, "O My Father, if it is possible, let this cup pass from Me" (Matt. 26:39). Jesus did not want the pain of being rejected and forsaken by His Father as He hung on the cross and took on the sins of the world.

Jesus is being tempted to not go to the cross and He is suffering. True submission happens when you are not in agreement with what you are being told to do. In the Garden of Gethsemane the will of Jesus was not the same as the will of the Father. If their will was the same Jesus could not have said, "Not My will, but Your will be done." Jesus submitted His will to the Father's will. He put His flesh down and submitted to the will of the Father. This was not easy and this was not agreement. There is much confusion in the body of Christ in this area. You only have the opportunity to truly submit when you don't agree. As long as you want to do what the person over you wants you to do there is no submission involved. Your will is their will. This is not submission, it is agreement. To submit when you don't agree, you must put your flesh under, bite your lip, and do what you don't want to do. Your attitude is "not my will but Your will be done."

There is no other way to grow and mature. Jesus learned obedience through the things He suffered, by not getting to do what He wanted to do and by yielding to the will of the One over Him. 1 Peter 5:6,7 says, "Therefore humble yourselves under the hand of God, that He may exalt you in due time, casting all your care upon Him, for He cares for you." Your cares are about yourself and Peter is saying to cast what you want on Jesus and go do what you've been told to do. He knows what you need and if you will walk in faith He'll provide it for you. Humble yourself and bring your flesh under submission. Be teachable, be willing to humble yourself and take correction. Be willing to submit. True submission involves suffering, the pain and discomfort of not getting your own way. You suffered being tempted to rebel and be disobedient. Rebellion is the very nature of the devil and if you yield to rebellion you are not suffering.

Submission is not a bad suffering, it's a good suffering. Some things need to be put to death in you. Paul said in Gal. 5:24,25, "And those who are Christ's have crucified the flesh with its passions and desires. If we live in the Spirit, let us also walk in the Spirit." The Message Bible says, "Among those who belong to Christ, everything connected with getting our own way and mindlessly responding to what everyone else calls necessities is killed off for good - crucified." When rebellion sets in you need to crucify your flesh and pull out the spikes and hammer. Is it easy? No! Jesus sweat blood doing this. Can you do it? Yes! You can do it by the grace of God. Should you do it? Yes! Is it worth it? Yes, a million times yes! Is there reward for doing it? Notice the results in 1 Peter 5:9,10, "Resist him, steadfast in the faith, knowing that the same sufferings are experienced by your brotherhood in the world. But may the God of all grace, who called us to His eternal glory by Christ Jesus, after you have suffered a while, perfect, establish, strengthen, and settle you."

When you put your flesh down and submit you become like a mighty tree whose roots go down deep. You become like the house that's built on the rock. You become perfected, matured, established, settled, and strengthened. You become Christ-like and are pillars of strength in a world filled with pride and rebellion. You're not moved by every wind of doctrine and every whim of your flesh and you don't give in to temptation. How do people get this way? They suffered not getting their own way. They suffered saying to God, "Not my will but Your will be done." God does not change because He doesn't have to change. He gets it right every time. He's right every time about everything. And since He's right all the time you must submit yourself to Him and to what He says is right and true. Submission is to do what you're told by those over you and smile while you're doing it. Submission goes to the heart of God and reveals how He operates. He could make you do anything but He allows you to obey willingly. If a person is forced to do something then it's not true submission.

You were not put on this planet just so you could make a living and raise a family. No, you are here to make a contribution to the kingdom of God. And when you step forward to do so, without a doubt the enemy will come knocking on your door. The devil wants to control you and he doesn't care if it's your will or not. Every day countless prayers are going up to God asking Him to make the devil stop harassing those who are saying the prayer. These people are ignorant of the Word for there is not one verse in the Bible telling you to pray and ask God to make the devil leave you alone. Not one! Yet people pray for this several times each day. James said "you" submit to God and "you" resist the devil. How do you submit to God? First, you submit to His Word. If the Word tells you to do something, you do it. Don't pray about what the Bible tells you to do. You're either going to do it or you're not.

Finally, you submit to God by submitting to those He has placed in positions of authority over you. God gives those in authority wisdom and grace that others don't get, not because of who they are personally but because of the position they hold. You may be more spiritual than those in leadership and know more Bible verses but not have the grace and anointing to lead like they do. Leaders are called and empowered by God to lead and when you submit to their authority you submit to God. Jesus told many of His disciples, "Come, follow Me" and they left what they were doing and followed Him. When you follow a person who says "come" you are in submission to that person. You drawing near to God reveals your submission to Him. You have come into His presence with thanksgiving in your heart and you have entered His courts with praise. The blessings of life come when you hearken to His voice, when you "come" when He calls you to do so, when you submit to His authority. Submission is a beautiful thing and has many, many rewards. Embrace it today.

-7-

"SEPARATE YOURSELF"

During the prime viewing season of any professional sport, advertisers will bombard the airwaves with various commercials trying to get the audience to become like the superstar athletes of their respective sport. They'll try to get you to drink what they drink and to wear the same shoes they wear. If a famous athlete drives a certain make and model of car, then you should drive one also. They are exploiting the people's admiration for these star athletes by suggesting if they'll buy their product, they'll then be like the person they so highly acclaim. What these advertisers and the viewing audience don't know is that people who inspire to be like a star athlete are setting their sights too low. Jesus is to be your example and every day you should endeavor to become just like Him. Never desire to be like any man or woman, past or present, because if you do you'll also duplicate their faults and weaknesses. Jesus is the person you should want to be like and this is why Paul wrote in 1 Cor. 11:1, "Imitate me, just as I imitate Christ."

Jesus should be your inspiration for what you want your life to become. Heb. 7:26 says, "For such a High Priest was fitting for us, who is holy, harmless, undefiled, separate from sinners, and has become higher than the heavens." The NLT says, "He is the kind of high priest we need because He is holy and blameless, unstained by sin. He has been set apart from sinners and has been given the highest place of honor in heaven." The thing that set Jesus above everybody else was that He was unstained by sin. He was holy and separate from sinners. To be like Jesus you must be the same way. 2 Cor. 6:17,18 says, "Therefore, 'Come out from among them and be separate,' says the Lord. 'Do not touch what is unclean, and I will receive you. I will be a Father to you, and you shall be My sons and daughters.' says the Lord Almighty." The Message Bible says, "So leave the corruption and compromise; leave it for good. Don't link up with those who will pollute you. I want you all to Myself. I'll be a Father to you; you'll be sons and daughters to Me."

Jesus is holy and to be like Him you need to cleanse yourself "from all filthiness of the flesh and spirit, perfecting holiness in the fear of God" (2 Cor. 7:1). The NIV says "let us purify ourselves from everything that contaminates body and spirit, perfecting holiness out of reverence for God." People believe that only Jesus can be holy and that no one person can reach such a high standard of living. These people do not understand that their conduct is not what makes them acceptable to God. Their best behavior could not make them righteous before God. It's His righteousness that makes you righteous and it's His blood that makes you holy. You don't cleanse yourself from all sin to become holy, you purify yourself because you are holy. You need to let what's inside of you dominate how you talk and act on the outside. Many people never try to better themselves because the enemy has convinced them that holiness is something they'll never achieve. Why climb the holiness mountain if you'll never be able to reach the top?

Paul said you have to cleanse yourself from all filthiness of the flesh and spirit. This is something you do and it begins when you separate yourself from the wrong people and the wrong environments that will contaminate and defile you. You are not of this world but you are in the world and there are a lot of bad things here that can pollute your life and bring you down. There are things that can contaminate you on the inside and there are things that will contaminate you on the outside. Jesus is your role model and as you strive to become just like Him you will walk away from those situations that have the potential to harm your life. Don't allow anything to hinder your faith and your confidence in God. Holiness plays a huge part to the answers you're looking for and to your development in God. It affects how sensitive you are to hearing His voice and being led by the Holy Spirit. He is a holy God and holiness is the realm and domain in which He lives and operates. He is holy and you need to be just like Him.

Jesus is to be your standard. If you will act like Him and talk like Him, you will be holy. Do not fall into the trap of trying to compare yourself to other people. Doing this will cause you to think you're better than they are and will give you a "holier than thou" superiority complex. Is. 6:5 says there are those who say, "'Keep to yourself, do not come near me, for I am holier than you!' These are smoke in My nostrils, a fire that burns all the day." The Message Bible says, "These people gag Me. I can't stand their stench." God does not like it when you compare yourself to anybody other than Him when determining what your life and behavior should be like. Your neighbor goes to church once a week and you go three times so this means you are holier than they are. Wrong! Do not compare yourself to other people to determine how holy you are. True holiness does not give you a feeling of superiority over other people. That is pride and Prov. 16:18 says, "Pride goes before destruction, and a haughty spirit before a fall."

Jesus taught about this in the parable of the Pharisee and the tax collector found in Luke 18:9-14, "Also He spoke this parable to some who trusted in themselves that they were righteous, and despised others: 'Two men went up to the temple to pray, one a Pharisee and the other a tax collector. The Pharisee stood and prayed thus with himself, "God, I thank You that I am not like other men - extortioners, unjust, adulterers, or even as this tax collector. I fast twice a week; I give tithes of all that I possess." And the tax collector, standing afar off, would not so much as raise his eyes to heaven, but beat his breast, saying, "God, be merciful to me a sinner!" I tell you, this man went down to his house justified rather than the other; for everyone who exalts himself will be abased, and he who humbles himself will be exalted.'" Jesus told this story to those who were complacently pleased with themselves over their moral performance and looked down their noses at the common people. He was telling people to not be this way.

You need to separate yourself from ungodliness, sin, and things that defile. Luke 6:14,15 says, "Do not be unequally yoked together with unbelievers. For what fellowship has righteousness with lawlessness? And what communion has light with darkness? And what accord has Christ with Belial? Or what part has a believer with an unbeliever?" Many associate these verses with marriage saying that a Christian should not marry a person who is not saved. This is true but what Paul is saying here goes way beyond that. He is also saying to not associate with family members and co-workers who use foul language all the time and always talk bad about other people. They don't want to hear what you have to say and, for sure, you don't want to hear what they have to say. Paul is telling you to separate yourself and come out from among them. If you don't, in time you'll find yourself doing the same things they are. It was Paul who said in 1 Cor. 15:33, "Do not be deceived: 'Evil company corrupts good habits.'"

Be aware of people who want to hear nothing about God. They don't want His name mentioned and they don't want Him talked about. They've taken God completely out of their lives and these are the people you are to separate yourself from. If God lives in your heart then He goes wherever you go. He's in you and you're in Him. If people don't want anything to do with Him, then neither do they want anything to do with you. Even Jesus said in Matt. 10:14, "And whoever will not receive you nor hear your words, when you depart from that house or city, shake off the dust from your feet." People may argue that Jesus ate with sinners. Yes, but they wanted to hear what He had to say. They were receptive to His words and not like those who cast God out of their lives forever. By all means, if somebody is willing to listen to you talk about Jesus, then do it with all your heart and soul. How else will the sinner hear the gospel message unless someone tells them about it? Share with those who want to hear about Jesus, separate yourself from those who don't.

To be holy you will have to confront the issue of sin. In many Christian circles this subject is almost never talked about and many are hesitant to even say the word. Instead of calling sin for what it is, they say a person has a problem and they're working on it. No, that person is sinning and it should be called such. This will make some people angry but you can't be vague when it comes to sin. You must call it for what it is. Jesus said in John 7:17, "The world cannot hate you, but it hates Me because I testify of it that its works are evil." Jesus called sin for what it was and the people wanted to kill Him for doing so. He confronted sin to the point of throwing the moneychangers out of the temple and turning over all their tables (Matt. 21:12). You need to hate and despise all sin. People try to minimize their wrongdoing by calling some sins small and other sins big. They say they told a "little white lie" but Rev. 21:8 says all liars will have their place in the lake of fire. How small is that?

Sin is just not an outward, physical act. Sin is what happens in your heart. Sin is serious and you can't sugarcoat it. Rom. 6:23 says the wages of sin is death. You're not told to separate yourself from sinners to spoil your fun, God says to separate yourself from sin because it will kill you. You may still be breathing but the Bible says Adam and Eve died spiritually the day they sinned. Every time you sin, something inside of you dies. People who don't repent and turn away from their sin are walking around half dead. They're no longer as happy as they used to be and things seem to always be going wrong in their lives. No longer do they act right and no longer do they think right. Their mind is cloudy and good decisions can no longer be made. Tempers flare up and jobs are lost and relationships are broken. There is no more joy and peace in the lives of the habitual sinner. They are dying on the inside and it's all because of the sin they didn't separate themselves from.

1 John 1:6 says, "If we say we have fellowship with Him, and walk in darkness, we lie and do not practice the truth." Light and darkness don't mix. You can't walk in full fellowship with the Lord and walk in sin. Sin is any action that displeases God, anything that is outside of His will. Vs. 7 says, "But if we walk in the light as He is in the light, we have fellowship with one another." When you are walking in the light you have, when your ways are pleasing to Him, you will have fellowship with God and He will have fellowship with you. Vs. 7 continues, "and the blood of Jesus Christ His Son cleanses us from all sin." This is not a past-tense cleansing but an ever-present washing away of those things you don't know and see. There is some light that hasn't been revealed to you yet and, when you miss the mark in that area, God is merciful and will cleanse you from that sin. This is an ongoing, continuous thing God does because if He didn't do it, there would always be something between you and Him.

God is not trying to find a reason to keep His distance from you. He loves you so much that He moved heaven and earth in an effort to get close to you. Now it's your turn to draw near to Him by walking in the light you've been given. When you don't walk in the light, you are in violation of the will of God. Sin is violation of light and God will not hold you responsible for something you haven't seen yet. He is a just God but He is merciful and fair. All He asks is that you walk in the light you've been given. If you will do that, then you will be cleansed of everything else you don't know. You'll be washed by the blood of Jesus and this is how God is able to see you as pure and clean. He could not see you as "the righteousness of God in Christ Jesus" except by this continual cleansing. When you walk in the light you have, God will look at you and see the manifestation of holiness. He sees righteousness and purity because He sees you in the blood of Jesus, the One who was spotless and without sin.

Sin is when you do something you know you're not supposed to do. It's a violation of the light you've been given. James 4:17 says, "Therefore, to him who knows to do good and does not do it, to him it is sin." This verse is not universal but is solely directed to the person who knows what he's supposed to do. What may be a sin to one person may not be a sin to another person. Some people have light in a certain area that other people may not have. God is saying that if a person has light but doesn't do it, to him it is sin. 1 John 1:8 says, "If we say that we have no sin, we deceive ourselves, and the truth is not in us." This verse appears to be contradictory to the preceding verse. How can a person be cleansed from all sin and be wrong in saying they have no sin? This verse is not talking about those who have been cleansed. It's referring to those in vs. 6 who say they have fellowship with God and continue to walk in darkness. People who are deceived are those who walk in darkness yet say they have no sin.

1 John 1:9 was written for those who violated the light they've been given, "If we confess our sins, He is faithful and just to forgive us our sins and to cleanse us from all unrighteousness." Here again is the importance of calling sin for what it is. Don't confess you have a problem and don't make a fool of God by saying maybe you missed it

somewhere and maybe you didn't. No, call it for what it is. Confess that you violated the light you've been given and that you willfully sinned. Period! No if's, and's, or but's about it. The key to successful repentance is bare-hearted, sincere honesty. You cannot play games with God and walk clean. People who lie and are dishonest can't be helped. Christians over the years have perfected the art of pretending they didn't know what they were doing was wrong even after the light was given to them in that particular area. This is when excuses are made and the tears flow. People who do that are not repenting and will not be forgiven.

The spirit of death is on the person who is not forgiven. With unforgiveness comes guilt and condemnation and this is why you have to be honest and call sin for what it is. Those who fall to pieces are not sorry for what they did but are sorrowful because they got caught. This is not a laughing matter. Those who make excuses for their sin are deceived and will turn around and try to deceive God. Adam blamed his wife and Eve blamed the serpent. There is nothing more serious in life than not speaking the truth. There never has been, and never will be, an acceptable and excusable lie. To lie and deceive is one of the most serious and worst things you can do in life. People are highly skilled in the art of deception. They'll tell you what somebody did wrong to them but won't tell you what they did to the other person. Children tell their parents they didn't put their hand in the cookie jar when crumbs are falling out of their mouths. God cannot help people who are not honest and will not confess that what they did was wrong. You must call sin for what it is.

Lying is the language of the devil and, when you won't admit you've done wrong, you're siding with the enemy. You're becoming just like he is for John 8:44 says "he is a liar and the father of it." It is the plan of the enemy to pull you into a sinkhole of sin and despair. Not only did you do wrong in the first place, you're now lying to cover it up. Don't do this. You can't fool God so be honest about it. Go before Him with humbleness and confess that you violated the light you've been given. The word "violate" means 'to break, to disregard, to fail to show the proper respect for.' When you confess your sin, you're admitting that God gave you some light but you did not regard it with the proper respect. This is how darkness sets in. If something is wrong in your life and things aren't going right for you, then somewhere along the line you didn't walk in the light you had. You need to separate yourself from sin and you can do this through the blood of the Lamb and prompt obedience.

It is a wonderful thing to hear from God and to walk in the light. If you will do what God tells you to do, your problems would be fixed and your life would be glorious. You'll be abundantly blessed and you'l be a blessing to others. This will happen when you separate yourself from sin and come out from among them that do. Do not subject yourself to unnecessary temptation. Don't watch programs you know you shouldn't watch and don't go to places you know you shouldn't go to. God will help you but He won't do it for you. You've got to get your will involved and give Him something to work with. Stay away from things that will pull you down and distract you from living a holy life. Paul said you have to cleanse yourself from all forms of darkness. Walk away from people who use foul language and tell dirty jokes. Stay away from that part of town where women stand on street corners offering to have sex with you for a certain amount of money. Stay away from those things that will bind you up and hold you captive. Walk away from such things and don't look back.

Sin is deceitful. Heb. 3:12,13 says, "Beware, brethren, lest there be in any of you an evil heart of unbelief in parting from the living God; but exhort one another daily, while it is called "Today," lest any of you be hardened through the deceitfulness of sin." The devil will only show you the pleasure side of sin. His biggest weapon is deception and he'll get people to believe it's okay to sin if nothing bad happens to them right away as a result of their wrongdoing. The deception and the sin are never far apart (1 Tim. 2:14). People who don't read the Bible and don't go to church have hardened their hearts to the things of God and have become unteachable and unchangeable. These people don't know the truth and have become prime targets of the enemy because they are easily deceived. The good news is that the more truth you know, the more difficult it will be for the devil to get you into sin. He can't deceive you because your heart is not hardened and you're walking in the light. You know the truth and the truth sets you free.

The devil is not as tough as he deceives people into thinking he is. He is a defeated foe and Jesus said in Luke 11:20, "But if I cast out demons with the finger of God, surely the kingdom of God has come upon you." God is all powerful yet all it takes to cast the enemy out is His little finger. You, also, have this same power if God lives in your heart. The next time the devil comes to tempt you, just flick your finger and watch him run. He knows you can do this and that's the reason he uses deception to sneak in the back door of your life. He'll try to get you to think that you're a wretched sinner when the Bible says you're dead to sin and have become a new creation in Christ. Jesus is the personification of holiness and you become holy when you become like Him. He was separate from sin and never once gave in to temptation. He was the ultimate example of how to live a holy, righteous life. As He is, so are you to be in this world.

You need to purpose in your heart to separate yourself from those things that displease God. The devil will deceive you into thinking that it's impossible to go a day without sinning. That's not true. You can go days and weeks without sinning. Rom. 6:11,12 says, "Likewise you also, reckon yourselves to be dead indeed to sin, but alive to God in Christ Jesus our Lord. Therefore do not let sin reign in your mortal body, that you should obey it in its lusts." Vs. 14 says, "For sin shall not have dominion over you, for you are not under law but under grace." The Message Bible says, "That means you must not give sin a vote in the way you conduct your lives. Don't give it the time of day. Throw yourselves wholeheartedly and fulltime into God's way of doing things. Sin can't tell you how to live." You are dead to sin and it shall not have dominion over you. Dead people do not commit adultery, and neither do they lie and cheat and manipulate. You are to consider yourself dead to sin because sometimes it will feel like your flesh is alive and well. Consider it dead anyway.

You can do this. You can treat your fleshly desires as though they're dead. Babes in Christ and the unsaved do not have the power to do this but in Christ you do. The Greater One is inside of you and your spirit is alive. The purpose of every temptation is to get you to believe you're no longer dead to that particular sin. If the devil can deceive you into believing that, you'll then miss the mark and sin will happen. Always remember that because of Jesus you are now dead to sin. Don't let the devil tell you differently. The power of suggestion is the only weapon he has but, if your mind is renewed with the Word of God, you'll be able to resist that temptation with a flick of your finger. Inside of you is the strength to do this. When you're in the light, darkness must flee. You are in control of your thoughts, feelings, and desires. You tell your body what it can and cannot do. Jesus was separate from sin and so are you.

You are a child of a holy God and all His children should also be holy. As you separate yourself from sin, holiness is being perfected in the fear of God. It's the blood of the Lamb that cleanses you of all sin before Him. Likewise, you cannot attain righteousness or holiness through your own works so you must receive His righteousness and His holiness. Rom. 5:17 says you receive from God grace and "the gift of righteousness." 2 Cor. 5:21 says, "For He made Him who knew no sin to be sin for us, that we might become the righteousness of God in Him." If you have been made righteous, then it only stands to reason that you should live righteous and holy lives. 1 Cor. 1:30 (NLT) says, "God has united you with Christ Jesus. For our benefit God made Him to be wisdom itself. Christ made us right with God; He made us pure and holy, and He freed us from sin." The Message Bible says, "Everything that we have - right thinking and right living, a clean slate and a fresh start - comes from God by way of Jesus Christ."

You being made the righteousness of God is the most exciting thing that will ever happen to you. Much more than forgiveness of sins happened when you gave your life to Christ. Eph. 2:6 (NLT) says, "For He raised us from the dead along with Christ and seated us with Him in the heavenly realms because we are united with Christ Jesus." In the eyes of the Father, you are seated at His right hand alongside Jesus. You are in the dwelling place of the Almighty and in this throne room is the seat of all power and dominion. It's the place where God rules over all principalities and powers, and reigns over the affairs of men. As surely as Christ was raised from the dead, you've also been raised up with Him by the Heavenly Father. And just as surely as Jesus was taken to the throne of glory, you've also been taken with Him to the same glorious place. Because you are in Him, you are also where He is at. In Jesus resides all wisdom and power and strength and, because you are seated with Him, you've been given access to all these riches and everything you need to live a victorious, fruitful life.

Because you are righteous, you will walk as Jesus walked and talk as Jesus talked. You will be holy as He is holy. He will be manifested in you each and every day. He is in you and will live through you wherever you go. The devil can't influence believers who are seated with Christ in heavenly places for it is a position of authority, honor, and triumph. People who are righteous do not sin because they love pleasing God more than they love pleasing their flesh. It's really very simple. What you love more is what you will do. John 3:19,20 says, "And this is the condemnation, that the light has come into the world, and men loved darkness rather than light, because their deeds were evil. For everyone practicing evil hates the light and does not come to the light, lest his deeds should be exposed." God loves you more than anything and He expects you to feel the same way about Him. He is a jealous God and He is unwilling to share first place in your life with anybody or anything. Think about that the next time the devil tempts you to sin.

Randall J. Brewer

-8-

"CONTROLLING THE FLESH"

The flesh is real, it is present in your life, and it must be dealt with. Paul said in 1 Cor. 9:27, "But I discipline my body and bring it into subjection, lest, when I have preached to others, I myself should become disqualified." Paul was a great man of God but still he had to discipline his body every single day. He knew that if he didn't control his body, then his body would control him. Millions of lives and relationships have been destroyed because somebody didn't control their flesh. Rom. 8:5 says, "For those who live according to the flesh set their minds on the things of the flesh, but those who live according to the Spirit, the things of the Spirit." It takes faith to please God and live a victorious life, and the more carnal a person is, the less faith they will have. People are deceived when they think they can yield to the flesh all the time and still have strong faith. Their lives are collapsing around them and this is proof that what they're thinking is not true. It takes a strong spirit to have strong faith.

Faith is of the heart and the more you yield to the flesh, the more it will undermine your confidence to receive from God. The devil doesn't play fair. He'll tempt you to sin and when you do, he'll cause you to feel condemned for what you did. He knows that condemnation is an enemy of faith because a person can't be confident and feel condemned at the same time. Nothing but harm comes to a person who walks in the flesh yet some believers do it continually. When their sin finds them out they'll cry and repent yet, before the sun goes down, they're doing the exact same thing all over again. Why does this happen? First of all, they weren't truly sorry in the first place and, secondly, they never determined in their heart to once and for all say no to their flesh. The flesh is always hungry for satisfaction and they just keep feeding it and feeding it until the bottom falls out of their life and the world around them comes crashing down. This happens because they are carnally minded and their spirit is weak.

You can control your flesh if you want to control your flesh. You can become strong in spirit so you don't give in to whatever your flesh wants to do. There is no such thing as a temptation you cannot resist for God promises that He will make a way of escape for you. Nothing is too hard for the Lord and, if you are strong in Him, you'll be able to resist the enemy when he comes knocking on your door. Babes in Christ give in to the lusts of the flesh and afterward will make excuses for why they did what they did. Unbelief always makes excuses and this is why they miss the mark and won't do what it takes to grow strong in the Lord. These people need to humble themselves and be honest with themselves and with God. They need to call sin for what it is and admit they did wrong. People who make excuses don't ask to be forgiven because they think it's always somebody else's fault for them doing what they did. This is why they need to train themselves to make the Bible the final authority in their life. If they're born again then they don't have the right to think whatever they want to think.

In order to control your flesh you must let the Word define what is right and what is wrong. It doesn't matter what the world says, it does matter what God says. If the Word says it's wrong, it's wrong. If you love God and people like you're supposed to, then you won't do anything that will bring them misery and harm. Those who give in to the flesh are selfish because they're more focused on what they want at the moment than how it will affect others afterwards. These are the ones who are on their third or fourth marriage and have health problems that never seem to go away. Selfishness is a killer. It steals and it destroys. It will cause your life to be cut short by decades. Your body is the most precious thing you have and you need to cherish it and take care of it. Don't eat all that cheesecake before you go to bed at night and don't fill it with alcohol and illegal drugs. Don't join your body to somebody you're not married to. These are the very things your flesh wants to do but don't give in to these wrong desires.

Don't be intimidated by your flesh. Never say it's got a mind of its own and does whatever it wants. No, you take charge and you control your flesh. You can do it! Phil. 4:13 says, "I can do all things through Christ who strengthens me." The Message Bible says, "Whatever I have, wherever I am, I can make it through anything in the One who makes me who I am." You can do all things through Christ and this means you can control how you spend your money, what and how much you eat, and all those wrongful sexual desires that come to you. Believe in the power of your words and start saying you can control these things. His grace is sufficient for you and in Him is the power to control your flesh. But you must do it! Those fleshly desires won't leave on their own but you can control them if you first believe that you can. Jesus said in Mark 9:23, "If you can believe, all things are possible to him who believes." Pass judgment on your flesh and make it stop doing what it wants to do. It's your body and your life, therefore, you must take control of what happens to it.

The reason many people don't control their flesh is because they don't want to do it bad enough. They want something else instead. To control your flesh you must have the desire to get it out of your life. Mark 11:24 says, "Therefore I say to you, whatever things you desire when you pray, believe that you receive them, and you will have them." You make choices every day and you must be honest about what you want the most. If you desire to look good more than you desire cheesecake, then you won't eat the cheesecake. Your flesh wants instant gratification but, if you desire the right things, you'll do what's best for you in the long run. Carnality sacrifices tomorrow for the pleasure it gets today whereas wisdom will cause you to control yourself today for the benefit it brings tomorrow. If you'll do what's right, you may not get what your flesh wants but you'll be better off tomorrow and in time will receive those things God says you can have.

A believer who walks in the light will control their desires and their feelings and their thoughts. Babes in Christ, on the other hand, are always yielding to the flesh and will say the first thing that crosses their mind. They may regret what they said later on but the damage has already been done. A person who is spiritual has power over his own will for he is standing steadfast in his heart. He doesn't yield to his emotions but lets the strength of God on the inside of him come out and control what he says and does. The question to be asked is if you're not in control, then who is? Who holds the steering wheel of your life? People make excuses and say the devil made them do it. That's not true for the devil can't make you do anything. People do what they yield to and, for the most part, what they can get away with. Don't be like those who are controlled by their flesh but be like Jesus who was in control of every situation He was in. People say God is in control but that's only true to the degree that you allow Him to be.

It matters what you think about because your mind is the doorway to your spirit. The mind is where the battle is won or lost spiritually. Things get in your mind through your five senses and things get in your spirit though your mind. If a thought comes to you and you think about it long enough, it will get down in your spirit and this is when it will affect your life. Be careful what you meditate on. Job 12;11 says, "Does not the ear test words and the mouth taste its food?" Physically you eat with your mouth and spiritually you eat with your ears. If you put something in your mouth and you don't like the taste of it and it doesn't agree with you, you spit it out. The same thing should happen spiritually. If a word or a thought comes to you and it doesn't agree with the Word of God, then cast it aside and think about it no more. Spit it out! As you exercise your senses this way, in time you'll be able to discern in your spirit what is good and what is bad. Babies will put anything in their mouth but not the grown up child of God.

Heb. 5:14 says, "But solid food belongs to those who are of full age, that is, those who by reason of use have their senses exercised to discern both good and evil." The Message Bible says, "Milk is for beginners, inexperienced in God's ways; solid food is for the mature, who have some practice in telling right from wrong." Spiritually, you are what you eat. If you feed on unbelief and the traditions of man, all you'll ever be is a babe in Christ. But if you'll feed yourself on what the Bible says and on words of faith, your spirit will grow and become strong. It will learn the ways of God and will be able to discern between good and evil. It matters what you think about. To be carnally minded is death, but to be spiritually minded is life and peace. If one day you find yourself frustrated and upset, then you've been thinking about the wrong things. You are losing the mind battle for in your mind is the arena where battles are fought and won. What you think about is what you chew on and, if you chew on it long enough, you'll eventually swallow it and it becomes a part of you.

God said in Josh. 1:8, "This Book of the Law shall not depart from your mouth, but you shall meditate in it day and night, that you may observe to do according to all that is written in it. For then you will make your way prosperous, and then you will have good success." The first thing God said to do is keep the Word in your mouth. Many people have thought if they could just control their mind, then they would confess the right things. They have it backwards. First you get the Word of God in your mouth, then you meditate on what you heard yourself say. God is saying here that you can use your mouth to control your mind. Bad thoughts will come but you can use your words to super impose the right thoughts into your mind. When the thoughts of God come in, the bad thoughts must leave. Don't sit in silence when wrong thoughts bombard your mind. This is not a silent battle. Your words are a powerful weapon which you can use to impart life and victory into your mind. Before long the thoughts of God will be the things you'll be thinking about all the time.

A person who walks in the light controls their thoughts and feelings. Spiritual people control their flesh, their desires, and the words they speak. When you're strong spiritually, you have a strong grip and control of all your being. You're not out of control, you're in control just like Jesus was in control of everything He did. He got mad at times but He was always in control. Mark 11:11 says, "And Jesus went into Jerusalem and into the temple. So when He had looked around at all things, as the hour was already late, He went out to Bethany with the twelve." Jesus went into the temple, He saw the moneychangers who were there, and He turned around and left. It was the next day that He went back to the temple and overturned the tables of the moneychangers and the seats of those who sold doves (vs. 15,16). Jesus was angry the first time He went into the temple but He was in control and didn't get mad and fly off the handle. He left, got direction from the Father, and then went back the next day and drove out those who bought and sold in the temple. He was in control and on purpose did what He did.

Gal. 5:16 says, "I say then: Walk in the Spirit, and you shall not fulfill the lust of the flesh." The NLT says, "So I say, let the Holy Spirit guide your lives. Then you won't be doing what your sinful nature craves." People who give in to the flesh, those who eat too much and sleep too long, are not walking in the Spirit as they should be. People who are consumed by alcohol and lust are not in control of their lives. They believe they can't control these fleshly appetites but that is not true. They can if they would commit themselves to walking in the Spirit every single day of their lives. The first thing you need to do to control the flesh is you've got to believe in your

heart and confess with your mouth that you can do this. Your words and your faith can change anything in your life so don't underestimate the power of walking in the Spirit. Nothing is too hard for the Lord, and nothing is impossible to the person who believes. When you walk in faith, you give God something to work with.

Jesus said in Matt. 16:19, "And I will give you the keys of the kingdom of heaven, and whatever you bind on earth will be bound in heaven, and whatever you loose on earth will be loosed in heaven." Keys denote access and use, and whatever you forbid on earth will be forbidden in heaven, and whatever you permit on earth will be permitted in heaven. You have the keys and you are in control of what happens in your life. The enemy is constantly working to convince people that they are helpless pawns, that they are powerless to do anything about their life and circumstances. This is not true because there is nothing that happens to you where you can't do something about it. It's all about control but people won't exercise it if they don't know they have it. James 4:7 says, "Resist the devil and he will flee from you." Who is in control of resisting the devil? You are! You have been given authority in the Name of Jesus to do this and, if you don't do it, then neither will the Lord because He will not override the authority He's given you.

The devil wants you to be carnal or in error all the time. This is why you need to read your Bible every single day and go to a church where the uncompromising Word of God is taught without fail. The devil doesn't want you to know that you have authority over him where you can bind him and make him stop in his operations against you. You have the keys of the kingdom and you are in control. If something is happening in your life that you don't agree with, then stand up and do something about it. If bad thoughts come your way, don't just sit there and meditate on them. No, bind them up and cast them away. Jesus said in Mark 11:23, "For assuredly, I say to you, whoever says to this mountain, 'Be removed and be cast into the sea,' and does not doubt in his heart, but believes that those things he says will come to pass, he will have whatever he says." This verse is not telling you to pray and ask God to remove the mountain. Jesus is telling you to do it because you have the authority and you are in control. If you don't do it, then neither can God.

Instead of praying for your problems, you need to start talking to them. Stop asking God to do something you're supposed to do. You have the keys and whatever you bind will be bound and whatever you loose will be loosed. Talk to your problems the same way Jesus talked to a fig tree, a fever, and the wind and waves. He's your example and you're supposed to do the same things He did. He was in control of every situation He was in and so are you to be. When a bad thought came to Him, He cast it out of His mind. When a bad thought comes to you, cast it out also. Your mind is your mind and you are in control of what you think about. The devil is very persistent and he will continually bring bad thoughts to your mind. Don't feel condemned when they do come. Recognize where they come from and follow the instructions of 2 Cor. 10:5, "Casting down arguments and every high thing that exalts itself against the knowledge of God, bringing every thought into captivity to the obedience of Christ."

Guard your mind. Don't watch wrong movies or listen to bad music. Don't spend hours on the phone gossiping about other people and don't laugh when a bad joke is told at work. Walk away from such things and stay focused on the Lord. This will bring peace to every area of your life. You'll have peace in your mind and in your emotions. You'll have peace in your home and with those you do business with. It matters what you let into your mind. You are in control of what thoughts you think, what words you say, and what actions you take. If you are in control of these areas, then the devil is not in control. The problem with many people is they have a "whatever will be, will be" mentality. They just take life as it comes. Whatever happens to them, so be it. It is what it is. No, these people are being deceived by the enemy into believing they have no control over their lives. If something bad happens, you don't have to lay down and play dead. Rise up and do something about it.

God, being who He is, has chosen not to control you but rather to put control in your hands. This is one of the things that makes being a Christian so wonderful. Who wants to be a mindless robot or a puppet on a string? He has given you a free will and a mind of your own with which to choose the direction your life will take. Yes, God has a plan for your life but you are the one to choose whether or not you will follow that plan. God is great and awesome, yet He refuses to make you do anything. He wants you to follow Him freely and willingly. To make that happen, He has given you the keys of the kingdom. He has given you control. God does not force anybody to do anything and has chosen to let you decide for yourself what you want to do with your life. This is why when Jesus was baptized the Holy Spirit came down in bodily form as a dove which is the universal symbol of peace. He could have came as an elephant because He's big or as a lion because He's strong but He didn't. He came as a dove. He is big and powerful, yet so gentle.

The devil will try to deceive you into thinking that God is in control of your life. If you think that way, then you won't do anything when something bad happens. Who are you to interfere with what God allows? This is precisely what the devil wants you to think. He knows that if you're not in control, then he can be in control. People are always asking God to do something about their problems but He says, "You've got the keys of the kingdom, you do something." God is saying that you have control. You can bind and you can loose. You can stop bad things from happening and you can permit good things to happen. You can do it with faith and the words you speak. God, in all His might, will back you up on this. He'll allow what you allow. Bad things are happening on the earth today because people have a free will and have chosen the wrong things too many times. And yes, God will allow them to do that. It's the devil who forces people to do things, not God. What's sad is that when something bad happens, people blame God and not themselves for allowing it.

God is your helper and when you decide to do something, He'll help you. He won't do it for you but he will help you do it. You've got to take control of your life and do something so He'll have something to help you with. You can't pray and ask God to take away your desire to eat two bowls of ice cream before you go to bed at night. It's your appetite and you are in control of what you do with it. God cannot help you if you're convinced there is nothing you can do about fleshly thoughts, desires, and appetites. There is a battle taking place inside of you between the flesh and the spirit and it's up to you to decide which one is going to reign in your life. Always giving in to the flesh will limit how high you can go in the things of God. It puts a roadblock on your path that prevents you from going forward in your spiritual walk. The good news is that if you can get over the temporary pain of not letting the flesh get what it wants, God will release more of His favor into your life and you'll rise higher and higher.

The flesh likes to be comfortable but, if you're always comfortable, you'll never grow. It's a fact of life that the harder something is to overcome, the more you'll grow in that area. No pain, no gain. Overcoming the uncomfortable is what causes growth to come. No discipline feels pleasant at the time but later on it will produce a great harvest. The flesh wants to be satisfied right now but a person who walks in the light will not get caught up in the emotion of the present moment. He looks beyond that and considers how what he does today will affect his life in the future. Before giving in to the flesh you need to step back and think about tomorrow. Think before you tell your boss off at work; think before you start flirting with somebody at the grocery store; think before you try to cheat on your taxes. There is a price to pay tomorrow for giving in to the flesh today. It may feel good to give your spouse a piece of your mind but don't be surprised if you're sleeping on the couch for the rest of the week. Before you act on fleshly desires, always consider what will happen tomorrow.

God speaks in a still, small voice whereas the flesh screams louder than a trumpet blast. God speaks in a whisper and this is why you have to discipline yourself to hear His voice. You need to make decisions based on godly wisdom for this is what causes the blessings of God to flow in your life. People who have a happy home and a successful business got that way because they were disciplined to do the right thing even when it was hard on their flesh. The people who reach their highest potential are the ones who are good at saying no to their flesh. These are the people who go home to their family after work instead of going out drinking with their friends. They will go to church on Sunday instead of playing two rounds of golf and will eat an apple instead of a candy bar. These people are disciplined and they will go far in life. Gal. 6:8 says, "For he who sows to the flesh will of the flesh reap corruption, but he who sows to the Spirit will of the Spirit reap everlasting life."

When you do the right thing when it's hard, when you sow to the Spirit, you will receive from God favor and increase. You'll fulfill your destiny and many will be blessed because you lived a disciplined life. Living by how you feel is a shallow way to live and this is why you need to take the keys of the kingdom and release the power of God in your life. This happens when you walk in the Spirit and not according to the dictates of the flesh. Always remember, the pleasures of the flesh are temporary while the blessings of God are eternal. Why destroy your life, home, and marriage for a few minutes of pleasure? Paul said in 1 Cor. 15:31, "I die daily." Everyday he had to say no to his flesh. Everyday he had to take his feelings off the throne of his life. Paul wrote over half of the New Testament but still he had to deal with his flesh. You will never reach a point where you'll get so mature and spiritual that you'll no longer have to deal with your flesh. Discipline is a daily happening in the life of the person who walks in the light.

Self-control is like a muscle that needs to be exercised in order to grow strong. Be disciplined and start saying no to your flesh. You have a destiny to fulfill but it will never happen if you are continually ruled by the flesh. Gal. 4:1 says, "Now I say that the heir, as long as he is a child, does not differ at all from a slave, though he is master of all." Spiritual maturity has nothing to do with how long you've been saved or how many times a week you go to church. It has everything to do with how you control your flesh. There are people who have been saved for decades yet have the spiritual maturity of a little child. These are the people who get angry all the time and gossip about others. They're always late for work, their grass is never mowed, and their clothes no longer fit around their waist. These are the people who do nothing worthwhile in the kingdom of God. They are too busy satisfying their own fleshly desires to have time to think about blessing somebody else.

Mountain climbers at the start of their journey have to be aware of poisonous snakes that are in the area. But the higher they climb they'll reach a point where the oxygen level is cut off thus preventing the snakes from following them to the top of the mountain. The more you discipline yourself, the more you rule over your emotions and take control of your flesh, the more you will grow to a higher level where the flesh will dominate you no more. The closer to God you get, the weaker the flesh becomes. Yes, the flesh is still there but because you are disciplined those thoughts and feelings have no control over you. Their oxygen has been cut off. You have the keys of the kingdom and you're in charge of what happens in your life. No longer are you a puppet on a string but are a vessel of honor who God can use to do great works in His kingdom. The inheritance is yours and you have stepped into your destiny and are becoming everything God predestined you to be.

Randall J. Brewer

-9-
"GODLY SORROW"

A long time ago God created a race of people made in His image with whom He could share an eternity of love and fellowship. He began by walking in the cool of the evening with His most perfect creation, Adam. How uplifting it would be to know the things they talked about. God loved His new friend so much that He created for him a wife taken from his own side. Then the day came when sin entered the world and the fellowship between God and man was broken. A mighty angel cast Adam and Eve out of the garden away from the tree of life because if they were to partake of its fruit they would become immortal sinners. Never again could man look upon God face-to-face because the very brilliance of His glory would cause the instant death of any sinner who looked upon Him. But God, in His unfailing love, did not give up on man and a plan was put into motion to return people to a right standing with Himself. This plan of redemption eventually led to the birth of Jesus Christ but, before it could unfold, communication first had to be restored between God and man.

Since God could no longer speak to man face-to-face as He had once done in the Garden of Eden, the great Jehovah was now forced to find new and different ways to correspond and converse with His people. Old Testament scripture records a variety of interesting and highly unusual methods in which this was accomplished.

One time God talked to a shepherd named Moses through a burning bush while another time He used a donkey to speak to a wayward prophet. Visions and dreams were a common occurrence and occasionally a message was personally delivered by an angel. More times than not, however, God chose to speak to His people through the voice of the prophet. As a prelude to the indwelling Holy Spirit, this vessel of honor received a special anointing to become a spokesperson for God. The first words out of a prophet's mouth were usually "Thus saith the Lord." And when the prophet spoke, people listened. Vast knowledge and wisdom can come from a careful study of the prophets and the messages God spoke through them.

Interestingly, Jesus in Matt. 11 tells us what the greatest of these messages was. John the Baptist, the "voice of one crying in the wilderness" (Matt. 3:3), has the unique distinction of being one of only a handful of men whose birth and ministry were foretold in scripture. Called by Jesus the greatest prophet of all time (Matt. 11:11), John the Baptist's mission is described in vs. 10, "For this is he of whom it is written: 'Behold, I send my messenger before your face who will prepare Your way before You.'" Jesus did not bestow this high honor on John because of who he was as a person but rather because of the message John brought to the people. It was a special time in history and the Son of God was about to be revealed. It was John's responsibility to prepare the people to receive Him. With a loud voice he would cry out, "Repent, for the kingdom of heaven is at hand!" (Matt. 3:2). The message of the greatest prophet of all time was a message of repentance.

2 Peter 3:9 says, "The Lord is not slack concerning His promise, as some count slackness, but is longsuffering

toward us, not willing that any should perish but that all should come to repentance." The Message Bible says, "He is restraining Himself on account of you, holding back the End because He doesn't want anyone lost. He's giving everyone space and time to change." God does not want anyone to be destroyed and repentance is how you prevent that from happening. In Greek the word means 'to care afterward' which refers to a person having regret for the wrong they did. It also means 'to think differently afterwards; to reconsider; to change one's mind or purpose.' Repentance is a lifestyle and involves much more than just saying you're sorry for committing some sin. It goes way beyond that. If change doesn't come then a person really hasn't repented. When John the Baptist told the people to repent, he was telling them to change. Jesus was soon to be revealed and if the people didn't change their heart, they wouldn't be able to receive what the Lord would say to them.

Repentance gets you ready to receive from God and this is very exciting. Getting ready for what God is about to do in your life should bring you joy unspeakable and much happiness. Repentance is a gift that comes from the grace of God. 2 Tim. 2:25,26 says "in humility correcting those who are in opposition, if God perhaps will grant them repentance, so that they may know the truth, and that they may come to their senses and escape the snare of the devil, having been taken captive by him to do his will." Repentance brings about recovery from that which was lost. If you would do this with sincerity of heart, you wouldn't need other people to pray for you. If you go to God with a repenting heart, the power that breaks every yoke and bondage will come on you and set you free. True repentance also brings change to your deeds and actions. If you don't change on the outside, then you really haven't changed on the inside. Change should always begin in the heart for out of it flow the issues of life. When change comes to your heart, mighty things begin to happen in your life.

When you repent, the devil loses his grip on your life. Babes in Christ who refuse to repent put themselves in a position where even God can't help them. They've been ensnared by the evil one whose sole purpose is to destroy their lives. Those who repent, however, have a miraculous turnaround in their lives. They started out carnal but end up spiritual. Old things have passed away, behold, all things become new. Change comes when you're willing to change, when you walk in humility by admitting not everything in your life is as it should be. Peter didn't want Jesus to wash his feet like He was doing to all the others. Jesus answered him, "If I do not wash you, you have no part with Me." What was Peter's response? He changed! He said, "Lord, not my feet only, but also my hands and my head!" (John 13:8,9). The man didn't want just a foot washing, he changed so much that he wanted a complete bath. This is the type of person God can use. This is the type of person who can help change the world.

Repentance is a gift from God and you need to thank Him for it. It is one of the greatest things He has ever given to mankind. It is the alternative to perishing and being forever separated from God. Repentance is what causes you to break free from the chains of bondage that have had you bound for many, many years. It's what brings you out from a life of destruction and devastation. It keeps you out of strife which is the manifested presence of the devil. Titus 2:11,12 says, "For the grace of God that brings salvation has appeared to all men, teaching us that, denying ungodliness and worldly lusts, we should live soberly, righteously, and godly in the present age." The Message Bible says, "God's readiness to give and forgive is now public. Salvation's available for everyone! We're being shown how to turn our backs on a godless, indulgent life, and how to take on a God-filled, God-honoring life." Vs. 14 (MSG) says, "He offered Himself as a sacrifice to free us from a dark, rebellious life into this good, pure life, making us a people He can be proud of, energetic in goodness."

A lot of people don't look at repentance as a positive thing, but it is. It's what brings you out of bondage caused by sin and ungodly living. God, in His infinite mercy, always provides a way out of the snare of the enemy. 1 Cor. 10:13 says He "will not allow you to be tempted beyond what you are able, but with the temptation will also make the way of escape, that you may be able to bear it." There is no such thing as an irresistible temptation because God will not allow it. No matter what comes your way, you have the power inside of you to resist it for God has provided for you the way of escape for that temptation. You need to believe this for the devil will try to convince you that there are some temptations too big for you to overcome. He'll get you to think you can't help yourself, causing you to not even try to resist the temptation. That is a lie because greater is He that is in you than he who is in the world. The devil can't make you do anything and he knows it. This is why deception is one thing you should always be aware of.

If the temptation is there, you can resist it for God has provided a way for you to overcome it. There is a way out. Still, many people don't follow this way of escape and sin anyway. They miss the mark. These are good people, they're born again, but one day their guard was down and sin entered in. For them, God has provided a way back to fellowship with Him. There is a way out, and there is a way back. If you take the way out, you won't need the way back but thankfully it is there. The way back to God is repentance and it is a glorious thing. There is nothing worse than severed fellowship with the God you serve. You don't stop being His child when you sin but fellowship is broken. When David sinned with Bathsheba he prayed in Ps. 51:11, "Do not cast me away from Your presence, and do not take Your Holy Spirit from me." The Message Bible says, "Don't throw me out with the trash, or fail to breathe holiness in me." Light and darkness don't mix and when Jesus took your sin on the cross, fellowship with God was broken and the Father looked away.

When you repent and confess your sin, God will cleanse you from all unrighteousness and fellowship will be restored. Be honest with Him and acknowledge you did wrong. You can't fool God so why make excuses and try to cover it up? David wrote in Ps. 32:5, "I acknowledged my sin to You, and my iniquity I have not hidden. I said, 'I will confess my transgressions to the Lord,' and You forgave the iniquity of my sin." When you sin, your heart will condemn you (1 John 3:20) but don't nurse that condemnation. Yes, you knew better and you didn't have to give in to that temptation. There was a way out but you didn't take it. You yielded to your flesh and now your heart is condemning you. What do you do? First of all, stop making excuses and acknowledge you did wrong. 1 John 1:8 says, "If we say that we have no sin, we deceive ourselves, and the truth is not in us." Don't pretend everything is okay just because you're under grace. It's not. You sinned and fellowship with God is broken. Don't hide your sin and try to cover it up. Acknowledge you did wrong and this will open the door for fellowship to be restored.

The blood of Jesus is on the mercy seat and it never stops cleansing you from all your sin. 1 John 1:9 says, "If we confess our sins, He is faithful and just to forgive us our sins and to cleanse us from all unrighteousness."
When you sin, don't run from God, run to Him. James 4:6 says, "God resists the proud, but gives grace to the humble." Pride runs from God, humility runs to Him. Repentance is the way back to fellowship with God and with it comes fullness of joy. Guilt and shame are gone and peace and comfort has come. It is not God's will for anybody to perish and repentance is what keeps this from happening. You are a Christian and you walk in faith and you walk in love. Sin has no place in your life and God has provided a

way out for you not to sin, and a way back if you do. His mercy endures forever and having unhindered fellowship with you is His top priority. He loves you so much. Your heart may condemn you of your sin but He won't. He sees your sin nailed to the cross with Jesus so don't run from Him when you sin, run to Him.

A terrible sin was taking place in the Corinthian church and Paul wrote them a letter reprimanding them for it. He spoke of this letter in 2 Cor. 7:8,9, "For even if I made you sorry with my letter, I do not regret it; though I did regret it. For I perceive that the same epistle made you sorry, though only for a while. Now I rejoice, not that you were made sorry, but that your sorrow led to repentance. For you were made sorry in a godly manner, that you might suffer loss from us in nothing." Sin can't be taken lightly and you need to have a genuine, godly sorrow when you've done something wrong. Some preachers teach that Christians are supposed to be joyful all the time and never feel sorrow. That's not entirely true. The NLT says in vs.9, "Now I am glad I sent it, not because it hurt you, but because the pain caused you to repent and change your ways. It was the kind of sorrow God wants His people to have, so that you were not harmed by us in any way." The Message Bible says, "You let the distress bring you to God, not drive you from Him."

Paul continues in vs. 10 (NLT), "For the kind of sorrow God wants us to experience leads us away from sin and results in salvation. There's no regret for that kind of sorrow. But worldly sorrow, which lacks repentance, results in spiritual death." Paul distinguishes two kinds of sorrow here, one that is good and one that is bad. Godly sorrow is a part of godly repentance. Your heart is condemning you and you are bothered because of the wrong you did. This is a good thing and Paul says it's not to be regretted. Vs. 11 says, "Just see what this godly sorrow produced in you! Such earnestness, such concern to clear yourselves, such indignation, such alarm, such longing to see me, such zeal, and such a readiness to punish wrong. You showed that you have done everything necessary to make things right." True repentance is more than a casual change of mind for it brings with it a change of heart. Godly sorrow is a good thing but it's not supposed to last a lifetime. You repent, you receive forgiveness, you then rejoice because you've been washed and cleansed by the blood of the Lamb.

There is a perversion in the church where the grace of God is distorted into a license to sin. Jude 4 talks about how "some ungodly people have wormed their way into your churches, saying that God's marvelous grace allows us to live immoral lives" (NLT). This is what happened at the Corinthian church. 1 Cor. 5:1 tells how a man was living in sin with his father's wife. Vs. 2 says, "You are so proud of yourselves, but you should remove this man from your fellowship." The Message Bible says, "And you're so above it all that it doesn't even faze you! Shouldn't this break your hearts?" The NKJV says the people are "puffed up." This was written to a church of believers who Paul said was "sanctified in Christ, called to be saints" (1 Cor. 1:2). Why were these people proud and puffed up because of this horrendous sin? They had a perversion of grace which brings with it a lack of moral restraint. They thought that because of grace they could still embrace this man and accept him in their fellowship in spite of what he was doing wrong.

These people in Corinth were in pride because they thought they were more enlightened than other churches. They were not walking in the light but were being deceived by the evil one. You're not supposed to be mean to people when they sin but you're not doing them any favors if you say it's okay if and when they do sin. It does matter whether or not you sin and people's lives are being destroyed because they're being taught that it's no big deal if they do. Because they're covered with grace, these people think they don't have to repent of their sins and, sad to say, there are preachers and other believers who are enabling their disillusion. This is what the church at Corinth was doing. They were allowing this man to continue sleeping with his stepmother while at the same time accepting him as one of their own. God is a holy God and what is acceptable to some people is not always acceptable to Him. What some people think does not change what is true in the eyes of God. The danger of not thinking right is that it stops you from repenting and changing the way you live your life.

Are you willing to change? Do you love God enough that if He shows you something is wrong in your life, you'll stop doing it? 1 Cor. 5:3 (MSG) says, "I'm telling you that this is wrong. You must not simply look the other way and hope it goes away on its own. Bring it out in the open and deal with it in the authority of Jesus our Master." God hates sin and is not as tolerant of it as some carnal people imagine Him to be. Paul continues in vs. 4,5 (NLT), "You must call a meeting of the church. I will be with you in spirit, and so will the power of our Lord Jesus. Then you must throw this man out and hand him over to Satan so that his sinful nature will be destroyed and he himself will be saved on the day the Lord returns." Rarely, if ever, is this taught from the pulpit as it should be. Many believers are sleeping with people they shouldn't be sleeping with and the church is refusing to deal with it openly. People who commit such atrocities are in danger of being lost and the church is standing idly by watching it happen.

The Message Bible says in vs. 6,7, "Your flip and callous arrogance in these things bothers me. You pass it off as a small thing, but it's anything but that. Yeast, too, is a 'small thing,' but it works its way through a whole batch of bread dough pretty fast. So get rid of this 'yeast.' Our true identity is flat and plain, not puffed up with the wrong kind of ingredient." God loves these people and this is why they are being confronted with their sin. If this wrong is not dealt with, it could spread throughout the entire church and before long even young teenagers will be doing the same perverted things. Sin spreads when it's not dealt with for, indeed, a little leaven leavens the whole lump. Sin not being dealt with is the reason over half of all Christian marriages end in divorce. Sin is happening and nobody is doing anything about it. After all, everybody is under grace, aren't they? This is perverted thinking. Somebody in the church has to stand up and boldly confront those who commit willful and habitual sin and tell them to either repent and change or leave the church. This isn't being harsh, this is tough love in action.

This is serious business. Christians tend to forget that the wages of sin is death (Rom. 6:23). The Message Bible says, "Work hard for sin your whole life and your pension is death." Not only are you not to do these things, neither are you to associate with people who do. Paul wrote in 1 Cor. 5:9-13 (NLT), "When I wrote to you before, I told you not to associate with people who indulge in sexual sin. But I wasn't talking about unbelievers who indulge in sexual sin, or are greedy, or cheat people, or worship idols. You would have to leave this world to avoid people like that. I meant that you are not to associate with anyone who claims to be a believer yet indulges in sexual sin, or is greedy, or worship idols, or is abusive, or is a drunkard, or cheats people. Don't even eat with such people. It isn't my responsibility to judge outsiders, but it certainly is your responsibility to judge those inside the church who are sinning. God will judge those on the outside; but as the Scriptures say, 'You must remove the evil person from among you.'"

Believers sin and believers must repent of their sin. Along with this is a godly sorrow that will lead them into the arms of a forgiving Savior. Sin will always be judged but 1 Cor. 11:31,32 says, "For if we judge ourselves, we would not be judged. But when we are judged, we are chastened by the Lord, that we may not be condemned with the world." The

Message Bible says, "If we get this straight now, we won't have to be straightened out later on. Better to be confronted by the Master now than to face a fiery confrontation later." Never should you judge a sinner for sinning for that's what they do. Sinners sin and you shouldn't be surprised and shocked when they do. The Bible says God will judge them. You are, however, supposed to judge yourself and the sinful believer who sits among you. The Bible says to remove that person from your midst. Don't sit with them, don't eat with them, don't associate with them. The Lord doesn't tell you to do this to be mean to them but rather that your actions will shake them to the core, to the point that they'll see the error of their ways.

Believers who engage in gross sin may not change if they're still allowed to sing in the church choir. If the church does not confront them and take corrective action, they will develop a false sense of believing that God is accepting them in spite of their sin. They're on the path to destruction but think everything is okay. Paul knew what was going on in the Corinthian church and it didn't please him to have to confront these people, but he did it anyway. 2 Cor. 2:4 says, "For out of much affliction and anguish of heart I wrote to you, with many tears, not that you should be grieved, but that you might know the love which I have so abundantly for you." Love will correct you even if you despise it. It's not love to let somebody blaze down the path of destruction without making an effort to get them to change their ways. Paul confronted these people, they listened to him, corrective action was taken. The man who slept with his father's wife was put out of the church and, thankfully, later repented of his wrong doing.

Now what? Paul wrote, "This punishment which was inflicted by the majority is sufficient for such a man, so that, on the contrary, you ought rather to forgive and comfort him, lest perhaps such a one be swallowed up with too much sorrow. Therefore I urge you to reaffirm your love to him" (2 Cor. 2:6-

8). Changes were made and now was the time to restore him which was God's plan all along. Repentance is the way back to fellowship with God and there is nothing more precious than that. If you will judge yourself and repent, you will be forgiven and will not be judged for your failure and sin. It is not His will for anybody to perish, or be destroyed, or to be consumed with the sinfulness of their ways. He's a good God and He's the God of victory. Through Jesus the power of sin and death was destroyed and, when you repent, the enemy loses his grip on your life. This is why Paul said, "Now is the time to forgive this man and help him back on his feet. If all you do is pour on the guilt, you could very well drown him in it. My counsel now is to pour on the love" (MSG).

Never think it's too late to repent and be forgiven. Nothing is too hard for God and nothing is impossible to Him. He can and will forgive you no matter how bad you think the sin was. After all, repentance is a gift from Him. He wants to forgive you and He's waiting with opened arms for you to come to Him. It breaks His heart when fellowship with you is broken but, thankfully, there is repentance, forgiveness, and restoration. Meditate on how wonderful it is that God would allow you to be forgiven. There is no greater expression of God's heart than His willingness to forgive you and cleanse you from all unrighteousness. The time to repent is now. Change needs to come to your life, a turning around from one attitude to another that produces a change in direction. God said to the church of Ephesus in rev. 2:5 (NLT), "Look how far you have fallen! Turn back to me and do the works you did at first. If you don't repent, I will come and remove your lampstand from its place among the churches."

Judgment comes when people don't repent, it's held back when they do. This should be some of the greatest news you've ever heard. It is not God's will that any should perish but sin is one thing He will not turn His back on if it is not repented of. In the church of Thyatira there was a false prophetess who was teaching the people to commit sexual immorality and to eat things sacrificed to idols. God said in Rev. 2:21-23, "And I gave her time to repent of her sexual immorality, and she did not repent. Indeed I will cast her into a sickbed, and those who commit adultery with her into great tribulation, unless they repent of their deeds. And I will kill her children with death. And all the churches shall know that I am He who searches the minds and hearts. And I will give to each one of you according to your works." Sin is nothing to scoff at. God takes it seriously and so should you. Repent while there is still time to repent for, indeed, it is a fearful thing to fall into the hands of the living God (Heb. 10:31).

Randall J. Brewer

-10-

"NO HIGHER PLACE"

Sin is here and it's the biggest problem humanity has ever had. Unfortunately, many people today consider it politically incorrect to even use the term, especially in church. They'd rather say that a person has an issue they're dealing with, or that there are problems in their life they're trying to solve. No, the people are sinning and they need to call it that. Don't sugarcoat sin by calling it something else. Sin is sin and there are gross consequences for those who let it run rampant in their life. Rom. 6:23 says, "For the wages of sin is death." This is a spiritual law that has been around since the Garden of Eden. God told Adam in Gen. 2:16,17, "Of every tree of the garden you may freely eat; but of the tree of the knowledge of good and evil you shall not eat, for in the day that you eat of it you shall surely die." If you sin, you die. Period. Sin is a violation of light, an open rebellion against the right thing you know you're supposed to do. 1 John 3:4 (MSG) says, "All who indulge in a sinful life are dangerously lawless, for sin is a major disruption of God's order."

People who don't believe in God have no morals. The course their life takes is based solely on what they think is right and wrong, and that can change daily. What's wrong today may be considered acceptable tomorrow. There was a time when it was abominable to have sex before marriage, now it's an accepted practice everywhere. This is why when a person believes less and less in God, the more immoral they will be. People will say that this is a new generation where the level of acceptability gives them the freedom to do whatever they desire. If it feels good, do it. But God never changes. He's the same yesterday, today, and forever (Heb. 13:8). It always has been, and always will be, God's will "that we may lead a quiet and peaceable life in all godliness and reverence. For this is good and acceptable in the sight of God our Savior, who desires all men to be saved and to come to the knowledge of the truth" (1 Tim. 2:2-4). The truth of God's Word will set you free for it reveals the standard for which people are to live their lives.

Sin is when you violate what the Bible says is right and wrong. 1 John 5:17 says, "All unrighteousness is sin" and Rom. 14:23 says "for whatever is not from faith is sin." The problem many Christians have is they're trying to live as close to their old life as they can without losing their salvation. These people are walking on dangerous ground because all sin leads to darkness. Heb. 3:12 says, "Beware, brethren, lest there be in any of you an evil heart of unbelief in departing from the living God." The Message Bible says, "So watch your step, friends. Make sure there's no evil unbelief lying around that will trip you up and throw you off course, diverting you from the living God." An evil unbelief is when you've seen the light but can't be persuaded to walk in it. This is why sin is called a violation of light. You've seen the light, you know the truth, yet you willingly refuse to change your life and follow the standard God revealed to you. If you don't walk in the light you have, everything around you will get darker and darker.

Heb. 3:13 says, "You must warn each other every day, while it is still 'today,' so that none of you will be deceived by sin and hardened against God." When you willingly walk in sin you will no longer be tender hearted and sensitive to the things of God. You'll become dull of hearing and all open communication with God will be lost. Hardness of heart causes you to not see the light and, the farther in life you go, the more blind you will become to the spiritual side of life. In time, you won't be able to discern right from wrong and will do things that even sinners would be ashamed of. This is what happened when a man in the Corinthian church began to sleep with his father's wife. 1 Tim. 4:1,2 says, "Now the Holy Spirit tells us clearly that in the last times some will turn away from the true faith; they will follow deceptive spirits and teachings that come from demons." This verse is talking about believers because you can't depart from the faith unless you've first been in the faith. How did this departure take place? They listened to false teachings that did not line up with the light of God's Word.

People whose hearts are hardened cannot distinguish between right and wrong. Be careful what you listen to because bad things happen when you listen to the wrong things. This is what opens the door for the enemy to come in and destroy your life. Understand that God is gracious and merciful and will not allow you to be taken captive by the enemy just because you're a helpless victim to the devil's deceptions. Those who get destroyed are the ones who see the light and willingly refuse to walk in it. There comes a point when people know better but decide to get off the beaten path anyway. As long as you're walking in the light you have, the blood of Jesus will cleanse you continually from all sin. When people refuse the truth there is nothing left to believe but a lie. In the last days the man of lawlessness will be revealed and Paul says in 2 Thess. 2:10 (NLT), "He will use every kind of evil deception to fool those on their way to destruction, because they will refuse to love and accept the truth that would save them."

These people will be destroyed because they will not receive the love of the truth. They will have seen the light but wouldn't walk in it. Vs. 11,12 says, "So God will cause them to be greatly deceived, and they will believe these lies. Then they will be condemned for enjoying evil rather than believing the truth." When you believe a lie you are deceived and, the farther you go from the light, the darker it gets. It is a dangerous thing to not walk in the light you have, to deny what you know to be true. Heb. 6:4-6 says, "For it is impossible for those who were once enlightened, and have tasted the heavenly gift, and have become partakers of the Holy Spirit, and have tasted the good word of God and the power of the age to come, if they fall away, to renew them again to repentance, since they crucify again for themselves the Son of God, and put Him to an open shame." This verse is referring to those who refuse to repent and turn away from a life of sin and darkness. They've turned their back on God and refuse to return to Him no matter how hard you try to persuade them otherwise.

A baby Christian cannot commit the unpardonable sin. These verses are referring to those who know better, believers who have seen the light and have walked in the counsel of God. They've experienced the anointing in their lives and have flowed in the gifts of the Holy Spirit. Then one day they decided they didn't want to serve God anymore and willfully turned their back on Him. These people knew what they were doing and what they did was not done in ignorance. On purpose they violated light and this is what makes their turning away so grievous and severe. They proclaimed that the blood of Jesus has no value to them and chose to walk in darkness rather than light. It is impossible to get a person to repent once they've done this. There is no such thing as once saved, always saved. The good news is that you can be saved as long as you want to be saved. Mental institutions are filled with people who think they've committed the unpardonable sin but they haven't. If they did something wrong but still want a relationship with God, they have not done what these verses is talking about.

The devil is always standing by hoping you will reject the truth because, if you do, that opens the door for him. For sure, he will give you something else to believe for he is the master of alternate choices. He is a liar and the father of it and when you listen to him you have started down the path that leads to death and destruction. The deceitfulness of sin hardens your heart and you reach a point where nobody can talk to you. Your trust in God is eroding and your conscious is severed to the point where it don't bother you when you sin. This is what happens when you don't walk in the light you've been given. You knew the truth but chose an alternate way to live. People who do this are nothing more than puppets on a string controlled by the devil as he tries to prevent you from fulfilling your destiny. Those who are deceived are cold-hearted believers who are unable to tell the difference between right and wrong. Their sin will dull their spiritual senses and will take away their ability to hear from God.

Before there is sin, there is temptation. James 1:14,15 (NLT) says, "Temptation comes from our own desires, which entice us and drag us away. These desires give birth to sinful actions. And when sin is allowed to grow, it gives birth to death." People are pulled away from God and pulled into sin by their own desires. The Message Bible says, "The temptation to give in to evil comes from us and only us. We have no one to blame but the leering, seducing flare-up of our own lust. Lust gets pregnant, and has a baby: sin! Sin grows up to adulthood, and becomes a real killer." The path to sin begins when you desire the wrong things. The devil then comes in and entices you with alternate choices contrary to the Word of God. The devil works with your desires for if you had no desire in a certain area, he would have nothing to entice you with. Desires grow strong when you feed them, they grow weak when you starve them. Never think you're too holy to be tempted. Everybody has desires and everybody gets tempted. Those who don't give in to sin are those who control their desires rather than letting their desires control them.

Heb. 11:24,25 says, "By faith Moses, when he became of age, refused to be called the son of Pharaoh's daughter, choosing rather to suffer affliction with the people of God than to enjoy the passing pleasures of sin." There is pleasure in sin for if there wasn't you wouldn't be tempted to do it. The devil offered Moses an alternate choice that would give him temporary pleasure. This shows how deceptive the devil is for there is no such thing as a sinful wrong that brings everlasting pleasure. It only brings short term gratification and afterward there will be consequences to pay. Never forget that the wages of sin is death. It can bring an end to your marriage, the demise of your health, and it can cause you to die an early death. Sin is a decision you make to put action to the wrong desires you have. There may be things you're very passionate about, but if God says it's wrong, it's wrong. Be like Moses who made a right choice. Put your flesh down and follow what's in your heart. This is how you control your desires. You are well able to resist every temptation that comes your way, if you choose to.

God hates sin and so should you. The Father said to Jesus in Heb. 1:9 (NLT), "You love justice and hate evil. Therefore, O God, Your God has anointed You, pouring out the oil of joy on You more than on anyone else." Jesus loved what was right and hated what was wrong and, because of that, He was anointed with joy and gladness above everybody round about Him. The devil does not want you to know that the happiest people on the planet are the holiest people. The most satisfied are the most sanctified. Like Moses, they choose to follow after God instead of the alternate choices the devil puts before them. The pleasure of sinners is temporary but the joy of God followers is eternal. The devil will lie to you and say the opposite is true. He'll try to convince you that the only way to have fun is to sin. Jesus never sinned and He was never depressed. No, He was filled with joy and gladness. He was the gladdest of the glad. There is no amount of temporary pleasure worth forfeiting your relationship with God for, or your family, your job, and even your life.

You have the responsibility to walk upright before God in what He has given you freely through the blood of Jesus. You need to be like Jesus who was holy, blameless, and unstained by sin. 1 John 2:6 says, "He who says he abides in Him ought himself also to walk just as He walked." That is a higher call that many are unwilling to believe is possible. They don't understand that God will not tell you to do something that was not possible for you to do. No person is righteous in and of themselves but, by faith, you believe that Jesus gave you His righteousness, and this is what makes you acceptable in the eyes of God. You need to be holy as He is holy. You need to walk in the light which is on the path of obedience. You need to do what you know you're supposed to do. Believe in your heart that you are separate from sin and that it's possible for you to go days, weeks, and even months without sinning. Don't listen to those who would tell you that it's human nature for a person to sin every day. That may be true for sinners but it's not true for a born again child of God.

If ever there was a reason not to sin, it would be to escape the condemnation that comes afterward. One of the most immediate results of sinning is the consequence of condemnation. It will strip you of your faith and will destroy your confidence to pray and to receive from God. It's the reason people are confused, in fear, and insecure. The word "condemn" means 'to be against; to judge against' and refers to a person being found guilty and sentenced to the punishment required for the wrong they did. If you are feeling condemned, then you are guilty of some wrong and believe you deserve to be punished. Fear is the result of knowing you're guilty and that punishment is coming. This is the reason Adam and Eve hid themselves when they ate of the forbidden fruit. Sin consciousness will cause you to run away from the presence of God. In Luke 5 Jesus performed a miracle for Peter and his fishing partners by providing for them an overflowing abundance of fish. Peter saw this and said, "Depart from me, for I am a sinful man, O Lord!" (vs. 8).

Condemnation will cause you to run away from God and push away the answer to all your problems. It causes you to draw back in fear and is the reason many people commit suicide. Peter felt unclean, dirty, and inferior standing next to Jesus. He was looking at a miracle and saw a manifestation of a holy God, yet he felt unworthy to be in the presence of Jesus. The devil is making people feel the same way today and he does it with condemnation. He is successful to a certain degree because righteousness is not being taught in the church as it should be. Week after week preachers point their finger at the members of their church telling them what wretched sinners they are. The people then go out and commit the very sin the preacher was talking about. Before long they're feeling condemned and decide not to go to church for a while, if ever at all. What these preachers should be telling the people is that the blood of Jesus cleanses them of all their sin and makes them acceptable to God in spite of all their failures and mistakes.

Jesus died to set you free from the law of sin and death. Heb. 10:10 (NLT) says, "For God's will was for us to be made holy by the sacrifice of the body of Jesus, once for all time." Vs. 14 says, "For by that one offering He forever made perfect those who are being made holy." The Message Bible says, "It was a perfect sacrifice by a perfect Person to perfect some very imperfect people. By that single offering, He did everything that needed to be done for everyone who takes part in the purifying process." What Jesus did, He did for you and what He says in vs. 17 is probably the greatest blessing of all, "Their sins and lawless deeds I will remember no more." If that don't make you shout, then nothing will. 1 John 1:9 says, "If we confess our sins, He is faithful and just to forgive us our sins and cleanse us from all unrighteousness." If your sins are cleansed and washed away by the blood of the Lamb, there is nothing to remember. When you're forgiven, you're forgiven. When you're clean, you're clean. Accept it and go on living a holy life.

Knowing you're forgiven takes away all guilt and shame and replaces it with holy boldness and confidence that rises up from inside of you. With this boldness you can enter into the Holy of Holies and fellowship with the Lord your God. Heb. 10:22 says, "Let us draw near with a true heart in full assurance of faith, having our hearts sprinkled from an evil conscience and our bodies washed with pure water." God has made you worthy to look directly into the eyes of Jesus which are like deep wells of living love. It takes faith to believe this and humility to yield to it. Forget about how you feel and all the mistakes you've made in the past. If God says you're righteous, then believe you are righteous. If He says you've been made holy, then you've been made holy. It matters not how you feel but it does matter what you believe. Fears melt away when you meditate on all that God has done and boldly confess out loud that you've been made the righteousness of God in Christ Jesus.

There is no higher place to go than to stand before the throne of grace. You can go there boldly when you know that God has made you worthy to do so. Heb. 10:19,20 (NLT) says, "And so, dear brothers and sisters, we can boldly enter heaven's Most Holy Place because of the blood of Jesus. By His death, Jesus opened a new and life-giving way through the curtain into the Most Holy Place." Sin and guilt causes you to draw back in fear because you're conscious of all your past mistakes and the times you missed the mark. But when you're conscious of the blood of Jesus, you can boldly draw near with a true heart in full assurance of faith. James 4:8 says, "Draw near to God and He will draw near to you." Heb. 4:16 says, "Let us therefore come boldly to the throne of grace, that we may obtain mercy and find grace to help in time of need." God responds when you draw near because it takes faith to do it. Faith pleases God and 1 John 3:22 (MSG) says, "We're able to stretch our hands out and receive what we asked for because we're doing what He said, doing what pleases Him."

There are things in this life that, if you participate in them, will contaminate and defile you both inside and out. This is why 2 Cor. 7:1 says you must cleanse yourself from all filthiness of the flesh and spirit. God is not going to make you avoid these bad things but He will give you the strength to resist them if you choose to. 1 John 5:18 says, "We know that whoever is born of God does not sin, but he who has been born of God keeps himself and the wicked one does not touch him." This does not mean that a believer cannot sin, it does mean "that God's children do not make a practice of sinning" (NLT). A born again believer who is in close fellowship with God does not keep on sinning as a way of life. A person who keeps yielding to sin is not as close to God as they should be. But if you will cleanse yourself and keep yourself, the enemy won't be able to touch you. This is why you have to keep yourself in the love of God, the faith of God, and the eternal plan of God. You're in trouble if you don't.

Consider what a great life you would have if the devil can't touch your body, your marriage, or your finances. You'll fulfill your destiny, your family will follow in the footsteps of Jesus, and all your bills will be paid. This is what happens when you keep yourself out of sin. It is sin that allows the devil to gain access to your life. It's what opens the door to calamity and destruction. There is a reason some people are blessed more than others. It is not random nor is it by accident. At the same time, there is a reason people are cursed and struggle day in and day out. If there is destruction in your life, then you've been touched by the evil one. God's touch brings healing, restoration, life and liberty. You need to know that the devil can't touch you just because he wants to. You stop him by keeping yourself from all sin and by overcoming all temptations. The devil tempts you because he wants to touch you. If you don't yield to the temptation, he has no right to enter your life.

There is a reason why good things happen, and there is a reason bad things happen. Just because you don't know what the reasons are does not mean they're not there. Jesus once healed an impotent man and later said to him, "See, you have been made well. Sin no more, lest a worst thing comes upon you" (John 5:14). It is not normal for a child of God to always be sick and never having enough to meet their needs. Many people have gotten used to being this way but this is not how God intended life to be. A believer should be victorious in every area and if they're not then they've been touched by the enemy. This happens when people don't walk in the light they have. A door gets opened and the devil comes in to steal, kill, and destroy. 1 Peter 5:8 says the devil roams around like a roaring lion seeking whom he can devour. This means he can't devour everybody. He can only devour those who open the door and let him in. You stop this from happening when you keep yourself from all sin.

God expects you to walk in the light you have. He never said to pray and ask Him to make the devil leave you alone. He told you to keep yourself from sin and this is what shuts the door on the enemy. When you walk in the light you have, you are in fact submitting to God. This is what allows you to resist the devil and he will flee from you (James 4:7). This verse doesn't say the devil will flee from God, it says he will flee from you. When you keep yourself you have the right to confront the devil and make him leave you alone. Storms may come but, when the wind stops blowing, you'll still be standing strong. The devil can't touch you if you keep yourself and walk in the light you have. If you want the perfect will of God in your life, then you have to do the perfect will of God. If you will keep yourself in the will of God and keep yourself from all sin, you will walk in victory every time. The devil won't touch you but God will. He'll put a hedge of protection around you that will keep you safe from all harm.

It is your responsibility to keep yourself from all contamination and defilement. There are movies you should not watch and places you should not go. There are business opportunities and other endeavors that you should not be a part of because it can contaminate you both on the outside and on the inside. Be a doer of the Word and walk in the light you have. Paul said in Gal. 5:16, "Walk in the Spirit, and you shall not fulfill the lust of the flesh." The NLT says, "So I say, let the Holy Spirit guide your lives. Then you won't be doing what your sinful nature craves." You keep yourself from sinning by walking in the Spirit every day of your life. It's when you choose to yield to what you know is true on the inside of you. When temptation comes, the Holy Spirit will rise up on the inside of you and tell you not to give in to it. When you yield to what He says, you are walking in the Spirit and sin won't have dominion over you. You can't be full of God and full of sin at the same time.

Many people are trying hard not to sin but God never said to do that. He knows that if you think about sin all the time, you'll probably end up doing it. What God said to do is walk in the Spirit. Instead of watching those bad movies, go pray and read your Bible. Make it easy on yourself and live a separated life. Walk in the Spirit so you won't fall into sin and spend the rest of your life paying the consequences for doing so. Listen to your heart for, when you do, you will not fulfill the lusts of the flesh. And don't wait an hour to do it. Respond immediately. If your heart tells you not to watch that television program, turn the channel right then and there. Don't wait until you see something you're not supposed to see. Listen to your heart and act accordingly for if you walk in the Spirit you won't carry out the desires of the flesh. This is how you conquer the sin problem. The Greater One is living inside of you and He's telling you what to do and what not to do. Whatever He says to you, do it.

Why do people override what's in their heart and go on and do what's wrong? 2 Tim. 3:1 says in the last days "men will be lovers of themselves" and vs. 4 says they are "lovers of pleasure rather than lovers of God." Paul wrote in 2 Tim. 4:9,10, "Be diligent to come to me quickly; for Demas has forsaken me, having loved this present world, and has parted for Thessalonica." The pleasures of sin are real and is the bait the devil uses to pull you into his snare. The attractions of the world with all its fleshly pleasures is amplified by the devil who is called the "ruler of this world" (John 12:31). You must continually walk in the Spirit and keep yourself from being pulled into the abyss of pleasurable sin. 1 John 2:15,16 (NLT) says, "Do not love this world nor the things it offers you, for when you love the world, you do not have the love of the Father in you. For the world offers only a craving for physical pleasure, a craving for everything we see, and pride in our achievements and possessions. These are not from the Father, but are from the world."

Why aren't churches filled to capacity every time the doors are open? Because people love something more. They love sleep more than spending time with God. They love golf more and love being lazy more. These people are not walking in the Spirit and are fulfilling the lusts of the flesh. There is a direct correlation between how much you walk in the Spirit and how much sin has a grip on your life. If you walk in the Spirit all the time, you'll sin none of the time. If you walk in the Spirit half the time, you'll sin half the time. And if, like these people, you walk in the Spirit none of the time, you'll sin all the time. It's not difficult to see how you can defeat sin in your life. All you have to do is follow what's in your heart and do what you know is right. When you do this, you are walking in the Spirit and won't give in to those evil temptations that come your way. You're more interested in pleasing God than in pleasing your own flesh. Your priorities are in order and this gives you the motivation to do what's right, those things that please God.

Everything in your life is centered around the choices you make. Even if something happens beyond your control, you still choose how you will react to it. Choices are made based on what you want more. If you want to be fit and trim then you must choose not to eat two pieces of cheesecake at midnight. It's no mystery why people fall into sin. They love the pleasures of sin more than they love God, and this is the basis on which their choices are made. John 3:19,20 says, "And this is the condemnation, that the light has come into the world, and men loved darkness rather than light, because their deeds were evil. For everyone practicing evil hates the light and does not come to the light, lest his deeds should be exposed." The Message Bible says, "They went for the darkness because they were not really interested in pleasing God." Whenever a decision has to be made, you will always choose what you love more. There is nothing in this universe that God loves more than you, and He is requiring you to love Him the same way. When you do, the problem of sin is forever defeated in your life.

-11-

"NOT GUILTY"

To conquer sin you must daily be walking in the light you have. James 4:17 says, "Therefore, to him who knows to do good and does not do it, to him it is sin." Sin is violation of light, and light is what you see and what you know. If you know you're supposed to be doing something, and don't do it, you're violating what you know. What may be sin to you may not be sin to another person if they had not seen the light in that particular area. Not everybody is walking in the same light and God tells you not to judge another person because you don't know how much light they have. What you should know is that the more light you have, the more God expects of you. "To whom much is given, from him much will be required" (Luke 12:48). Do not look down on or condemn another person if they don't have the same amount of light as you. John 3:17 says, "For God did not send His Son into the world to condemn the world, but that the world through Him might be saved."

The word "condemnation" means 'to be down and against.' To be condemned means you've been found guilty of committing some wrong and are deserving of punishment. The trial is over, the verdict is in, you've been found guilty of violating light. The good news is that God did not send His

Son into the world to find it guilty. Never point a finger at another person and tell them how guilty they are. That is not good news to the person you're talking to. Under the law of the old covenant people were made aware of their sin but, under the new covenant and the shed blood of Jesus, people are being made aware of righteousness. 2 Cor. 3:9 (NLT) says, "If the old way, which brings condemnation, was glorious, how much more glorious is the new way, which makes us right with God!" Instead of talking about sin all the time, you need to be talking about 2 Cor. 5:21 which says, "For He made Him who knew no sin to be sin for us, that we might become the righteousness of God in Him."

God is righteous and in Jesus you are also righteous and justified. This is the opposite of being condemned because the blood of Jesus makes you innocent and not guilty. The slate is wiped clean and you've been cleared of all charges from any wrong doing. You've been declared innocent and are undeserving of any punishment. That is the good news of the gospel message. The righteous have a right to go boldly into the throne room with no sense of guilt and shame. The righteous have a right to be free from all sickness and disease. They have a right to get all their needs met. The righteous are redeemed from the curse of the law and everything that would hinder them from living a rich, full life. Jesus came to make you aware of the freedom you have in Him from the chains of sin. If He didn't condemn, then neither should you, especially with members of your own family. Why look at the speck in their eye when you have a plank in your own? No, tell them about the blood of Jesus and how righteous they are in Him.

When you walk in the light, you confess your sin and God will cleanse you from all unrighteousness. Jesus died for everybody so never make somebody feel bad about themselves for what wrong they may have done. Condemnation is the business of the devil and you want no part of that. You don't want people shattered for what they've done, you want them to be cleansed and restored. You're supposed to build people up, not tear them down. John 3:18 says, "He who believes in Him is not condemned." The NLT says, "There is no judgment against anyone who believes in Him." Jesus did not come to condemn and, because you're made in His image, you should have no desire to condemn anybody. Love covers a multitude of sins (1 Peter 4:8) and it should bother you when you see a person broken and shattered over something they did wrong. You don't approve of the sin but you also don't want the person condemned for what happened. You want them forgiven just like God forgave you when you repented of the wrong you did.

Rom. 8:1 says, "There is therefore now no condemnation to those who are in Christ Jesus, who do not walk according to the flesh, but according to the Spirit." Why is there no condemnation? "For the law of the Spirit of life in Christ Jesus has made me free from the law of sin and death" (vs. 2). Sin is very real and it's not to be mocked or made light of. The wages of sin is death which means you can't play with fire and not be burned. You must take sin seriously because, if you don't, then the work Jesus did on the cross won't mean anything to you. He didn't deal with the problem of sin as something remote and unimportant. No, He came to earth as a man and "entered the disordered mess of struggling humanity in order to set it right once and for all" (vs. 3 MSG). What Jesus did was serious and very significant. On the cross He became sin with your sin so that you may become the righteousness of God. You didn't become righteous on your own but became righteous with His righteousness. He took on your sin and you took on His righteousness.

It is possible to live a life free from condemnation with no sense of guilt and shame. Not only is it possible, it is also necessary in order for you to live a victorious life. If you want to walk in overcoming faith where miracles happen in your life, you will have to first overcome the chains of guilt and condemnation. This is not an option. Because of sin there is coming a day of judgment, a day of wrath where the guilty will be judged and punished. This is a sobering thought but those who are in Christ Jesus do not have to fear this day of reckoning. Soon, and very soon, all of creation is going to stand before God on the great day of judgment. On that day the guilty will be condemned and the justified will enter into the eternal joy of the Lord. It is of utmost importance as to whether you're guilty or innocent on that day. What's at stake here is where you will spend eternity. Are you guilty or innocent, condemned or justified? If you're guilty you go one way, if you're innocent you go the other way. You, and only you, are the one who decides which direction you will go.

You have an adversary who Rev. 12:10 calls "the accuser of our brethren, who accused them before our God day and night." The devil is seeking judgment to come against you so that he can gain access to your life. He accused Job before God when he said, "You have blessed the work of his hands, and his possessions have increased in the land. But now, stretch out Your hand and touch all that he has, and he will surely curse You to Your face!" (Job 1:10,11). The devil is bringing accusations against Job the same way a prosecuting attorney would do in a court of law. In like manner, he is seeking a judgment against you and if you're found guilty he will gain the right to come in and steal, kill, and destroy. Every day and night he is trying to find a way to get you to be judged. The good news is that you have a say in the matter. In a court of law you're allowed to take the stand and defend yourself. Rev. 12:11 says, "And they overcame him by the blood of the Lamb and by the word of their testimony." What you say matters. Are you a guilty sinner or an innocent believer whose sins have been washed away by the blood of Jesus?

What is your testimony? Are you condemned or are you righteous? You can't be both. The devil is doing everything he can to convince you that you're a no good sinner and deserve the wrath of God. Don't listen to him. He is the accuser but Jesus is your advocate, a defense attorney who never has, and never will, lose a case. After all, His Father and your Father is the Judge presiding over the court room. John writes to the church, "My little children, these things I write to you, that you may not sin. And if anyone sins, we have an Advocate with the Father, Jesus Christ the righteous" (1 John 2:1). If you do sin, don't say you're guilty. Bring before the court vs. 2 as proof of your innocence, "He himself is the sacrifice that atones for our sin - and not only our sins but the sins of all the world" (NLT). Jesus says you're not guilty so don't you say anything else. Only say what Jesus says about you. He says you're righteous, you're healed, you're redeemed. He says you've been set free from the law of sin and death. This is your testimony which you should be confessing every day of your life.

John 3:18 says, "He who believes in Him is not condemned; but he who does not believe is condemned already, because he has not believed in the name of the only begotten Son of God." Those who believe in Jesus are not guilty, those who don't are. The devil is the accuser of the brethren and he's always accusing you of being guilty so you'll accept condemnation, shame and guilt. Don't listen to him because as a believer you have the right to be blameless and shameless. Most religious folks don't believe this but this is what belongs to the born again child of God. Jesus asked the woman caught in adultery, "Woman, where are those accusers of yours? Has no one condemned you?" She said, "No one, Lord." And Jesus said to her, "Neither do I condemn you; go and sin no more" (John 8:10,11). Jesus did not make light of the wrong she had done. It was a horrible sin but Jesus didn't judge her for it. He found her not guilty and told her to not do it again. He fixed the problem. He removed the burden of blame and shame and the woman walked away different than she was before.

How innocent are you? You're just as innocent as Jesus because it's His innocence and His righteousness that you have. What He did on the cross, He did for you. Rom. 8:31-34 (NLT) says, "What shall we say about such wonderful things as these? If God is for us, who can ever be against us? Since He did not spare even His own Son but gave Him up for us all, won't He also give us everything else? Who dares accuse us whom God has chosen for His own? No one - for God himself has given us right standing with himself. Who then will condemn us? No one - for Christ Jesus died for us and was raised to life for us, and He is sitting in the place of honor at God's right hand, pleading for us." God is not bringing any charges against you because it is He who finds you not guilty and it is He who finds you innocent. Jesus is in the high court of heaven representing you and the great Judge is listening to Him. You have an Advocate with the Father and you can be sure of victory every time. The Message Bible says, "Do you think anyone is going to be able to drive a wedge between us and Christ's love for us? There is no way!"

The devil is forever seeking whom he can devour. Ps. 37:32 says, "The wicked watches the righteous, and seeks to slay him." The devil is watching you and is seeking to bring a charge against you. He wants you to be condemned, judged, and destroyed. All his efforts are in vain because vs. 33 says, "The Lord will not leave him in his hand, nor condemn him when he is judged." God is on your side and that is all you need to know to walk in victory every time. Ps. 56:9 says, "When I cry out to You, then my enemies will turn back; This I know, because God is for me." Ps. 118:5,6 says, "I called on the Lord in distress; The Lord answered me and set me in a broad place. The Lord is on my side; I will not fear. What can man do to me?" God is on your side and you need to be on your side also. Many believers don't like themselves and are always saying negative things about who they are. They're on the witness stand in the heavenly court room and they're testifying against themselves. They're shooting themselves in their own foot. It is foolishness to be against your own self when the Bible says God is on your side.

God is on your side but whose side are you on? Are you for yourself or against yourself? What you think and what you say will determine the direction your life will take. Jesus said in Matt.12;37, "For by your words you will be justified, and by your words you will be condemned." Listen to your words and take notice of what you're saying about yourself. It's a matter of life and death, guilt or innocence. Choose this day to be on whatever side God is on. Since God is on your side, you also should be on your side. Put a smile on your face and say out loud, "I'm a winner! I'm victorious! I'm free from blame and shame! I'm redeemed and I'm not guilty!" Stop talking bad about yourself and quit making jokes at your expense. Some people are their own worst enemy while Jesus is trying to be their best friend. Never talk about your failures but change sides and talk about your victories. Don't give the enemy anything to work with. Instead, confess the Word continually and give God something to work with. After all, He is on your side.

Your words carry more weight in your life than what anybody else says against you. It's by your words that you will be found innocent and it's by your words that you will be found guilty. Never say condemning words about yourself but only say words that show you are justified. Is. 50:7-9 says, "For the Lord God will help Me; Therefore I will not be disgraced; Therefore I have set My face like a flint, and I know that I will not be ashamed. He is near who justifies Me; Who will contend with Me? Let us stand together. Who is My adversary? Let him come near Me. Surely the Lord God will help Me; Who is he who will condemn Me? Indeed they will all grow old like a garment, the moth will eat them up." The accusations of other people will be here today and gone tomorrow. Never concern yourself with what other people say or think. Prov. 17:15 says those who condemn the just are an abomination to the Lord. Nothing they say matters because you serve a God who will never put you to shame. Jesus is your advocate and vindicator and He is on your side. If He says you're innocent, you're innocent.

If God says you're not guilty, then who are you to argue with Him? Never say a bad thing about yourself or any other believer. The Lord once told Peter, "What God has cleansed you must not call common" (Acts 10:15). Don't call guilty what God has justified. It's an abomination if you do. Is. 54:4 says, "Do not fear, for you will not be ashamed; Nor be disgraced, for you will not be put to shame." Vs. 14 says, "In righteousness you shall be established; You shall be far from oppression, for you shall not fear; And from terror, for it shall not come near you." If you're innocent, act like it. Vs. 15, "Whoever assembles against you shall fall for your sake." Vs. 17, "No weapon formed against you shall prosper, and every tongue which rises against you in judgment You shall condemn. This is the heritage of the servants of the Lord, and their righteousness is from Me." You are established in righteousness and in court you will deny and discredit every false accusation. Nothing anybody says can be used against you because you are identified with Christ. If God be for you, who can be against you?

When a believer sins it is wrong to say to that person, "Shame on you." Get those words out of your vocabulary for when you say them you are ministering condemnation to the person who sinned. This is not of God for He did not send His Son to condemn the world. When you accuse somebody of wrong doing you're acting just like the devil for he is the accuser of the brethren. Don't do it. Don't condemn other people and don't condemn yourself. In Christ there is no blame and no shame. Many preachers use guilt to motivate church goers. They think a sign of being a good Christian is to always be conscious of sin and to confess how guilty they are. These ministers may be sincere but they're sincerely wrong. They lack the mentality of knowing you've been made the righteousness of God in Christ Jesus. There was a time when sin condemned people but Jesus came and condemned sin. Because of the cross there is now no condemnation to those who are in Christ Jesus. If you feel condemned then for you the death of Jesus was in vain.

You are righteous and James 5:16 (AMP) says, "Therefore, confess your sins to one another [your false steps, your offenses], and pray for one another, that you may be healed and restored. The heartfelt and persistent prayer of a righteous man (believer) can accomplish much [when put into action and made effective by God - it is dynamic and can have tremendous power]." Tremendous power is available to a person who is righteous and not guilty. They pray and get results. Prov. 28:1 says, "The wicked flee when no one pursues, but the righteous are bold as a lion." The wicked flee because they have fear on the inside of them. No person can hope to escape what he carries with him on the inside wherever he goes. But the righteous are different. They're bold as a lion. When a lion looks you in the eye, you can tell they're not afraid of you or anything else. They're bold and they're powerful. Nothing intimidates them and this is how the righteous are. They have no sense of fear or inferiority and are able to go boldly into the throne room of God.

The Young's Literal translation says, "The righteous, as a young lion, is confident." To be bold is to be confident and this is a faith term. 1 John 3:21 says, "Beloved, if our heart does not condemn us, we have confidence toward God." Condemnation will give you an inferiority complex that will turn you into a coward. The devil will use condemnation to rob you of your faith in God and in yourself. Sin consciousness will hold you in bondage and prevent you from living a good life and fulfilling your destiny. Cowards pray desperate prayers but righteous believers pray bold prayers, prayers filled with faith and confidence. They act and talk like Jesus to the point that people marvel in their presence. How does a person get righteous? Rom. 10:10 says "For with the heart one believes to righteousness, and with the mouth confession is made to salvation." With your heart you believe that Jesus took your sin and gave you His righteousness. His blood washed away your sins and this is why you're righteous. You are clean in Him and have no blame and no shame.

If Jesus could be made righteous after taking on the sin of the world, then everyone who accepts Him as Lord and Savior will become as righteous as He is. 2 Cor. 5:21 says, "For He made Him who knew no sin to be sin for us, that we might become the righteousness of God in Him." This righteousness allows you to stand before God with no sense of guilt and condemnation. It also allows you to confront the devil without fear and any sense of inferiority or intimidation. If you're bold enough to stand before God, then you can be bold enough to stand before the devil and tell him to get out of your life. The righteous submit to God and are bold to resist the enemy. They're confident of who they are in Christ and what they've become. This is why they're bold as a lion. They have the same liberty and freedom that Jesus had with the Father when He walked the earth. Those who are righteous act just like Jesus. 1 John 2:1 calls Him, "Jesus Christ, the righteous." Put your name in that verse and never hesitate to call yourself "the righteous" for this is who you are in Christ.

Those who are righteous are "strong in the Lord and in the power of His might" (Eph. 6:10). They are able to stand against the wiles of the devil because they put on the whole armor of God, one of the pieces being the breastplate of righteousness (vs. 11-14). You put this piece of armor on because the enemy is trying to pierce your heart with guilt and condemnation. He is seeking whom he can devour and he will kill you if he can. Rom. 7:11 says, "For sin, taking occasion by the commandment, deceived me, and by it killed me." Never play games where the devil is concerned and never make light of sin. You are a soldier in the army of God and at your disposal are weapons of righteousness. 2 Cor. 6:7 (AMP) says, "In [speaking] the word of truth, in the power of God; by the weapons of righteousness for the right hand [like holding the sword to attack] and for the left [like holding the shield to defend]." These weapons are not imaginary but are very real for the pulling down of strongholds. Sin is real, the devil is real, and so are your weapons of righteousness real. They are so real that they are able to stop the devil from piercing your heart.

Those who are always sin conscious are vulnerable to the attacks of the enemy and are easily pierced. These people need to put on the breastplate of righteousness. They need to know that Jesus took their sins and gave them His righteousness. When this happened, the Judge slammed the gavel down and pronounced them not guilty. Those who walk in the light have learned this truth. They have overcome guilt and shame and condemnation. They are more than conquerors in Christ Jesus because they have put on the breastplate of righteousness. If you don't put this piece of armor on, your confidence will erode and you'll never be as bold as a lion. You can't go through life thinking about every mistake you've ever made and every sin you've ever committed. Some people will think this is being humble but it's not. This is foolishness because it's making light of what Jesus did on the cross. Hanging your head in shame is saying that for you Jesus died in vain. It's time to rise up and put on the whole armor of God. It's time to put on the breastplate of righteousness.

Those who are bold don't keep quiet for one weapon they have at their disposal is the word of their testimony (Rev. 12:11). They are a witness for God and openly declare all the good things He has done in their life. Before Jesus ascended on high He said in Acts 1:8, "But you shall receive power when the Holy Spirit has come upon you; and you shall be witnesses to Me in Jerusalem, and in all Judea and Samaria, and to the end of the earth." Don't keep quiet but go on record and testify that you are a witness for the Lord Jesus Christ. Be bold and tell people how He's met all your needs and paid all your bills. Tell them that once you were lost but now am found. Be willing to stand up and testify any time, any where. Some people may not like it but do it anyway. Jesus said in Matt. 10:32-34, "Therefore whoever confesses Me before men, him I will also confess before My Father who is in heaven. But whoever denies Me before men, him I will also deny before My Father who is in heaven. Do not think that I came to bring peace on the earth. I did not come to bring peace but a sword."

Never be ashamed of who you are in Christ. This doesn't mean you have to force your beliefs on people who don't want to hear it. What it does mean is that you're bold as a lion and are always talking about the goodness of God and all that He's done in your life. Sinners don't keep quiet so why should you? The devil knows that you overcome him by the blood of the Lamb and the word of your testimony. You've got a testimony but nobody will know what it is unless you give voice to it. What you say matters, so much so that Jesus said in Matt. 12:36,37 (AMP), "But I tell you, on the day of judgment people will have to give an accounting for every careless or useless word they speak. For by your words [reflecting your spiritual condition] you will be justified and acquitted of guilt of sin; and by your words [rejecting Me] you will be condemned and sentenced." This has not been believed by most Christians. They're not careful about the things they say and just rattle off whatever comes to their mind. They speak first and think later. This is wrong and the Bible says they'll be judged for it.

Believe that what you say matters. There are some things that should never come out of your mouth. If you hear yourself say the wrong thing, quickly correct yourself and say the right thing. Your words carry weight both in your life and in the court room of heaven. Heb. 4:14 says, "Seeing then that we have a great High Priest who has passed through the heavens, Jesus the Son of God, let us hold fast our confession." Your words and your testimony gives God something to work with. You don't overcome the devil by keeping quiet and this is why you're told to hold fast your confession. You've got a testimony and you're supposed to speak it out of your mouth. The words you speak is what Jesus presents to the Father when He makes intercession for you (Heb. 7:25). You do the speaking and Jesus will back you up all the way. This is why you can't go around confessing what a no good sinner you are. Is this what you want Jesus to tell the Father? No, confess you're saved by grace, you're redeemed and, above all else, you're not guilty.

Randall J. Brewer

-12-

"JUDGE NOT"

God takes sin serious and so should you. As the return of the Lord draws near, the world is growing darker and darker. People are sinning freely and willingly with no regard to the fact that a day of judgment will soon be upon them. A stern warning is given in Heb. 10:31, "It is a fearful thing to fall into the hands of the living God." Yes, God is loving and kind and generous but He is also holy and just. He is the great Judge of the universe who is angered by injustice every day (Ps. 7:11). Still, in the midst of these threats of judgment and wrath comes a generous offer of grace and mercy. Ps. 103:8 says, "The Lord is merciful and gracious, slow to anger, and abounding in mercy." God loves the people of the world so much that He sent Jesus to die on a cross for them and to take upon Himself all the wrath and indignation reserved for sinful man. God gives sinners warning of what's to come and a chance to prevent it from happening. When a person receives Jesus into their heart, He becomes their Advocate and in turn the great Judge declares them not guilty of their sin.

Since you have not been judged of your sin, be careful not to judge others of theirs. There is only one judge in the universe and it's not you. Ps. 50:6 says, "Let the heavens declare His righteousness, for God Himself is Judge." A verse that all Christians should pay close attention to is Matt. 7:1 where Jesus said, "Judge not, that you be not judged." Almost all believers know this verse, and a lot of non-believers as well. Everybody knows you're not supposed to judge another person and, at the same time, nobody will admit they're doing it. The truth of the matter is that people are judging others all the time but they're calling it something else. They're denying the fact that they've taken on the role of judge and jury when it comes to the actions of other people. Jesus is telling you not to do this. The Amplified Bible says, "Do not judge and criticize and condemn [others unfairly with an attitude of self-righteous superiority as though assuming the office of a judge], so that you will not be judged [unfairly].

It matters if you get judged or not. Many ministers preach today that it's not possible for a believer to be judged, but Jesus said you would be if and when you judge another person. It is a serious thing to be judged and you do not want this to happen to you. Matt. 7:2 says, "For with what judgment you judge, you will be judged; and with the same measure you use, it will be measured back to you." The Amplified Bible says, "For just as you [hypocritically] judge others [when you are sinful and unrepentant], so will you be judged, and in accordance with your standard of measure [used to pass out judgment], judgment will be measured to you." God will deal with you the way you deal with other people. This is just and fair although many people may not think so. They want others to be condemned but want mercy for themselves. God says differently. The NLT says, "For you will be treated as you treat others. The standard you use in judging is the standard by which you will be judged." Be careful what you think and say about other people.

Most Christians don't believe they're in a position to be judged. If they did, it would change the way they treat other people immediately. They act like they're caring for people when they point out their faults when the truth is they are judging them. Matt. 7:3 says, "And why do you look at the speck in your brother's eye, but do not consider the plank in your own eye?" It is wrong to point out and magnify the defects in other people, especially when you life is in worse shape than the person you're pointing your finger at. When you see the wrong in other people the first thing you should do is check up on yourself and make sure you're not doing the same thing. This is what prevents judgment from coming. Examine yourself and be honest about it. Vs. 4 says, "Or how can you say to your brother, 'Let me remove the speck out of your eye'; and look, a plank is in your own eye." People always want to straighten out the lives of others when their own life is in a mess. They want to correct others when they have serious problems they won't deal with themselves. Jesus calls these people hypocrites.

"Hypocrite! First remove the plank from your own eye, and then you will see clearly to remove the speck from your brother's eye" (Matt. 7:5). Doing this will give you a different attitude about other people and the things they're dealing with. It will motivate you to help them and not judge them. You won't be harsh and judgmental if you've gone through the same thing. And, if you don't judge others, you yourself won't be judged. Your problems will be solved and you'll be spared from going through many of the difficulties of day to day living. This is why 1 Cor. 11:31 says, "For if we would judge ourselves, we would not be judged". The Amplified Bible says, "But if we evaluated and judged ourselves honestly [recognizing our shortcomings and correcting our behavior], we would not be judged." This is some of the best news you'll ever hear in your life. You can prevent judgment in your life by simply judging yourself and not judging others. James 2:13 (ASV) says, "For judgment is without mercy to him that hath showed no mercy: mercy glorieth against judgment."

The NIV says, "Speak and act as those who are going to be judged by the law that gives freedom, because judgment without mercy will be shown to anyone who has not been merciful. Mercy triumphs over judgment" (vs. 12,13). Judgment is coming and, if you expect to receive mercy on that great day, it is only right that you show mercy now. It is hypocritical for God to show mercy to you and then for you to turn around and be harsh and critical to someone else. You must show mercy to others for, if you don't, God will not show mercy to you when you are judged. But the one who shows mercy can stand without fear before God on that day. What do you want? Mercy or judgment? What you do for others is what God will do for you. Jesus said in Matt. 6:14,15, "For if you will forgive men their trespasses, your heavenly Father will also forgive you. But if you do not forgive men their trespasses, neither will your Father forgive your trespasses." This is serious business. What you say and do does matter.

Job 1:7 says that Satan is continually "going to and fro on the earth, and from walking back and forth on it." What's he doing? He is seeking whom he can devour and destroy. Sad to say, there are many Christians who are being devoured and their lives are being destroyed. This is not the will of God and there are many other believers who are not experiencing the same destruction. Those who think this is not fair better be careful for what they're doing is judging God. This is what Job did. He judged God for not being fair because of the supernatural destruction that came on his life. Job did not know what was going on behind the scenes but still he judged God for being unfair and unjust. You need to trust God with all your heart because everything He does and does not do is righteous, just, and fair. If you don't understand what's going on in your life then there is something wrong with the way you're looking at it. Job later repented for his judgment of God and as he sat in dust and ashes his life got turned around.

Paul said in Eph. 4:27 to not give place to the devil. One way to do that is to judge other people. It is a reality that you have been and will be tempted to judge. Before the day is out somebody may want to talk to you about somebody else in a negative way. If you join in that conversation then you are guilty of passing judgment on the person you're talking about. Make a decision right now to walk away from such conversations so you won't fall into the devil's trap of judging other people. Remember, how you judge others is how you will be judged. There is more involved here than two people having a conversation. The devil is listening to you and he's looking for a way to come in and destroy your life. He will try to influence you and get you to do and say things that are judgmental against that other person. He is trying to build a case against you so he can get you judged. He is looking for a door to get into your life so that he can bring calamity and destruction to you and your family. He is a despicable foe and this is how he operates.

If you don't show mercy, it's only right that you don't receive mercy. If you judge, it's only right that you get judged. If that happens, the destroyer will come in and devour your life. You need to close the door on being judgmental and give the devil no place and no access into your life. It doesn't matter what the other person did wrong and how obvious it is, it still isn't your place to pass judgment on them. You don't know all the facts about their situation, you don't know how much light of God's Word they've been given, so don't allow yourself to have a negative opinion about that person. Remember, there is only one judge and it's not you. If you want mercy, show mercy. Even if that other person did you wrong and hurt you in a bad way, show mercy and be kind to them. Don't grumble and complain and pass judgment. This is when you show what you're made of, a time to reveal who and what is on the inside of you. If it's God, then show mercy and act accordingly.

Judging is everywhere and most people can't go a day or a week without saying something bad about another person. Why is there so much judging going on? The enemy, the god of this world, will tempt you every day to judge somebody because he wants you to be judged. The only way he can gain access to your life to hurt you and destroy you is to get judgment passed against you. The devil accused Job before God and the man got judged. The judgment against Job is what gave the devil access to his life. Before judgment came there was a hedge of protection around Job and the enemy couldn't touch him (Job 1:10). After Job's life went into a tailspin his friends came to comfort him but ended up judging him as well. In the midst of all this, Job got mad and began to judge God believing it was unfair what happened to him. Thankfully, Job later repented and God had mercy on him, and when he prayed for his friends they were forgiven also. Be careful who you talk about because they may be the person you need something from later on.

If you're a Christian you can't judge without being hypocritical. Some people judge every day but cover it up by saying they're speaking the truth in love. Who do they think they're fooling? God knows what they're doing and so does the devil. These people then wonder why their life is in the mess it's in. They judged and they got judged. A door was opened and the devil gained access to their life. James 2:4 (NLT) says that people who judge "are guided by evil motives." When you judge somebody, you are not showing love toward that person. If you can't say something good about somebody, don't say anything at all. This is how you keep from being judged. If you show mercy, you will be shown mercy. If you don't, then you will forfeit the mercy provided for you at the cross and will fall back into judgment. James 2:13 (ERV) says, "Yes, you must show mercy to others. If you do not show mercy, then God will not show mercy to you when He judges you. But the one who shows mercy can stand without fear before the Judge."

If you're standing in faith over what Jesus did for you, if your sins are washed away by the blood of the Lamb, then you won't have to worry about what will happen once this life is over. You won't have to be afraid when judgment comes on all people. You can be bold because mercy has triumphed over judgment. Determine today to never judge again. Open your heart and mind and be quick to recognize the temptations to judge that come your way. James 4:10 says, "Humble yourselves in the sight of the Lord, and He will lift you up." People who judge are proud and full of themselves. You have to be prideful to judge another person. Vs. 11 (NLT) says, "Don't speak evil against each other, dear brothers and sisters. If you criticize and judge each other, then you are criticizing and judging God's law. But your job is to obey the law, not to judge whether it applies to you." The Message Bible says, "Don't bad-mouth each other, friends. It's God's Word, His Message, His Royal Rule, that takes a beating in that kind of talk. You're supposed to be honoring the Message, not writing graffiti all over it."

James 4:12 asks the question, "Who are you to judge another?" The Amplified Bible says, "Who are you to [hypocritically or self-righteously] pass judgment on your neighbor?" Who are you to set yourself up as the standard by which everybody should live their life? Who do you think you are? This is what this verse is asking. People who judge are fault-finders. This means they're actively looking for things wrong in other people. You can't find a fault unless you're first looking for one. In order to stop being a judge you've got to stop looking for the shortcomings in those around you. What's going on with them is none of your business. There are enough deficiencies in your own life to keep you busy where you won't have the time to look at the speck in your neighbor's eye. James 5:9 (BBE) says, "Say no hard things against one another, brother, so that you will not be judged; see, the judge is waiting at the doors." Titus 3:2 says, "They must not slander anyone and must avoid quarreling. Instead, they should be gentle and show true humility to everyone."

Love builds people up but judgment pulls them down. This is why Paul said in Eph. 4:29, "Let no corrupt communication proceed out of your mouth, but what is good for necessary edification, that it may impart grace to the hearer." Gossip and critical words don't minister grace to anybody. Don't speak evil about other people and at the same time don't allow others to say bad things about other people to you. Your ears are not garbage cans so don't allow others to fill them with rubbish. Walk away from such talk and don't you talk this way either. People are not helped when you talk about them behind their back. Instead of judging them, pray for them and go out and buy them a love gift. Tell them how special they are and that you and God thinks they're important. Do this because if you judge them you're taking the devil's side who is trying to take them down. And, while he's at it, since you're walking in judgment, the devil will turn around and take you down also. Nobody wins when you talk bad about other people so don't do it.

If you don't want to be judged there are two things you must do: stop judging others, and start judging yourself. If you are full of pride and are unwilling to humble yourself and repent, you will not be able to judge yourself. It takes humility to admit you've missed the mark and done something wrong. If you're walking in pride, the devil doesn't have to yield to you because you're yielding to him. You must humble yourself in order to resist the devil. 1 Peter 5:5,6 says to be clothed with humility for "God resists the proud, but gives grace to the humble." When you humble yourself you are willing to repent and this is what it means to judge yourself. This is God's will for your life. 2 Peter 3:9 says He is "not willing that any should perish but that all should come to repentance." Judging yourself is what stops the devil from gaining access to your life. It's what allows you to come boldly to the throne of grace. It's what allows you to live a rich, full life and, more importantly, it clears the roadblocks and allows you to fulfill your destiny.

1 Peter 4:17 says, "For the time has come for judgment to begin at the house of God; and if it begins with us first, what will be the end of those who do not believe the gospel of God?" This verse clearly says that a born again believer can be judged in this life, in the here and now. Acts 4:32-37 tells how a great multitude of those who believed went and sold their possessions and brought all the proceeds and laid them at the feet of the apostles who then distributed to each as anyone had need. This is what happens when people are walking in the light and are being led by the Spirit of God. They're full of love and faith and are generous givers. All was well but little did the people know that judgment would soon fall in the house of God. Acts 5:1,2 says, "But a certain man named Ananias, with Sapphira his wife, sold a possession. And he kept back part of the proceeds, his wife also being aware of it, and brought a certain part and laid it at the apostles' feet." These were Christian people who were part of the church, so much so that Peter knew him by name.

"But Peter said, 'Ananias, why has Satan filled your heart to lie to the Holy Spirit and keep back part of the price of the land for yourself?" (Acts 5:3). You can try to fool man but you can't fool God. He is everywhere and He sees and hears everything you do. The thoughts of Ananias and Sapphira were not on God but instead was on how they could fool the leaders in the church. They disrespected God by disrespecting the leadership who was there. God takes it personally when people do this. Vs. 4, "While it remained, was it not your own? And after it was sold, was it not in your own control? Why have you conceived this thing in your heart? You have not lied to man but to God." In the midst of this great move of God this Christian man stood up in church and lied in front of everybody. Now was the time to repent but this he did not do. Judgment came and it came immediately. "Then Ananias, hearing these words, fell down and breathed his last. So great fear came upon all those who heard these things. And the young men arose and wrapped him up, carried him out, and buried him" (vs. 5,6).

Ananias was judged because he didn't judge himself. The same thing happened to his wife three hours later (vs. 7-11). This is not to say they went to hell for 1 Cor. 11:32 says, "But when we are judged, we are judged by the Lord, that we may not be condemned with the world." The Message Bible says, "Better to be confronted by the Master now than to face a fiery confrontation later." Ananias and Sapphira got judged that day in church but they're not going to be judged with the rest of the sinful world at the great judgment to come. It's better to be judged now rather than later, it's even better to not be judged at all. This is what happens when you judge yourself. You'll receive grace and mercy and you won't be judged. In Acts 8 Simon the sorcerer wanted to buy the power to lay hands on people so they'll receive the Holy Spirit. Peter rebuked him for this evil thought and said in vs. 22, "Repent therefore of this your wickedness, and pray God if perhaps the thought of your heart may be forgiven you." Simon repented (vs. 24) and judgment was avoided. He judged himself and did not get judged.

Before you try to help somebody else with their shortcomings, Jesus said to first take the plank out of your own eye. This is another way of saying you've got to judge yourself. The Lord told you to do this so it must be important. The question is, are you doing it? Daily you need to prayerfully examine yourself and your relationship with God. Check up on your motives and test your heart to see if you're doing things for the right reason. Doing this shuts the door on the enemy and stops him from coming into your life. If you will judge yourself and not make a practice of sinning, 1 John 5:18 says "the wicked one does not touch him." This is the only verse in the Bible which contains such a declaration.

Stopping the devil from hindering your life depends more on what you do than on what God or anybody else does. You must judge yourself. Luke 6:36,37 says, "Therefore be merciful, just as your Father also is merciful. Judge not, and you shall not be judged. Condemn not, and you shall not be condemned. Forgive, and you will be forgiven." This is the key to continual happiness.

Jesus said in Luke 6:39, "Can the blind lead the blind? Will they not both fall into the ditch?" If you've got a plank in your eye then you cannot see and Jesus is asking, "How can the blind help the blind?" They can't and this is why you have to judge yourself so you'll be able to see clearly to help the other person. It all comes down to honesty. You need to look at yourself in the mirror of God's Word and be honest about what you see. Sin is violation of light and you must be honest about what you know and how much light has been revealed to you. Don't say you didn't know something was wrong if the light has been revealed to you in that particular area. Not admitting the truth about what you know is pride. You don't want people to know you missed the mark so you make excuses and plead ignorance. This is a failure to judge yourself and now judgment has come on you. This is why you need to humble yourself and, in honesty, judge yourself and repent. When you do, God will give you grace and mercy and wash your sins away.

How do you judge yourself? It's not complicated. You acknowledge that you knew better but you did it anyway. You missed the mark so humble yourself and make no excuses for doing so. Be honest about what you did. 1 John 1:8 says, "If we say that we have no sin, we deceive ourselves and the truth is not in us." If you're walking in darkness and aren't honest about it, John says you're deceiving yourself. This ties in with James 1:22 that says, "But be doers of the word, and not hearers only, deceiving yourselves." There is a danger in not being honest with yourself because in time you will come to believe that the wrong you're doing is acceptable in the eyes of God. You've been deceived and this will pull you farther away from the light of God's Word. You won't judge yourself because you don't think you need to and now you will be judged. There is, however, good news to be found in 1 John 1:9, "If we confess our sins, He is faithful and just to forgive us our sins and cleanse us from all unrighteousness."

Nobody likes to be judged and it's for your benefit that Jesus told you not to judge other people. Even if people are judging you, you can't judge them for doing that. Two wrongs don't make a right. You need to judge yourself and consider whether or not you're doing the same thing they are. Yes, you will be supernaturally persuaded and tempted to judge other people. It is no accident that this will happen because the enemy is forever looking for an open door into your life. On a regular basis you have to watch what you think and say or else you will fall into the same trap other people are falling into. The enemy will actively bring thoughts and feelings to you in an attempt to hurt you and bring you down. He wants you to get judged and, in order for that to happen, he's got to get you to judge other people. Don't let this happen. Take your eyes off them and put them on yourself. Rom. 12:2 (NLT) says, "Don't copy the behavior and customs of the world, but let God transform you into a new person by changing the way you think."

In humility you need to be honest about who you are. Paul said in Rom. 12:3 (NLT), "Don't think you are better than you really are. Be honest in your evaluation of yourselves, measuring yourselves by the faith God has given us." You can and should think highly of yourself, just don't think more highly than what is actually true. This is where pride comes in. It's when you believe things about yourself that are not true. Pride and deception always go together. Obadiah 3 says, "The pride of your heart has deceived you." Judging people will cause you to think you're better than they are and this is called pride. Don't do it. In like manner, you can't separate humility from honesty. Paul continued to say in Rom. 12:14-16 (NLT), "Bless those who persecute you. Don't curse them; pray that God will bless them. Be happy with those who are happy, and weep with those who weep. Live in harmony with each other. Don't be too proud to enjoy the company of ordinary people. And don't think you know it all!"

Don't carry on your shoulder an attitude of superiority where you think you're better than other people. You're not, so never put yourself so high on the scale that you're always looking down on those around you. Having a spirit of humility is what will cause you to not judge them. Yes, your life may be more blessed than some folks but this is all because of the grace of God and not your own doing. Living a good life does not give you the right to judge those who aren't. Don't look at their circumstances because, if you do, you won't see the value God places on them as people. Jesus ate with sinners and these people knew He cared about them. He didn't come to condemn the world but to show people the love of the Father and the road to eternal life. Rom. 13:10 says, "Love does no harm to a neighbor; therefore love is the fulfillment of the law." The Amplified Bible says, "Love does no wrong to a neighbor [it never hurts anyone]. Therefore [unselfish] love is the fulfillment of the law."

When you love somebody you don't want anything bad to happen to them, and this includes them being judged. If you're judging someone, you're not loving them. It is not your responsibility to point out every speck-sized problem they have. What should you do? Rom. 14:1 (MSG) says, "Welcome with open arms fellow believers who don't see things the way you do. And don't jump all over them every time they do or say something you don't agree with - even when it seems that they are strong on opinions but weak in the faith department. Remember, they have their own history to deal with. Treat them gently." If your life is going better than others, don't judge them but rather be an example to them. Show them the scriptures you used to get you to where you're at today. Don't look down on people but build them up and show them how to see the same goodness of God that you see. Judging people will only make matters worse, especially for yourself, but always remember that love covers a multitude of sins (1 Peter 4:8).

-13-

"CALLED TO BE SAINTS"

You are here for a purpose. God has a plan for your life, an assignment from on high, and the top priority of your life should be to discover that plan and to fulfill it to completion. Yes, God wants you blessed beyond measure but you must understand that the kingdom of God is not about getting what you want when you want it. Paul says in Rom. 4:17,18 that "the kingdom of God is not food and drink, but righteousness and peace and joy in the Holy Spirit. For he who serves Christ in these things is acceptable to God and approved by men." The Message Bible says, "God's kingdom isn't a matter of what you put in your stomach, for goodness' sake. It's what God does with your life as he sets it right, puts it together, and completes it with joy. Your task is to single-mindedly serve Christ. Do that and you'll kill two birds with one stone: pleasing the God above you and proving your worth to the people around you." The secret to fulfilling your purpose is to put God first in everything you do.

Knowing who you are in Christ is the most valuable thing you will learn in life. There is nothing better than to have the confidence that God loves you and to know you don't have to impress people in order to have a sense of self-worth. As a member of God's holy family you are being offered righteousness, peace, and joy in the Holy Spirit, and these are the things you must pursue with all your heart and soul. Matt. 13:44 says, "Again, the kingdom of heaven is like treasure hidden in a field, which a man found and hid; and for joy over it he goes and sells all that he has and buys the field." This man pursued this treasure and paid a great price to get it. Are you willing to do the same? Are you willing to lay aside the cravings of the flesh in order to be holy as God is holy? Are you willing to do whatever it takes to pursue those things that matter most in the eyes of God? The things you actively pursue in life has everything to do with your joy and the fulfillment of your destiny, so make sure you are pursuing the right things.

Matt. 6:33 says, "But seek first the kingdom of God and His righteousness, and all these things will be added to you." The Amplified Bible says, "But first and most importantly seek (aim at, strive after) His kingdom and His righteousness [His way of doing and being right - the attitude and character of God], and all these things will be given to you also." The world is seeking ways to be rich and famous but God is telling you to seek His way of doing things. People in the world are wasting their lives trying to do the very thing God said He would do if they would seek first His kingdom. Jesus prayed in vs. 10 of the same chapter, "Your kingdom come. Your will be done on earth as it is in heaven." Jesus is saying that God's kingdom is the place where His will is done, the place where the King reigns and has dominion over all things. To seek first the kingdom of God means to seek the advancement of those things He reigns over. As you do that, He will add everything you need to fulfill your destiny here in this life.

Today's headlines reveal that God's will is not being done all over this planet. Why is that? Ps. 115:16 says, "The heaven, even the heavens, are the Lord's; But the earth He has given to the children of men." The free will of man is what determines whether or not God's will gets done on earth as it is in heaven. God gave the earth to Adam and he turned the authority of ruling it over to the devil when he sinned. In the wilderness the devil said to Jesus, "All this authority I will give You, and their glory; for this has been delivered to me, and I give it to whomever I wish. Therefore, if You will worship before me, all will be Yours" (Luke 4:6,7). 2 Cor. 4:4 calls the devil "the god of this age" and this shows that the kingdom of God is not reigning over all this world. God is not in control of everything that happens here like most people would think. But He can and will reign over your life if you will exercise your free will and allow Him to do so. This is not automatic. He will only reign in your life to the degree that you are yielding to Him.

Once you surrender your will to the will of the Father, your mission in life is to help others see the light so that they'll allow Him to reign in their life as well. This is what it means to seek first the advancement of God's kingdom. You can help change the world by touching the lives of those around you one by one. But first you must allow Him to reign in your life. You must face and deal with the problem of sin and then set out on a journey where you are continually being led by the Spirit of God. John the Baptist brought a message of repentance to the people and so did Jesus. He said in Mark 1:15, "The time is fulfilled, and the kingdom of God is at hand. repent, and believe in the gospel." The Amplified Bible says, "The [appointed period of] time is fulfilled, and the kingdom of God is at hand; repent [change your inner self - your old way of thinking, regret past sins, live your life in a way that proves repentance; seek God's purpose for your life] and believe [with a deep, abiding trust] in the good news [regarding salvation]."

The Bible in its entirety reveals to you the will of God for your life. Each and every page points to a central theme which is clearly expressed in 1 Peter 1:15,16, "But as He who called you is holy; you also be holy in all your conduct because it is written, 'Be holy, for I am holy.'" The Message Bible says, "As obedient children, let yourselves be pulled into a way of life shaped by God's life, a life energetic and blazing with holiness." Born as a man, Jesus brought from the Father a message of repentance which, in turn, leads to a life of holiness. God said in Lev. 20:7,8 (MSG), "Set yourselves apart for a holy life. Live a holy life, because I am God, your God. Do what I tell you; live the way I tell you. I am the God who makes you holy." You were made in the image of God and, since it is His desire for you to be like Him, a life of holiness should be the ultimate goal of your life. Consider what Paul said in Eph. 1:4, "Even before He made the world, God loved us and chose us in Christ to be holy and without fault in His eyes."

Paul wrote in 1 Cor. 1:2, "To the church of God which is at Corinth, to those who are sanctified in Christ Jesus, called to be saints, with all who in every place call on the name of Jesus Christ our Lord, both theirs and ours." The Message Bible describes saints as "Christians cleaned up by Jesus and set apart for a God-filled life." You are called to be a saint in God's kingdom and Heb. 12:14 (NLT) reveals how important holiness truly is, "Work at living in peace with everyone, and work at living a holy life, for those who are not holy will not see the Lord." The Bible records the story of two people who were perfectly holy and without sin in their lives. They enjoyed a unique and almost unheard of relationship with their Heavenly Father. They walked with Him and shared their most intimate feelings and desires, and He did the same with them. Theirs names were Adam and the one called "the second Adam," Jesus. Nothing could separate them from the close and ultimate fellowship they had with their God. Nothing, that is, except sin.

The book of Genesis tells how Adam ate the forbidden fruit and, along with his wife, was forced out of the Garden of Eden. On the cross, Jesus was made to be sin on behalf of man and the Almighty was forced to turn His back on His beloved Son. The Lord's greatest pain was upon Him as He cried out, "My God, My God, why hast Thou forsaken Me?"

(Matt. 27:46). Since light and darkness don't mix, sin will always separate you from having close fellowship with your Heavenly Father. Because he loves you so much, it is His greatest desire that you get sin out of your life so you can "be holy as He is holy" and fellowship be restored. It was for this reason that Jesus came to earth. Because you are born again, God no longer sees you by yourself but rather sees you united with His Son. A marriage, a heavenly covenant, was performed the moment you asked Jesus into your heart. A wonderful and exciting journey now takes place as you begin a lifetime of letting God reign in your life as you allow Him to mold and shape your life "until Christ be formed in you" (Gal. 4:19).

Your main concern in life is to seek first the expansion of God's kingdom and this is what the fulfillment of your destiny is all about. Christianity is not just about getting God to help you live a better life, to help you build your own personal kingdom. No, you are here to help build His kingdom and it all begins with you actively dealing with the issue of sin in your life. Nobody has to tell you that there is an enemy arrayed against you, a thief who comes to steal, kill, and destroy (John 10:10). The name of that enemy is Satan and his biggest weapon is sin. It cannot be emphasized enough the alarming words of Is. 59:2, "But your iniquities have separated you from your God; and your sins have hidden His face from you so that He will not hear." Sin has a dire effect in the life of a believer in that it hinders his fellowship with God. It is hard to believe that a Christian man will have a close relationship with God if he is committing adultery on his wife. Habitual and gross sin in the life of a believer is a terrible thing and is not to be tolerated.

While it is true that all believers will trip and fall into sin, some more than others, it is never necessary for them to do so. Jesus broke the power of sin on the cross and showed the world how to live a sin-free life. 1 John 2:1 says, "My little children, these things I write to you, that you may not sin."

This should be the goal of every believer. God's desire for you is to be holy as He is holy and this means to be without sin. Since He commanded you to be holy, you can rightfully surmise that a life of holiness, a life where sin does not have a stronghold on your behavior, is an achievable goal. In order to attain a life of holiness you need to purge yourself from all sin. 2 Cor. 7:1 says, "Therefore, having these promises, beloved, let us cleanse ourselves from all filthiness of the flesh and spirit, perfecting holiness in the fear of God." The Message Bible says, "With promises like this to pull us on, let's make a clean break with everything that defiles or distracts us, both within and without. Let's make our entire lives fit and holy temples for the worship of God."

The way to be released from the bondage of sin is through the gateway of repentance. As you walk and grow in the Christian faith a deep love relationship develops between you and your loving Savior. A wholesome dread of displeasing Him begins to grow in your heart and this in turn will compel you to face head-on the problem of sin. Daily you are to crucify the flesh and to become a slave of righteousness. Gal. 5:24,25 says, "And those who are Christ's have crucified the flesh with its passions and desires. If we live in the Spirit let us also walk in the Spirit." Heb. 6:1 lists "repentance from acts that lead to death" as the first of many basic foundations for Christian living. You should never condone or attempt to excuse your sin. The two things you should do is confess your sin and then forsake it all together. Forgiveness comes when you confess your sin (1 John 1:9) while repentance is the act of forsaking your sin. Forgiveness is an attitude of the heart whereas repentance is an action. If corrective action is not taken then one will wonder if you were truly sorrowful in the first place.

The road to holiness always begins with a godly sorrow for having sinned. David wrote in Ps. 38:18, "For I will declare my iniquity; I will be in anguish over my sin." James 4:9 also says to, "Lament and mourn and weep. Let your laughter be turned to mourning and your joy to gloom." The Message Bible says, "Quit dabbling in sin. Purify your inner life. Quit playing the field. Hit bottom and cry your eyes out. The fun and games are over. Get serious, really serious. Get down on your knees before the Master; it's the only way you'll get on your feet." Do not confuse a genuine godly sorrow with the prideful sin of feeling sorry for yourself. When a person fells sorry for themself they regret having sinned but doesn't do anything about it. Basically, they're just sorry they've been caught and regret that they have to pay the consequences for their sin. It is pride that causes a person to feel sorry for themself whereas humility will push a person to the point where they'll strive to prevent sin from becoming a stronghold in their life.

Godly sorrow will cause a heaviness to come to your heart and this is what compels you to rise up and do what's necessary to get the sin out of your life. After telling you to mourn for your sins, James next tells you to "Humble yourself in the sight of the Lord, and He will lift you up" (James 4:10). Before you ask for forgiveness you must first humble yourself and admit you have sinned. You must own up to what you did wrong and take upon yourself the responsibility of doing something to change your sinful behavior. Humility is the ability to hear the truth about yourself. David said in Ps. 32:5, "I acknowledged my sin to You, and my iniquity I have not hidden. I said, 'I will confess my transgressions to the Lord, and You forgave the iniquity of my sin.'" The word "confess" means 'to acknowledge or say the same thing as.' The worst thing a person can do is run away from God when a sin has been committed. Acknowledge your sin and run to God because He is merciful and is able to cleanse you completely from anything that is inconsistent with His own moral character.

God is faithful and just and can be counted upon to keep His word. He is just in forgiving you of all your sins because Jesus paid the price for them on the cross. There is no sin too great or too small that is not covered by the blood of Jesus which He willfully poured out for you. One of the most remarkable chapters in the Old Testament is Psalm 51 which records the actual words of David's confession after being confronted with the sin of adultery and murder. Like David you must admit you sinned, regret the actions of your sin, plead the blood of Jesus over your sin and, most important of all, you must forsake your sin. As you do these things you must believe that God has indeed done what He promised, namely, to cleanse you from your sin and restore you back to fellowship and service. Having received forgiveness and cleansing you are next to forsake your sin and yield yourself completely to God. This is what repentance is all about and in doing so you will be restored to full fellowship with God.

Remember, forgiveness is an attitude whereas repentance is an action. Forgiveness will not do you much good if no action is taken to remove the sin out of your life. Your deep sorrow and remorse for having sinned should make you so contrite in your heart to the point that you are willing to change your sinful ways. Repentance always brings change and Is. 1:16 tells what the actions of a repentant believer are, "Wash yourselves, make yourselves clean; Put away the evil of your doings from before My eyes. Cease to do evil." The Message Bible says, "Go home and wash up. Clean up your act. Sweep your lives clean of your evil doings so I don't have to look at them any longer. Say no to wrong." Also, James 4:7,8 says, "Therefore submit to God. Resist the devil and he will flee from you. Draw near to God and He will draw near to you. Cleanse your hands, you sinners; and purify your hearts, you double-minded." Do not play games with yourself and God by thinking you can ask Him to forgive you without the willingness to change.

The devil is trying to rule over you and everybody else on this planet. If you are not submitting to God then you won't be free from the influence of the enemy. If you're not in submission to God, don't expect the devil to submit to you. With submission comes authority and the ability to reign in life. In Acts 19:13-16 the sons of Sceva were not submitted to God and tried to cast an evil spirit out of a man. They tried to exercise dominion over this spirit and failed miserably. The spirit laughed in their face and "leaped on them, so that they fled out of that house naked and wounded." The enemy knows that if you're not submitted to God, he doesn't have to be submitted to you. If you don't submit to God and perform the proper actions that true repentance demands, you are only hurting yourself. If you refuse to change your ways and habitual sin becomes a stronghold in your life, you will not "escape the snare of the devil, having been taken captive to do his will" (2 Tim. 2:26). There is always a price to pay for habitual sin for whatever a man sows, that he will also reap (Gal. 6:7,8).

The only way to walk in authority like Jesus walked is to walk in submission to God. Jesus said to the Father, "Not My will, but Yours be done" (Luke 22:42) and you must say the same thing. Allow God to reign in your life. Focus on what He wants more than on what you want. You are a soldier in the army of the Lord and a soldier follows the orders of the Commander-In-Chief. God said in Job 11;14 (NLT), "Get rid of your sins, and leave all iniquity behind you" and this is what you must do. If you don't do this you won't be successful in resisting the enemy and causing him to flee from you. A special promise is given to the church in 1 Cor. 10:13, "No temptation has overtaken you except such as is common to man; but God is faithful, who will not allow you to be tempted beyond what you are able, but with the temptation will also make the way of escape, that you may be able to bear it." This verse clearly shows that there is no reason for any born again believer to sin. No, the devil didn't make you do anything. When you sin, you do it knowingly and willingly.

Jesus walked the earth as a man and if He can walk daily without sinning then so can you. He came to be your example and when tempted to sin in the wilderness the first words out of His mouth were "It is written." A walk of holiness is accomplished by daily absorbing the Word of God into your heart. Ps. 119:9-11 says, "How can a young man cleanse his way? By taking heed according to Your word. With my whole heart I have sought You: Oh, let me not wander from Your commandments! Your word I have hidden in my heart that I might not sin against You." Repentance is always coupled together with obedience to God's Word. Is. 1:19,20 says, "If you are willing and obedient you shall eat the good of the land. But if you rebel you shall be devoured by the sword; for the mouth of the Lord has spoken." Your primary goal in life is to become as Christlike as you possibly can be and for that to happen you must put your spiritual gears in motion and with great determination and tenacity hook up with God as He leads you on the road to perfection.

There will be times when you miss the mark and fall short of your goal. Paul tells you precisely what your attitude should be during those times when you do fall. Phil. 3:12-14 says, "Not that I have already attained or am already perfected, but I press on, that I may lay hold of that for which Christ Jesus has also laid hold of me. Brethren, I do not count myself to have apprehended; but one thing I do, forgetting those things which are behind and reaching forward to those things which are ahead. I press toward the goal for the prize of the upward call of God in Christ Jesus." When you fall, the apostle Paul says to press on with your walk with the Lord. Go forward and don't look back at past failures. 2 Cor. 5:17 says, "Old things have passed away, behold, all things become new." Lot's wife looked back to Sodom and Gomorrah and was turned into a pillar of salt. Be like Joseph who despite all his setbacks always looked forward to the blessings he knew God would one day give him. Keep going forward knowing in your heart that God also has a planned destiny for your life.

Don't seek for the things the world is searching for but rather seek for the will of God to be done on earth as it is in heaven. Seek for Him to rule and reign in your life, seek for His kingdom to come. And where is His kingdom at? Jesus said in Luke 17:21, "For indeed, the kingdom of God is within you." God is reigning in every heart that has yielded to Him and has confessed Him as Lord and Savior. God allows people to choose whether He reigns over them or not. If they're not yielding to the God of heaven then they are being governed by the god of this world. It's one or the other. There is no other choice even though millions are being deceived into thinking they're in charge of their own life. They wish. No, if they're not being ruled by God, they are being ruled by the evil one. If you've made Jesus the Lord of your life then you can wake up each morning knowing that God's eternal kingdom is inside of you. Where you go, the kingdom goes. This is great news for it's in God's kingdom where His will is done on earth as it is in heaven.

The kingdom of God exists but is not yet manifested in its fullness on the earth. He is not reigning over all of mankind but only in the hearts of those who will receive Him and yield to Him. He reigns in the hearts of those who are called to be saints. If you've made Jesus the Lord of your life then His kingdom is inside of you and yet it is a kingdom that is not of this world (John 18:36). There are other kingdoms on the earth but not all of them are God's kingdom. This is why the first thing Jesus told you to pray for in the Lord's prayer is "Thy kingdom come." You want God's kingdom to rule in your heart and not some other kingdom. In heaven there is no sin, no sickness, and no poverty because God is in complete control there. His will is being done in that glorious place and He wants the same thing to happen in your life. It's up to you to make the right choice that allows Him to reign in your life, the proof being that His will is being done in you, through you, and round about you. Making Him Lord and dealing with sin shows that your heart is in the right place.

God told Nicodemus, "Most assuredly, I say to you, unless one is born again, he cannot see the kingdom of God" (John 3:3). Young's Literal says, "Verily, verily, I say to thee, if any one may not be born from above, he is not able to see the reign of God." To get into the kingdom from above, you must be born from above. Jesus said to the Pharisees in John 8:23, "You are from beneath; I am from above. You are of the world; I am not of this world." When you get born again you also will not be of this world. The kingdom of God is inside of you and good things will happen in your life as a result of that. As you yield to the God of the universe, He will reign in your life the same way He reigns in heaven. Your part is to seek first the kingdom of God and His part is to add all these blessings to your life. When you get healed of your diseases and get your bills paid, God's kingdom has come because His will is being done in your life just like it is in heaven. These blessings are favorable in His eyes and they now belong to you.

Paul quotes Isaiah in 1 Cor. 2:9, "Eye has not seen, nor ear heard, nor has entered into the heart of man the things which God has prepared for those who love Him." The Amplified Bible says these blessings are prepared for those "who hold Him in affectionate reverence, who obey Him, and who gratefully recognize the benefits that He has bestowed." The kingdom of God is a valuable thing. It's like treasure hidden in a field and, when you see how valuable it is, you are willing to sacrifice whatever it takes to get it. Those who are spiritual value the things of God more than anything else in their life. On the other hand, those who are carnal value the things of the world more than they value things which are spiritual. 1 Cor. 2:14 says, "But the natural man does not receive the things of the Spirit of God, for they are foolishness to him, nor can he know them, because they are spiritually discerned." Those who play golf on Sunday instead of going to church don't know what's really important. These people are carnal and don't even acknowledge how precious and valuable the kingdom of God actually is.

Jesus said in Matt. 13:45,46, "Again, the kingdom of heaven is like a merchant seeking beautiful pearls, who, when he had found one pearl of great price, went and sold all that he had and bought it." The kingdom of God is valuable and the cost cannot be too great for you to pursue it and take possession of it. You are called to be saints and are willing to lay aside all your personal plans in order for His will to be done in your life as it is in heaven. The things of God mean more to you than the things of the world. This world is quickly passing away but the kingdom of God lasts forever. Why sacrifice your eternal future for a temporary pleasure that is here today and gone tomorrow? Get sin out of your life and begin to walk in the light. Be led by the Spirit and seek first His kingdom every day of your life. You are in the world but are not of this world. You're different from most people because you have a higher value system than they do. You value the kingdom of God so much so that you'll do whatever it takes to get it. After all, that's what saints do.

Randall J. Brewer

-14-

"IT'S TIME TO GROW UP"

Getting saved is not all there is to the salvation experience. Many who have confessed Jesus as their Lord and Savior believe that once they're born-again they can eat, drink, and be merry until Jesus comes back to take them home to heaven. These people are greatly deceived and will not fulfill their destiny if they continue to believe and act this way. Every person who has made Jesus the Lord of their life has an assignment from on high for which they will be held accountable at the judgment seat of Christ. The end is upon us and now is the time to work and not play because life is a vapor and is quickly passing us by. Jesus is coming soon and the kingdom must be advanced and the work of the ministry must be done. God is raising up an army of believers right now who are being trained and will soon be receiving assignments from above. Pay attention, listen well, and put into practice that which you have learned. Take advantage of every opportunity to learn and grow because your training is very important and will soon be complete.

You are a soldier in the army of the Lord and soldiers are not in training forever. They're trained and then they're sent on an assignment. Without a doubt God gives us all things to enjoy and we are to be happy and joyful in our every day lives. However, having fun all the time is not what we're here for. There will be plenty of time for fun in the afterlife but in the here and now we've got a heavenly calling on our lives and the fulfillment of that call is what living the good life is all about. Everybody has a call, everybody has a place, but you must be trained until you reach a level of maturity where you can perform and operate in the graces and abilities God gives you. In other words, you have to grow up. It is the will of God for you to be perfected, developed, and matured for the work of the ministry. You can't serve God fully and completely unless you are spiritually grown up. You don't give a five year old a grenade launcher and send him into battle. But the more grown up and mature you are, the greater your development in the things of God, the greater and more effective your contribution to the overall building up of the body of Christ will be.

It is a commandment in the Word of God that you become like Jesus for He is the perfect example of being grown up and mature. 1 John 4:17 says, "As He is, so are we in the world." Jesus was not a whining baby nor was He childish. He is the King of kings and Lord of lords! When you grow up and become a mighty warrior like He is, you'll be able to endure hardness like a good soldier. You'll fight on the front lines of battle and push through the adversary. You'll complete the mission you were commissioned to do. God needs warriors who don't sit around and think about how they feel all the time. He needs grown up and mature believers who press on in battle whose war cry is "Greater is He that is in me than he that is in the world! I can do all things through Christ which strengthens me!" Everybody has a call on their life to advance the kingdom of God. He gives you special gifts and abilities to help fulfill that call but you have to grow up to see the manifestation of those gifts. If you remain a baby you won't see the full potential your spiritual gifts can achieve. For this reason God gave to the church anointed ministers to help all believers become all they were meant to be.

Eph. 4:11-16 says, "And He Himself gave some to be apostles, some prophets, some evangelists, and some pastors and teachers, for the equipping of the saints for the work of ministry, for the edifying of the body of Christ, till we all come to the unity of the faith and the knowledge of the Son of God, to a perfect man, to the measure of the stature of the fullness of Christ; that we should no longer be children, tossed to and fro and carried about with every wind of doctrine, by the trickery of men, in the cunning craftiness by which they lie in wait to deceive, but, speaking the truth in love may grow up in all things into Him who is the head - Christ - from which the whole body, joined and knit together by what every joint supplies, according to the effective working by which every part does its share, causes growth of the body for the edifying of itself in love." God uses people who surrender to the call on their life to do the work of the ministry and He has positioned you to be His answer to the needs of those around you.

You are called to build up and edify the church but first you must grow up to the full stature of Christ. The Message Bible says we are to be "fully mature adults, fully developed within and without, fully alive like Christ. No prolonged infancies among us, please. We'll not tolerate babes in the woods, small children who are an easy mark for impostors. God wants us to grow up, to know the whole truth and tell it in love - like Christ in everything." You must see the need to grow up before you can begin the journey to spiritual maturity. There is an over exaggeration of one's own maturity and most Christians won't admit they're spiritual babies. People who get upset when they're told to grow up think they already have but the fact that they are upset proves that they have not. One characteristic of being immature is to think you're more mature than you actually are. There are Christian babies everywhere and this can be confusing to new believers because there are spiritual infants in fifty year old bodies.

It is God's will for you to grow up and He has anointed people to tell you where you actually are in your spiritual development and what needs to happen next. You need to be told the truth in love and this truth will set you free from the restrictions of childhood. Babies can't do much. They have things decided for them. They don't have the freedom and the responsibilities and the rewards that adults do. Babies live in a small world that they are the center of. The only thing they are aware of is what pertains to them. Babies have themselves on their mind all the time. They like to vent and it's not pretty and it's not nice. Babies need somebody to do things for them. Spiritual babies look to somebody else for everything. They want their problems fixed and be told what to do. More than half the believers in the world want other people to pray for them and believe for them. These people need to be confronted and asked, "Why can't you pray for yourself?" Babies need to grow up and learn to put on their own clothes and start doing things for themselves. They need to work and carry their own weight and take on their responsibility to the body of Christ.

The majority of your learning comes from you doing the work of the ministry. You need to learn how to grow up and not burden other people with what you're dealing with. You need to deal with things for yourself. Paul said in 1 Cor. 3:1, "And I, brethren, could not speak to you as to spiritual people but as to carnal, as to babes in Christ." Babies can't handle much. Babies will ask you things you can't tell them because they don't have the maturity and understanding to comprehend the answer to their questions. You can't feed a baby a T-bone steak. Everybody has room to grow. You need to grow up from where you are right now and you need to do it quickly. It is not okay to be a childish baby for thirty years. Paul writes in 1 Cor. 2:14, "But the natural man does not receive the things of the Spirit of God, for they are foolishness to him, nor can he know them, because they are spiritually discerned." You need a mature, well developed spirit to evaluate and discern the things of God.

When you grow up you get very interested in the things of God for no longer is it foolishness to you but instead is the source of life. Don't be fooled into thinking you can discern the things of God with a great intellect. It doesn't matter how smart you think you are. A good education only goes so far for it can't tap into the realm of the Spirit. Some people are so dumb and ignorant that they actually think they're smart, that they know more than anybody else, including God. They'll dispute over doctrine or any little thing that comes up like what color the carpet should be at church. They complain if the church service went too long and they'll stay home if it's too cold out to go to church. You say up, they say down. You say left, they say right. You say white, they say black. It is time for these spiritual babies to grow up! Paul said, "When I was a child, I spoke as a child, I understood as a child, I thought as a child; but when I became a man, I put away childish things" (1 Cor. 13:11).

The Message Bible says, "When I was an infant at my mother's breast, I gurgled and cooed like any infant. When I grew up, I left those infant ways for good." Those who are deceived into thinking they're more grown up than they actually are become rebellious to the point where they won't let anybody show them where they're missing the mark and failing to grow up. It is shameful for a person to while away the years of their life and not grow up and reach their full potential. Jesus said in Matt. 5:48, "Therefore you shall be perfect, just as your Father in heaven is perfect." People often neglect this verse because they falsely believe the manifestation of it is not possible. They assume the fulfillment of what Jesus said is beyond them so they pass right over it and move on to the next verse. The truth of the matter is that Jesus did not say try to be perfect, He said do it! Be ye perfect. He would not tell you to do something were it not possible for you to do so.

In the Bible the word "perfect" does not mean 'flawless.' Everything and everybody in the natural realm is flawed in some way because of sin and the curse that is on the earth. God is a Spirit and He's not holding a magnifying glass on your flesh. Thank God for that. He looks at the heart (1 Sam. 16:7). His eyes roam to and fro across the earth to show Himself strong on behalf of those whose heart is perfect and loyal toward Him (2 Chron. 16:9). That does not mean 'flawless.' People say "nobody's perfect" so they don't even try but the Word commands you to be perfect and therefore you must be able to be perfect. The Hebrew word for "perfect" is 'complete' and a composite of both Hebrew and Greek means 'brought to its end, complete, lacking nothing necessary to completeness, brought to its completion.' Phil. 1:6 says, "being confident of this very thing, that He who has began a good work in you will complete it until the day of Jesus Christ." According to scripture a person who is perfect is mature, fully grown, and completely developed. The more mature you are, the more you'll be like Jesus.

God intends for you to reach your full potential and for that to happen you must grow beyond where you are now. You know you're grown up when you become like Jesus. 1 John 2:6 says, "He who says he abides in Him ought himself to walk just as He walked." Jesus emptied Himself and walked the earth as a perfect and mature man proving it can be done. He is now calling you to do the same thing and it is exciting to believe that you can. You grow up and get perfected so you can do the work of the ministry. When you do something for God He requires that you do it perfectly in a sense of following a thing through to its completion. You see it through to its end. You work on it, you continue on it until you have the satisfaction on the inside of you that the task is completed. Shortly before his death Paul told

Timothy, "But you be watchful in all things, endure afflictions, do the work of an evangelist, fulfill your ministry" (2 Tim. 4;5). He then said in vs. 7, "I have fought the good fight, I have finished the race, I have kept the faith."

Every believer has a job to do and the more complete and mature you are the better you'll be able to fulfill your ministry. You need to grow in faith and walk as Jesus walked and say what Jesus said and do the things Jesus did. Even Jesus said, "Most assuredly, I say to you, he who believes in Me, the works that I do he will do also; and greater works than these he will do, because I go to My Father" (John 14:12). When you begin something, see it through to the end. Jesus said, "No one, having put his hand to the plow, and looking back, is fit for the kingdom of God" (Luke 9:62). Be led by the Spirit and follow what's in your heart until you get a release in your spirit to stop and move on to something else. The Bible calls this "perfection." When Jesus said "be ye perfect" He was telling you to be complete just as your Father in heaven is complete. God created man in His own image (Gen. 1:27). He patterned you after His own self and He is perfection. Eph. 5:1 (AMP) says, "Therefore, be imitators of God, copy Him and follow His example as well beloved children imitate their fathers."

The Message Bible says, "Watch what God does, and then you do it, like children who learn proper behavior from their parents." Paul did this and wrote in 1 Cor. 11:1 (AMP), "Pattern yourself after me, follow my example as I imitate and follow Christ." People will imitate who and what they respect and imitation is the way God gives you to develop your spirit and your involvement in the things of God. 2 Thess. 3:11 says, "For you yourselves know how you ought to follow us, for we were not disorderly among you." 3 John 11 states, "Beloved, do not imitate what is evil, but what is good. He who does good is of God, but he who does evil has not seen God." Heb. 13:7 says, "Remember your leaders, who spoke the word of God to you. Consider the outcome of their way of life and imitate their faith." You must position yourself to be in the presence of strong, well developed believers who can show you how to grow up and be more mature and complete. We learn by observation. We imitate what we see people do, not what we hear them say.

In today's world there is too much "do as I say, not as I do." Paul addressed this when he wrote in Phil. 4:9, "The things which you learned and received and heard and saw in me, these do, and the God of peace will be with you." The Amplified Bible says, "Practice what you have learned and received and heard and seen in me and model your way of living on it and the God of peace will be with you." Jesus, of course, is the ultimate example of whom we are to follow. Every day press toward the mark of being like Jesus. Luke 2:40 says, "And the Child grew and became strong in spirit, filled with wisdom; and the grace of God was upon Him." Vs. 52 says, "And Jesus increased in wisdom and stature, and in favor with God and man." Jesus grew up! He is your example and you are to pattern your life after His. At age twelve Jesus was in the temple "sitting in the midst of the teachers, both listening to them and asking them questions. And all who heard Him were astonished at His understanding and answers" (Luke 2:46,47).

Every year His parents went to Jerusalem at the Feast of the Passover. The previous year and the years before that Jesus went home with the rest of His earthly family. But this year, at age twelve, He stayed behind and went to the temple. A change had taken place. Jesus began to grow up at age twelve. His focus began to change. His interests and priorities were different than they were the year before. Instead of playing with the other children He chose to go sit in the temple to learn spiritual truths. He's asking questions about the Word and sharing what He knows. As your example Jesus is showing you that children at age twelve should be hungry for and pursuing the things of God. They should want to learn more about Jesus than they want to go outside and play. It is not acceptable for a teenager to sit on the couch and play video games all day long. In times past sixteen year old boys were putting on armor and going into battle and fourteen year old girls were getting married.

This generation is expecting far too little from their children. They let them act like children all through their teenage years and when they turn eighteen they're not developed as an adult and can't handle the pressures of an adult world. How do you know if you're grown up? You know when it's time to play and when it's not time to play. God believes in vacations but not every week. Heb. 11:24,25 says, "By faith Moses, when he became of age" - when he grew up - "refused to be called the son of Pharaoh's daughter choosing rather to suffer affliction with the people of God than to enjoy the passing pleasures of sin." The prodigal son was an impatient young man who wanted his inheritance and he wanted it now! His father gave it to him "and not many days after, the younger son gathered all together, journeyed to a far country, and there wasted his possessions with prodigal living" (Luke 15:13). A characteristic of youth is waste and when his money was gone the prodigal son had no friends. Many people are users who will hang around you if you're popular and have money but scatter when the going gets rough.

Young people are easily influenced. They want to be like their peers and don't discern if they are doing good or not all for the sake of being accepted. It's popular today to get tattoos all over your body and body piercings and to dress in a certain way. They smoke and take drugs and have sex. Youth are impatient and wild and act insane and insecure. They have wrong priorities. Jesus wanted the rich young ruler to sell everything he had and come follow Him. "But when the young man heard that saying, he went away sorrowful, for he had great possessions" (Matt. 19:22). Jesus wanted him to grow up and mature and He was showing him how. Jesus wanted him to put God first and offered him a place with Him in the ministry right then and there. The young man thought his money and earthly pleasures were more important so he turned and walked away. It is time for the body of Christ to wake up and grow up! You have to change the way you think, talk, and act. You have to put away childish habits and behaviors. Paul said, "When I became a man, I put the ways of childhood behind me" (1 Cor. 13:11 NIV).

You are not supposed to go through a second childhood. The outward man is perishing but the inner man is being renewed day by day and growing stronger and stronger (2 Cor. 4:16). A characteristic of one who is grown up is to be self-disciplined and self-motivated. You've got to make yourself turn off the television and read your Bible. Force yourself to pray and visit the elderly and help the widow. Babies always express what they feel but a mature person learns the value of words and only speaks when necessary. He doesn't spew out of his mouth every lame thought or feeling that comes to his brain. Good listeners are not as common as they should be. Even a fool is considered wise if he keeps his mouth shut. Believers who are grown up don't use words to vent their feelings. They don't chat and say things that have no substance but instead use words as tools to build up and edify. What comes out of your mouth reveals the level of your maturity and development.

Children and those who are grown up speak differently. Adults don't talk about their problems nor do they gossip about other people and judge them. They talk about love and important things that have to do with the kingdom of God. Babies are carnal and ruled by their feelings but there will come a time when you feel one way but act another. You'll want to tell somebody off but you'll love them anyway. You'll endure hardness like a good soldier as you act in faith and talk in faith. You'll stir yourself up in the spirit as you press on and take that hill. Jesus is the standard by which all spiritual growth should be measured. He is the perfect example of the perfect spiritual man. He is the complete one, the fully developed one. When you grow up you are to be just like Him. You can operate like Jesus. You can think like Him, talk like Him, act like Him, pray like Him, love like Him, be led like Him, live like Him. Most of the church don't believe this. For them it is a reality not to be grasped but Jesus said in Luke 6:40, "A disciple is not above his teacher, but everyone who is perfectly trained will be like his teacher."

The Amplified Bible says, "A student who is completely trained will be just like his teacher." You can be just like Jesus. In fact, you're commanded to. You can grow up and be just as honest and faithful and genuine as Jesus. You're bridging the gap as the days go by. You'll never surpass Him but when you're grown up and fully developed you'll be just like Jesus. He was the brightness of the Father's glory (Heb. 1:3) and the image of His person. When you've seen Jesus, you've seen the Father. His plan for you is that when people see you, they've seen Jesus. And when they see Jesus, they've seen the Father. After the ascension the people said about the disciples, "They've been with Jesus." They trained under Him and they acted like Him and sounded like Him. We are living in the last days and there is a work to be done and little time to do it. He needs all of us to grow up and stop acting like babies. You need to put away childish things and operate in your full potential and do the job and let the Lord come back. Babies don't get to rule and reign but only those who are perfect, complete, and whole. It is imperative that you grow up and become just like Jesus.

Randall J. Brewer

-15-
"THE GIFT OF CORRECTION"

The goal of every believer should be to walk in the light they've been given and to attain perfection in their lives as defined in the Word of God. Phil. 3:12 (NLT) says, "I don't mean to say that I have already achieved these things or that I have already reached perfection. But I press on to possess that perfection for which Christ Jesus first possessed me." In the Bible the word "perfect" means 'to be complete, to develop to its end, to finish to full development or full maturity.' According to scripture, there are many who are called to be saints who have reached this spiritual level of perfection. Vs. 14-16 (AMP) says, "I press on toward the goal to win the [heavenly] prize of the upward call of God in Christ Jesus. All of us who are mature [pursuing spiritual perfection] should have this attitude. And if in any respect you have a different attitude, that too God will make clear to you. Only let us stay true to what we have already attained." You are called to perfection which means you are called to develop until you are completely mature, until you finish your course, and are fulfilled in what God has called you to do.

Many people don't begin the journey to perfection because they believe it's an unattainable goal. To them Paul writes in vs. 13, "Brethren, I do not count myself to have apprehended; but one thing I do, forgetting those things which are behind and reaching forward to those things which are ahead." Paul is saying you need to press on to Christlike perfection which means to be like Jesus in every area of your life. People make excuses and say "nobody's perfect" with the implication that nobody can be, not knowing that scripture says you can. They reason that if nobody can be perfect, then why try? This is precisely how the devil wants them to think. People who say nobody's perfect forget that Jesus was perfect and He lived a perfect life. His ministry was perfect and His relationship with the Father was perfect. They also forget what John said in 1 John 2:6, "He who says he abides in Him ought himself also to walk just as He walked." If Jesus walked in perfection, then so should you. Don't be foolish and tell the Lord you can't do this when He said you can.

If you don't believe it's possible to be perfect as Jesus is perfect then you need a fresh revelation of what's possible. You need to renew your mind and start believing what the Bible says more than the traditions of man which implies nobody can be perfect. You need to understand that God is not talking about the perfection of the flesh, He's talking about spiritual perfection. He is talking about having a heart that is perfect toward the things of God. Not only is this possible, it's your call in life. You are called to perfection. It's what you're called to do and what you're called to be. The Lord is looking for people to be this way. 2 Chron. 16:9 says, "For the eyes of the Lord run to and fro throughout the whole earth, to show Himself strong in the behalf of them whose heart is perfect toward Him." A perfect heart is a heart that is fully committed to Him. Don't get sidetracked thinking you've got to get your mind and your flesh in order before you can be perfect in the eyes of God. No, He's looking at your heart and this, indeed, can be perfect every day of your life.

Called To Be Saints

Those who walk in the light are wholehearted toward God, those who are halfhearted are lukewarm and these are the people God will spew out of His mouth (Rev. 3:15,16). Being halfhearted is what makes you imperfect, not a lack of knowledge or for sins committed in the past. There is no excuse or any justifiable reason for any born again believer to be halfhearted toward the Lord. It's a choice you make and, if you'll choose to follow God wholly and completely, you'll be on the path to perfection in His eyes. God does not look at your flaws and mistakes but rather looks at the condition of your heart. If you're doing everything you know to seek Him and please Him and follow Him, God will look at you and call you perfect. Your flaws are not as important to Him as they are to the carnal person who judges all the time. Yes, getting sin out of your life is important for it hinders your fellowship with the Father, but the person who is wholehearted will not live a life of gross and habitual sin.

Jesus said in Matt. 5:48, "Therefore you shall be perfect, just as your Father in heaven is perfect." This is Jesus talking but still most Christians don't believe this. You've got to make up your own mind as to whether you believe what He said or not. The Amplified Bible says, "You, therefore, will be perfect [growing into spiritual maturity both in mind and character, actively integrating godly values into your daily life], as your heavenly Father is perfect." The Lord has asked you to come up to a higher level from where you now are, so ask Him to renew your heart and mind and reveal to you what His definition of perfection is. Even if you don't yet understand it, you can still accept it by faith. Jesus also said in Luke 6:40, "A disciple is not above his teacher, but everyone who is perfectly trained will be like his teacher." The reason you follow the Master is because you want to be like the Master, you want to be perfect as He is perfect. The path to perfection is a daily journey where you grow and strive to be more and more like Jesus.

Randall J. Brewer

Many people who go to church have not had a life changing experience with Christ. Instead of becoming like Jesus they foolishly choose to follow the trends of the world which is getting darker and darker by the day. Instead of trying to bring change to the sinful world, they choose instead to become like the world to the point that homosexual ministers are now being ordained to lead the local church. It is easy to follow a God who they think makes no demands on them to change their sinful ways. They think God will accept them just the way they are but this is not the God of the Bible. The devil has deceived these people into thinking they can believe in Jesus without being changed. These people are walking on dangerous ground for the wages of sin is death. They're mocking God because they think they can sin and get away with it. They're trying to modernize the church to go in the direction the world is now going. Instead of changing the world, they're allowing the world to change them. These people have been called to be saints but instead are living like the devil himself.

You come to Jesus just as you are but that doesn't mean you stay that way. God hates sin and so should you. Immediately you should embark on the path to Christlike perfection. You need to renew your mind so you'll think like Him and you need to get your body under control. Don't sit around saying nobody's perfect but rise up and press on to the high calling of Christ. You need to do everything you can to become more like Jesus today than you were yesterday. You've been recreated in your spirit and this is what allows you to walk as the Master walked. His footsteps are on the path to perfection and so are yours. You can talk like Jesus and act like Jesus. Ps. 37:23 says, "The steps of a good man are ordered by the Lord, and He delights in his way." The Amplified Bible says, "The steps of a [good and righteous] man are directed and established by the Lord, and He delights in his way [and blesses his path]." You please the Father when you're on the path to perfection. If you miss the mark and fall down you immediately repent, get back on your feet, and keep moving forward.

Never think you are on this path alone. Jesus is by your side loving you, encouraging you and, if necessary, correcting you. There is no shame in being corrected by the Lord for it is evidence of His great love for you. Heb. 12:5,6 (NLT), "My child, don't make light of the Lord's discipline, and don't give up when He corrects you. For the Lord disciplines those He loves, and He punishes each one He accepts as His child." The Message Bible says, "My dear child, don't shrug off God's discipline, but don't be crushed by it either. It's the child He loves that He disciplines, the child He embraces, He also corrects." Those who are halfhearted think it's an insult when they get corrected and often respond with denial and anger. Their arrogance and pride is blinding their eyes to the love that is being shown. Those who are weak and timid hang their head in shame and walk away. Being corrected shines a little more light on your path and this is what everybody needs in order to walk as Jesus walked. Perfection is achieved when you embrace the correction given by those who love you most.

If you have not yet arrived at Christlike perfection then correction is needed in your life, sometimes a lot of correction. There are wrong doctrines and sinful temptations that are continually trying to get you off course and daily corrective adjustments have to be made. If you're not being corrected then you won't reach your destination. How far off course you are determines how much correction you need. If you're on the straight and narrow path to perfection then little correction is needed. If not, if you're way off course, then the correction may be somewhat harsh and traumatic. David was guilty of adultery and murder and a major correction took place when he was confronted by the prophet Nathan (2 Sam. 12:1-15). The good news is that David received this correction and repented of his sin. Some people need a lot of correction and there is no shame in this if your heart is in the right place. The important thing is to receive the correction when it is given. This won't be a problem if your heart is right toward God because you know these corrections will help you achieve Christlike perfection.

There is no such thing as a child or an adult who does not need correction. Whether or not you receive correction is based on how you view it. Is it a good thing or bad? Is it given to help you or condemn you? The condition of your heart determines the answer. Those who are wholehearted receive correction as a good thing coming from the Lord while those who are halfhearted avoid it like the plaque. God corrects you because He loves you, and love will always tell you the truth even when it's not desired. The truth is not always pleasant but it's the truth that will set you free. Those who receive it are the ones who mount up with wings as eagles and soar high above the clouds of gloom and despair. Those who don't receive it will stay in their immaturity all the days of their life. Their house is built on sinking sand and when the rain falls and the winds blow, their lives will collapse and great will be the fall of it. They did not receive correction when it was given and paid a heavy price for rejecting it.

People like to talk about the love of God but never want to talk about His correction. The two go hand-in-hand for whom the Lord loves, He corrects. He loves you and now He's going to correct you. Get ready for it for surely it's coming. Heb. 12:7,8 (NLT) says, "As you endure this divine discipline, remember that God is treating you as His own children. Who ever heard of a child who is never disciplined by its father? If God doesn't discipline you as He does all of His children, it means that you are illegitimate and are not really His children at all." When the Lord corrects you there is no condemnation attached to it. He is here to lift you up and not tear you down. He is always looking out for your good and knows that if these corrective adjustments are not made then the enemy can come in and bring havoc into your life. What type of Father would He be if He didn't try to stop this from happening? This is what godly correction is all about but still it is your responsibility to receive it and respond to it.

It takes a humble heart to receive the gift of correction. It's a manifestation of the love God has for you and should be received with opened arms. Don't run away from correction but embrace it with all that is within you. This is not to say it will be a joyful experience for you. It won't be. Heb. 12:11 says, "Now no chastening seems to be joyful for the present, but grievous; nevertheless, afterward it yields the peaceable fruit of righteousness to those who have been trained by it." The Message Bible says, "Later, of course, it pays off handsomely, for it's the well-trained who find themselves mature in their relationship with God." There is no justification for you to not receive correction if the need is there for it to be given. You missed the mark so humble yourself and repent. Correction is not pleasant as you're going through it but afterward it yields a great blessing. It's through correction and repentance that you are able to attain Christlike perfection. This should be the goal of every born again believer.

Jesus said in Matt. 11:29, "Take My yoke upon you and learn from Me, for I am gentle and lowly in heart, and you will find rest for your souls." Jesus has a humble heart and, when you yield to Him, you will become as He is. A humble heart is meek and gentle and is forever faithful. It is submissive and obedient. To become humble you must rid yourself of all that is prideful and defiant, and it may take some correction to do it. This is why you can't despise the chastening of the Lord. To get to where you want to be is going to require some correction yet millions of believers are offended when it happens. They need it yet don't have enough sense to receive it. Pride is blocking their ability to receive correction and soon hard times will come. Prov.

16:18 says, "Pride goes before destruction, and a haughty spirit before a fall." People who don't receive correction need to be confronted and rebuked because they're about to have some major problems. The motive of godly correction is always love for the Lord only has what's best for them on His heart and mind.

It's correction that causes you to become like the Master. Humble yourself and receive it quickly and willingly. Correction is not condemnation for God did not send His Son into the world to condemn the world. God is correcting you because He loves you and wants to have close, intimate fellowship with you. Jesus told the woman caught in adultery, "Go and sin no more" (John 8:11). He corrected her but did not condemn her. Jesus loved her and told her to do what was best for her. There is no excuse for getting angry and despising those who correct you in a godly manner. Don't accuse them of not knowing what they're talking about because if you do, you'll be like the devil who's called the accuser of the brethren (Rev. 12:10). You need to humble yourself, slow down, and take a deep breath. Then prayerfully consider that what they told you might be true and ask the Lord to help you get back on the path to perfection. God is forever ready to forgive you and give you the direction you need. Admit that you are not yet perfected but believe in your heart that you can be.

Be thankful when you're corrected. This means you're that much closer to being like Christ. Those who get hurt and offended all the time are spiritual babies and have not developed in the things of God. Those who don't receive the correction of the Lord will eventually be rebuked by Him, and this is far worse. The good news is that if you're receiving a lot of correction, this means you are well loved. Correction is a gift from on high and you should be forever grateful for God's love toward you. Heb. 12:1 says, "Let us lay aside every weight and the sin which so easily ensnares us." This is something you should do on your own but when you don't do it, God will step in with godly correction. He is only doing what you should have done in the first place, and He's doing it because of the love He has for you. You are in a curse-filled world and sin will contaminate you and weigh you down and hinder your pursuit to be like the Master. This is why you have to get sin out of your life, whether it be on your own or with the Lord's correction.

God loves you so much that He is unwilling to leave you in the condition you are currently in. Jesus said in John 15:1,2, "I am the true vine, and My Father is the vinedresser. Every branch in Me that does not bear fruit He takes away; and every branch that bears fruit He prunes, that it may bear more fruit." Notice that even if your walk with the Lord is flourishing and you're bearing much fruit, there is still some corrective pruning that is taking place. Why is that? So that you can bear more fruit. If the primary desire of your heart is to be used by God in a special way, then get ready for some pruning. He'll point out things in your life that have to change, things that could be slowing you down and preventing you from doing even more. Many people at this time will be expecting a pat on the back for all the good they've done, but the truth is they're just getting started. There is more work to be done and to help you fulfill your destiny God will tell you to change this and to change that. This is far more important than a pat on the back.

Don't be foolish and think you can reach a point in your life where correction is no longer needed. There is always sin to get rid of and weights to be removed. In your heart you know what these things are and, when they're dealt with, your productivity in the kingdom of God will rise to a higher level. This is why godly correction should be desired and not despised. Paul said in Eph. 4:15 (NLT), "Instead, we will speak the truth in love, growing in every way more and more like Christ, who is the head of His body, the church." The Message Bible says in vs. 14-16, "No prolonged infancies among us, please. We'll not tolerate babes in the woods, small children who are an easy mark for impostors. God wants us to grow up, to know the whole truth and tell it in love - like Christ in everything. We take our lead from Christ, who is the source of everything we do. He keeps us in step with each other. His very breath and blood flow through us, nourishing us so that we will grow up healthy in God, robust in love."

You are to be a light in a dark world. People are to see what Jesus is like by the things you say and do. If you are not acting like God's personal representative on the earth, then there are some things you need to be corrected on. Godly correction is not a bad thing but is a display of God loving you. To not be corrected is to not be loved. Job 5:17 says, "Behold, happy is the man whom God corrects; Therefore do not despise the chastening of the Almighty." Correction gives you freedom for it deliverers you from the bondage of doing things the wrong way. God can and will do this for you in every area of your life. You should desire this correction and receive it with gladness even though it may not be enjoyable at the time. You can take comfort knowing that God has your best interests in mind and that His only purpose in correcting you is so you can become more like Him. As He shines, so do you shine when you walk in the light of godly correction. All good things come with a price and the good benefits of being corrected is well worth the price to go through it.

A question that is often asked is who should correct whom? Who has the right to speak godly correction into the life of another? Aaron and Miriam tried to correct Moses in Num. 12 and paid a heavy price for it. Does anybody have the right to correct somebody else? As a whole, the church has been ignorant in this area and many people have been quick to judge and criticize others and pass it off as correction. They're looking at the speck in their brother's eye and considered not the plank in their own eye. For this reason many have been judged by God much like Aaron and Miriam. Their judgment opened the door to the enemy and gave him access to their lives. Never should a person correct their spiritual elders, those who are over them in the Lord. Even if you don't agree with everything they do and say, you need to respect the fact that God has chosen them to be in the position they're in. To disrespect your elders is to disrespect God because He's the one who put them there. God takes this personally and Aaron and Miriam learned this lesson the hard way.

Paul said in 1 Thess. 5:12,13 (NLT), "Dear brothers and sisters, honor those who are your leaders in the Lord's work. They work hard among you and give you spiritual guidance. Show them great respect and wholehearted love because of their work. And live peacefully with each other." A part of spiritual guidance is godly correction. God is saying here that spiritual leaders can correct those who are under their care, and not the other way around. The same principle is true in the Christian home. Children should never correct their parents and a wife should never correct her husband. This is unpopular with some people but not in the eyes of God. He said in Eph. 5:22,23, "Wives, submit to your own husbands, as to the Lord. For the husband is the head of the wife, as also Christ is the head of the church; and He is the Savior of the body." If the husband is missing the mark somewhere then the wife should pray and ask the Lord to reveal it to him. It is the Lord's place to correct the husband, not the wife's. The same is true with children in regards to their parents.

Those who are in a leadership role have been anointed by God to fulfill that call. This applies to pastors in the church and husbands in the home. This is not about what gender they are but rather the position they hold in God's eternal plan. There is no man who is any better than any woman, but the role of husband is the position God has chosen to be the leader in the home. You are to respect the position even if at times you don't respect the person who holds that position. The same thing holds true with your boss at work and those who hold government offices. Those whom God puts in leadership positions have been anointed to lead and correct. This means they have an advantage over those who are not in those positions. God has put an anointing on the husband to lead the home and give godly correction when necessary. The wife may know more than the husband in certain areas but this does not mean she's anointed to lead and correct. A lot of responsibility goes with any leadership role and this is why those who fill those positions should be honored and respected.

Correction is a good thing and you need to receive it from the Lord and from those He places over you. You need to know who these people are and be willing to submit to the anointing that is on them. You need to give them the respect they've earned and the honor they deserve. A truth in life is that you will listen more to the people you respect than to the people you don't. And listen you must do because you will need instruction and correction to become more and more like Jesus. You're in training and you must see it through to the very end. There are spiritual coaches and trainers assigned to you who will help and encourage you to stay the course. Perseverance and endurance is needed and as you discipline yourself to receive godly correction it will be there. Day by day you will find yourself growing into Christlike perfection. It won't always be easy but be like Jesus who "though he was a Son, yet He learned obedience by the things which He suffered" (Heb. 5:8). No, it's not easy but it is the only path that leads to perfection.

1 Peter 5:10 (AMP) says, "After you have suffered for a little while, the God of all grace [who imparts His blessing and favor], who called you to His own eternal glory in Christ, will Himself complete, confirm, strengthen, and establish you [making you what you ought to be]." Perfection comes as

you learn to endure those temptations to rebel and give up. You need to overcome these attempts by the devil to bring you down and submit yourself to godly instruction and correction. This is how you grow and get perfected. The Message Bible says, "So keep a firm grip on the faith. The suffering won't last forever. It won't be long before this generous God who has great plans for us in Christ - eternal and glorious plans they are! - will have you put together and on your feet for good. He gets the last word; yes, He does." Those who don't get perfected are the ones who don't overcome their own stubbornness and rebellion. These are the people who always want to hear how much God loves them but refuse to listen when He corrects them. Little do they know that with God love and correction always go together.

One of the worst mistakes you can ever make is to reject God's correction when He gives it to you. To reject His correction is to reject His love. A sobering truth is that you can wait too long to repent and then it will be too late. Heb. 12:16,17 (NLT) says, "Make sure that no one is immoral or godless like Esau, who traded his birthright as the firstborn for a single meal. You know that afterward, when he wanted his father's blessing, he was rejected. It was too late for repentance, even though he begged with bitter tears." To repent means to change so, if your life hasn't changed, then you haven't repented. You can kneel at the altar and cry your eyes out but if you don't change then all your tears are in vain. Esau never changed and because of that it was too late to turn his situation around. Jesus referred to this truth in Rev. 2:5, "Look how far you have fallen! Turn back to Me and do the works you did at first. If you don't repent, I will come and remove your lampstand from its place among the churches."

Jesus says again in Rev. 2:21, "And I gave her time to repent of her sexual immorality, and she did not repent." The Young's Literal says, "I gave her time to reform, but she did not reform." God will give you a window of time to receive godly correction and to repent. If you don't change in the time frame you've been given, you won't have the opportunity to turn your situation around. This may be hard to accept but it's the truth nonetheless. You've been given a set time to repent so you best make the most of it. Listen to godly correction and stop doing the wrong you've been doing. Turn your life around and get on the road to perfection. If you don't then bad days are ahead. Vs. 22,23 says, "Indeed I will cast her into a sickbed, and those who commit adultery with her into great tribulation, unless they repent of their deeds. And I will kill her children with death. And all the churches shall know that I am He who searches the minds and hearts. And I will give to each one of you according to your works." That is a sobering thought and, indeed, it should be.

-16-
"A CLEAR CONSCIENCE"

God is light and in Him is no darkness at all. Since you are made in His image, your primary responsibility is to walk in the light as He is in the light. Sin is a major roadblock that prevents this from happening and is the main reason it must be dealt with every day of your life. Paul knew this was so and said in Acts 24:15,16 (NLT), "I have the same hope in God that these men have, that He will raise both the righteous and the unrighteous. Because of this, I always try to maintain a clear conscience before God and all people." Paul is saying the condition of your heart is what determines whether or not you receive the Word which allows you to walk in the light you've been given. In explaining the parable of the sower Jesus said in Luke 8:15, "But the ones that fell on the good ground are those who, having heard the word with a noble and good heart, keep it and bear fruit with patience." Not everybody who hears the Word get results. That blessing is reserved for those with a good heart who have a clear conscience toward God and man.

A person with a good heart hears the Word and keeps it. They don't allow "cares, riches, and pleasures" (Luke 8:14) to choke the Word that's been planted in their heart. When trials come they persevere with patience and are able to bear much fruit. They get results because they have a good and honest heart. In Greek the word "honest" means 'honorable' and Jesus is saying that good ground is honest ground. Heb. 13:18 (AMP) says, "Keep praying for us, for we are convinced that we have a good (clear) conscience, that we want to walk uprightly and live a noble life, acting honorably and in complete honesty in all things." Your conscience is the voice of your spirit and it's through your conscience that God talks to you. To be dull in your conscience is to be dull in hearing from God. The Lord is talking to you or, at the very least, He is trying to. God does communicate with His people and it's all a question as to whether or not you hear Him when He does. You need to be able to identify His voice and this goes back to the condition of your heart.

1 Cor. 14:10 (KJV) says, "There are, it may be, so many kinds of voices in the world, and none of them is without signification." Every voice has something to say but that does not mean you should listen to every one of them. The voice of the flesh is feelings and this is one voice you shouldn't listen to. Paul said in Phil. 3:3 that he had "no confidence in the flesh" and this is why he wrote in 2 Cor. 5:7, "For we walk by faith, not by sight." Smith Wigglesworth was famous for saying, "I am not moved by what I see. I am not moved by what I feel. I am moved only by what I believe." Your mind also has a voice and it is reason and logic. Your mind will ask what's logical about loving your enemies or to confess those things that be not as though they were. This also is a voice you shouldn't listen to. The one voice you should be listening to is the voice of your spirit, and you identify this voice through your conscience. Rom. 8:16 says, "The Spirit Himself bears witness with our spirit that we are the children of God."

God communicates with you through your spirit, the inner man. The word "conscience" means 'co-knowing' or 'knowing with.' God is inside of you and His Spirit is bearing witness with your spirit. The two of you are knowing things together. When you got born again you had a witness inside of you that it really happened. Your conscience, the voice of your spirit, was bearing witness with God's Spirit confirming without a doubt that you are indeed a child of the living God. If God can let you know you're born again, He can let you know other things as well and He does it the same way. There is a witness inside of you that knows something God knows. This witness is your conscience and it is bearing witness with what God is revealing to you. This is why you need to listen to what your conscience is saying and take heed to it immediately. God is speaking to you and you need to stop and listen to what He's saying. It could be a matter of life and death. He is telling you to not do this or not do that. Or else He'll say don't go here or don't go there. Listen to Him and whatever He says, do it.

You are led internally so never ask God for an outward sign. If God wants you to do something, don't ask Him to confirm it by making a red car pass in front of you. People are misled by these sort of things and many have gotten off the beaten path. Yes, Gideon put out a fleece but He wasn't born again and the Spirit of God was not inside of him. He couldn't be led the same way you can. He didn't have that option and this is why he asked for an outward sign. Don't you do that. You can't be led by external things because this is where the devil is and he can do things that can cause you to do the wrong thing. He can make that red car pass in front of you all the while making you think it was God who did it. Some believers are very gullible and are easily deceived by things that are not scriptural. They then get mad when things don't go right and all along it was their own fault. These people have the same Bible you do and it's Author is living in their heart just like He is yours. There is no excuse for not being led the proper way.

Never do something because somebody told you to do it, even if they say they heard from the Lord. No, it's your responsibility to hear from the Lord yourself. The God in them is the same God in you and, if He told them something about your life, then He will tell you also. If He doesn't, then disregard what anybody else says. If it really is Him then you will have a witness down in your heart. The Spirit of God will rise up and bear witness with your spirit confirming that this indeed was from Him. This is how you are to live your life and how every decision gets made. Prov. 3:5,6 says, "Trust in the Lord with all your heart and lean not on your own understanding. In all your ways acknowledge Him and He will direct your paths." You trust God with a good and honest heart. This doesn't mean you turn your mind off, you just don't trust it more than what's in your heart. If something looks good on the outside but your heart is saying don't do it, listen to your heart and walk away.

The Spirit of God is inside of you so you don't have to let other people make decisions for you. At the same time, don't allow others to lean on you all the time expecting you to tell them what to do. Point them to the same God you follow and surely He will direct their paths also. Paul said in Rom. 9:1 (NLT), "With Christ as my witness, I speak with utter truthfulness. My conscience and the Holy Spirit confirm it." Here is another example of co-witnessing, of your spirit knowing what the Holy Spirit knows. The WET says, "Truth I speak in Christ. I am not lying, my conscience bearing joint-testimony with me in the Holy Spirit." God is in you and, if you'll listen to Him, He will lead you to do what's in the Bible even if you haven't learned it yet. Rom. 2:14,15 (NLT) says, "Even Gentiles, who do not have God's written law, show that they know His law when they instinctively obey it, even without having heard it. They demonstrate that God's law is written in their hearts, for their own conscience and thoughts either accuse them or tell them they are doing right."

God speaks to you through your conscience and this is why you must always strive to keep it clear. A clear conscience helps you to hear clearly whereas a contaminated conscience dulls your sense of hearing and will bring confusion into your life. There is so much dishonesty in the world today that most times people don't know what's true and what isn't. People have a tendency to tell people what they want to hear and not what's really on their mind. Don't get caught up in all this dishonesty for it will hinder your ability to hear from God. Speak the truth in love or, better yet, walk away and say nothing at all. The bottom line is that you must keep your conscience clear at all times. Every day walk in the light you've been given and this will keep open the door of communication between you and God. Your conscience bothering you is a sign that something is not right and you need to stop what you're doing and listen to what it is saying. This is what keeps you sensitive to the voice of God and makes you aware of what's going on.

You are to walk in the light you have and it is a dangerous thing to say you don't know something when in truth you do. To have a clear conscience you've got to be honest with yourself. If you're not then you will be self-deceived and you won't hear the voice of God. What's worse is that if you lie to yourself long enough you'll come to believe the lie is true. This will stop your faith from working and will prevent you from having any open communication with God. You are in the world but are not of the world so don't get caught up in the dishonesty of this evil generation. The devil is the father of lies but Jesus is the way, the truth, and the life. You've been delivered from the kingdom of darkness so never again should you be dishonest about anything. If you want your faith to be strong and the voice of God to be crystal clear to you then you must have a clear conscience at all times. Get rid of everything that is false and not true and this will allow you to hear the voice of God.

Always be aware of the deceptive practices of the enemy for he is forever roaming about seeking whom he can devour. 1 Tim. 4:1,2 says, "Now the Spirit expressly says that in latter times some will depart from the faith, giving heed to deceiving spirits and doctrines of demons, speaking lies in hypocrisy, having their own conscience seared with a hot iron." Many people have left the faith because they listened to the voice of the enemy more than the voice of their own conscience. There is nothing more devilish than lies and deception just like there is nothing more godly than truth. It is hard to imagine why these fallen believers would put their faith in a creature who does nothing but lie and deceive. True believers, on the other hand, put their faith in the living God for it is impossible for Him to lie (Heb. 6:18) and this gives them a solid foundation to stand on. This is the anchor of your soul which means you can base your eternal destiny on whatever God says to you. He has never lied, He never will lie, and throughout the Bible He warns against deception.

Jesus said in Matt. 24:4, "Take heed that no man deceive you." He is telling you to be on guard at all times so that nobody will deceive you. People will try to convince you that a lie is true and this is what deception is. If you knew what they were telling you was a lie you wouldn't be deceived. This is where a clear conscience comes in. It allows you to hear from God who always speaks the truth, and it is the truth that will set you free from all manner of lies and deception. Truth will liberate you and whom the Son sets free shall be freed indeed (John 8:36). People who are deceived don't hear from God. They believe things that are not true and this can make them bitter and angry for many, many years. In time their conscience will get seared and people with a sin-filled conscience don't hear the voice of God. 1 Tim. 4:2 (AMP) says these people will be "[misled] by the hypocrisy of liars whose consciences are seared as with a branding iron [leaving them incapable of ethical functioning]."

Paul said that people get deceived by listening to doctrines of demons. These teachings don't come from some satanist church, they come from the pulpits of local churches where the preacher has been deceived and influenced by religious spirits. The Living Bible says, "But the Holy Spirit tells us clearly that in the last times some in the church will turn away from Christ and become eager followers of teachers with devil-inspired ideas. These teachers will tell lies with straight faces and do it so often that their consciences won't even bother them" (1 Tim. 4:1,2). The CEV says their "consciences have lost all feeling." People who are deceived make excuses for their wrong behavior and this leads to more dishonesty. One lie leads to another and this is why some people don't know if they're coming or going. Their conscience has been seared and they don't know what's true and what's not true. These people are believing lies and the father of lies has become a god to them. What's worse is they don't even know it because they've been deceived.

A seared conscience is a bad thing because it's through your conscience that you hear from God. When you sin, your conscience will tell you that you did wrong. If you ignore these warnings your conscience will still speak but its voice gets softer and softer until eventually it gets seared and you don't hear it at all. You are now an open target for the enemy to come in and destroy your life. You'll become so dull and insensitive that God could be yelling at you and you wouldn't hear Him. You have now become a habitual sinner and are no longer bothered by the wrong you do. You are now on your way to death and destruction because you've opened the door to the devil who comes to steal, kill, and destroy. This is what happens when you listen to doctrines of demons and have a seared conscience. This is why Heb. 3:13 says, "But exhort one another daily, while it is called 'Today,' lest any of you be hardened through the deceitfulness of sin."

The NLT says, "so that none of you will be deceived by sin and hardened against God."

What should be happening? Paul said in Eph. 4:14,15 (NLT), "Then we will no longer be immature like children. We won't be tossed and blown about by every wind of new teaching. We will not be influenced when people try to teach us with lies so clear they sound like the truth. Instead, we will speak the truth in love, growing in every way more and more like Christ, who is the head of His body, the church." You must always speak the truth in love. The devil created lying and that in itself should cause you to despise it. Once and for all, make up your mind that you will never again tell another lie no matter what you may have to go through by telling the truth. Lying is not an option. Ever! The Bible says there are horrific consequences for people who do. Rev. 21:8 says "all liars shall have their part in the lake which burns with fire and brimstone, which is the second death." Your only option is to be honest and to speak the truth in love. This will clear the muddy waters of a sin-stained conscience and will allow you to hear God when He speaks.

Your conscience is important and you need to honor it as such. Paul wrote in 2 Tim. 1:3, "I thank God, whom I serve with a pure conscience, as my forefathers did." He also said in Titus 1:15, "To the pure all things are pure, but to those who are defiled and unbelieving nothing is pure; but even their mind and conscience are defiled." The word "defiled" means 'to be smeared' and is the opposite of being clean and crystal clear. The world is getting darker by the day and the conscience of many people is smeared and dirty. This is not so with those who have been called to be saints. On the inside their conscience is pure and sparkling clean. Heaven is pure and when you have a clear conscience you can have a touch of heaven on earth. Rev. 21:18 says, "And the construction of its wall was of jasper, and the city was pure gold, like clear glass." When something is pure, it is clear.

Vs. 21 says, "And the street of the city was pure gold, like transparent glass." Your conscience is the voice of your heart, and the condition of your heart is what determines the condition of your conscience.

Eph. 4:30,31 says, "And do not grieve the Holy Spirit of God, by whom you were sealed for the day of redemption. Let all bitterness, wrath, anger, clamor, and evil speaking be put away from you, with all malice." The Holy Spirit can be grieved and it's the sins of the flesh that do it. People get hurt, they get mad, and when they don't deal with it properly they get a hard heart. They no longer hear the voice of God and go on to teach their children to be mean and hardhearted like they are. A hardened heart can affect an entire generation and this is how it happens. How should they be? Vs. 32 says, "And be kind to one another, tenderhearted, forgiving one another, just as God in Christ also forgave you." What would the world be like if everybody was kind to one another? God lives inside of you and this is how He is telling you to live. Being kind is the greatest life you will ever live. You're made in the image of God and you're living how He lives. This is what causes you to have a good conscience that is clean and clear. You are able to talk to God and He is able to talk to you.

It takes a clear conscience to hear from God. It takes a heart that is kind and tenderhearted, a heart with no impurities in it, a heart that is not defiled and smeared. Jesus said in Matt. 5:8, "Blessed are the pure in heart, for they shall see the kingdom of God." Paul said "I myself always strive to have a conscience without offence toward God and men" (Acts 24:16). The word "offence" means 'that which causes to stumble' and can mean anything that stands in the way of forward progress. To be clear means to be free from obstacles that are in the way, things that will trip you up and slow you down. Sin, guilt, and condemnation will slow you down and this is why you need to get these roadblocks out of your life. Don't sin but if you do sin, repent and go on. If you repent, you can be restored. Your conscience will be wiped clean and will be clear to hear from God. This is why you need to repent as soon as your heart is convicted of wrong. Don't put it off. Repent as soon as you can and allow that door of communication between you and God to remain open.

God is speaking to people but most don't know they have a responsibility to listen to Him. They're more interested in what other people are saying, hoping to be liked and accepted by their peers. Don't let this happen to you. Pay attention and daily listen for the voice of God as He speaks through your conscience. Train yourself to spend time alone with Him on a regular basis. Read your Bible every day and have faith in the cleansing power of the blood of Jesus. When you get forgiven of your sins, your conscience will be clear. His blood is the only thing that can cleanse a conscience that has been defiled. Heb. 9:14 (NLT) says, "Just think how much more the blood of Christ will purify our consciences from sinful deeds so that we can worship the living God. For by the power of the eternal Spirit, Christ offered Himself to God as a perfect sacrifice for our sins." You're forgiven and your conscience is now clear, therefore, there is nothing to trip over and nothing to slow you down. You are now free to hear from God so take the time to listen.

Getting forgiven is not the end of the story. Once your conscience gets made clear you next need to walk in the light you've been given. If you know something is wrong, you need to stop doing it. Jesus did not condemn the woman caught in adultery but He did tell her to "go and sin no more" (John 8:11). Being forgiven does not give you a license to go on sinning. It is a diabolical thing when Christians willfully give in to the sins of the flesh thinking they can be forgiven tomorrow. These people are making a mockery of what Jesus did for them on the cross. Little do they know that those who wait until tomorrow to get right with God usually get in trouble today. God does not play these type of games where sin is concerned and this is why He says what a person sows, he shall also reap (Gal. 6:7). If you don't stop sinning you will never have a clear conscience. You must walk in the light as He is in the light and sin no more. James 4:17 says, "Therefore, to him who knows to do good and does not do it, to him it is sin."

The blood of Jesus will give you a clear conscience but to keep it clear you must walk in the light you've been given. You must be honest about what you know and understand, and then do what's right. If you know it's wrong to gossip, don't do it. If you know it's wrong to let the sun go down on your wrath, make peace with that other person and go to bed with a clear conscience. You need to do what you know is right. It's a simple concept. It's not always easy, but it is simple. There is a war going on between your spirit and your flesh. To maintain a clear conscience you daily need to overcome temptation and control your flesh. You do this by walking in the light and by always doing the right thing. After telling the woman to sin no more Jesus spoke to the people and said, "I am the light of the world. He who follows Me shall not walk in darkness, but have the light of life" (John 8:12). You need to feed your spirit and starve your flesh. When you do this your inner man will rise up and take charge when temptation comes your way.

Jesus is light and you need to follow Him every day. He won't make you follow Him but like a good shepherd will lead you in the way you should go. If you follow Him, never again will you walk in darkness. You will walk in light and you will hear His voice. You then do what He tells you to do and this is how you live a good life and fulfill your destiny. Sin is no longer a stronghold in your life. The light you're walking in is getting brighter and brighter. Every day you are fulfilling the command to be holy as He is holy. Jesus is described in Heb. 7:26 (NLT), "He is the kind of high priest we need because He is holy and blameless, unstained by sin. He has been set apart from sinners and has been given the highest place of honor in heaven." When you walk in the light you also will be holy and blameless, unstained by sin. Paul confirms this in Rom. 8:1, "There is therefore now no condemnation to those who are in Christ Jesus, who do not walk according to the flesh but according to the Spirit." This means you have no guilt and no shame. You are holy as He is holy.

To be holy is to be like Jesus who said in John 8:29, "I always do those things that please Him." When you walk in the light you've been given you also will please the Father. You'll be like Jesus and will be holy as He is holy. This is when God will show up and work miracles in your life. You are a child of the living God and 1 Thess. 3:13 says Jesus will "establish your hearts blameless in holiness before our God and Father at the coming of our Lord Jesus Christ with all His saints." Jesus is holy and His light is holy light. Ps. 36:9 says, "For with You is the fountain of life; In Your light we see light." His light and His holiness go together. When you walk in light, you walk in holiness. This light is like a flaming fire that burns away the impurities from your life. Col. 1:22 (NLT) says, "Yet now He has reconciled you to Himself through the death of Christ in His physical body. As a result, He has brought you into His own presence, and you are holy and blameless as you stand before Him without a single fault." You can now hear the voice of God.

God is talking to you and you need to be like young Samuel who responded when God spoke to him. 1 Sam. 3:10 says, "Then the Lord came and stood and called as at other times, 'Samuel! Samuel!' And Samuel answered, 'Speak, for Your servant hears.'" With a clear conscience you need to say the same thing. Jesus is the light of the world and He is speaking to you. Your sins have been washed away, there is nothing blocking your path, so say to Him, "Speak, Jesus. I am listening to you." And speak to you He will because Eph.

5:8 is now a reality in your life. "For you were once darkness, but now you are light in the Lord. Walk as children of light." Children of light have a clear conscience and are the people who hear God when He speaks. In Christ you are getting brighter and brighter which means you can hear God more clearly with each passing day. There is nothing more glorious than to have the Creator of the universe speak personally to you. When this happens you will do everything you can to keep the doors of communication open. You will walk in the light you have and will always do the right thing.

Randall J. Brewer

-17-
"ATTEND TO MY WORDS"

God is merciful and forever ready to direct your steps as you journey on the road to perfection. You should always seek the Lord's direction but first you need to understand that you have a vital role to play that determines whether you get it or not. Prov. 3:6 says, "In all your ways acknowledge Him, and He shall direct your paths." The Lord will direct your paths but first you must acknowledge Him. The Amplified Bible says, "In all your ways know and acknowledge and recognize Him, and He will make your paths straight and smooth [removing obstacles that block your way]." There is a part you have to play in order to receive divine direction. Prov. 4:1 says you are to "give attention to know understanding." Prov. 4:10 says, "Hear, my son, and receive my sayings, and the years of your life will be many." You need to pay attention to what's in your heart because that's where God is. To be led by God you've got to be aware of what's in your heart. God is there and that's where divine direction comes from.

Prov. 4:20-23 (NIV) says, "My son, pay attention to what I say; turn your ear to my words. Do not let them out of your sight, keep them within your heart; for they are life to those who find them and health to one's body. Above all else, guard your heart, for everything you do flows from it." Many people get mad at God when hard times come thinking He is silent and doesn't hear their prayers. They are pointing their finger at the wrong person. They need to stand in front of a mirror and ask themselves why they weren't paying attention. Just because they didn't hear anything doesn't mean God wasn't talking to them. You need to learn how God speaks to people and then pay attention to what He says. God tells people to pay attention because they're not doing it. Their hearts and minds are elsewhere and they then wonder why they're not hearing from God. He is speaking but they're not listening and yet God gets the blame for this lack of communication. The answer to all this is that you've got to pay attention when He speaks.

The world is a place full of distractions. All kinds of electronic games and devices were created to distract you from the realities of life. If you allow it, you can be continually distracted from those things that are really important in life, things like hearing from God. You can't hear Him when He speaks if your eyes are glued to some smart phone twenty-four hours a day. God will not force you to pay attention to the important things in life but, if you're wise, you will put that phone down and follow the instructions of Prov. 5:1, "My son, pay attention to my wisdom; Lend your ear to my understanding." Doing this will protect your life from destruction and will cause you to succeed in life. There are no Spirit led disasters and those who experience such things were not paying attention to God as He was talking to them. This is hard for some people to accept because it's easier to blame God than themselves but it is the truth nonetheless. God was talking but they weren't listening. The good news is that they can pay attention now and God will lead them from chaos to total restoration.

Prov. 4:20 (KJV) says, "My son, attend to my words; incline thine ear unto my sayings." The YLT says, "To my words give attention." You can give attention to things other than God. You can focus too much on the trial you're facing and not pay attention to God and His solution to the problem. You can't receive a healing if all you do is focus on the symptoms of whatever it is that's attacking you. If you're doing that then you're not hearing from God. He is not leading you to focus on how you feel or to despair over a bad report. What He will do is tell you to not look at the problem but to pay attention to Him. He'll say, "Attend to My words and listen to what I'm saying." Wake up and take your eyes off the evening news and give attention to the words of God. Rom. 8:5 says, "For those who live according to the flesh set their minds on the things of the flesh, but those who live according to the Spirit, the things of the Spirit." It matters what you think about, who and what you pay attention to.

Is. 26:3 says, "You will keep him in perfect peace, whose mind is stayed on You, because he trusts in You." You need to become more aware of God's presence inside of you, and that He goes wherever you go. You need to pay attention to what He's saying and what He's doing. Heb. 2:1 (AMP) says you "must pay much closer attention than ever to the things that we have heard, so that we do not [in any way] drift away from truth." More times than not, people have heard the answers they're searching for but they didn't pay attention to it and it drifted away. What they need today is the same solution God gave them last year, but because they didn't pay attention to it they've wasted several months looking for a different answer. They're not going to find it because God does not change. The answer He gave them last year is the same answer they need now. God is good and He doesn't make people wait on the answers they're looking for. The problem is that people are not focused on Him and are paying attention to other things.

God is telling you what to do. "My son, pay attention to what I say. Attend to My words. Take heed to what I'm telling you." God is speaking but people are not listening because the devil is the master of distraction and he's continually trying to take your focus away from God. He will bombard your mind with thoughts and suggestions and feelings in an effort to get your attention away from where it should be. This is why Prov. 3:5 says, "Trust in the Lord with all your heart, and lean not on your own understanding." God is in your heart and this is from where He will lead you and direct your path. You need to train yourself to pay attention. Go off by yourself and get still before Him. Be quiet and listen for those divine promptings that come to you down in your heart. You are listening and surely He will speak. You will know that you know you've heard from Him. Jesus said the sheep follow the shepherd "for they know his voice" (John 10:4). Never follow any voice other than the one you know is His.

Stop thinking so much and start to listen more. What you need is not in your mind, it's in your heart. Knowledge and understanding are good things but the answer you're looking for will come from your heart and not your mind. You've got to have a hunger to hear Him better and then you must put forth some effort to help make this a living reality in your life. Never think you can reason yourself out of every predicament that comes your way on intellect alone. It's not going to happen. More times than not you will be in situation after situation where you don't have the answer you need and you're unable to figure the solution out on your own. You don't know as much as you think you do so if all you're doing is relying on what's in your mind then you will soon experience a rude awakening. What you need is help from above, divine direction that will come to your heart and from there will bring enlightenment to your understanding. God knows everything and He lives in your heart so why try to figure things out on your own? It doesn't make sense if you do.

Those whom you think are super spiritual are, in truth, not all that much different from you. What sets them apart is they've learned how to listen to God. To hear from God you've got to first acknowledge Him in all your ways. This means you've got to be continually aware of God's presence inside of you, and you need to be looking to Him night and day. You need to check in with Him concerning everything you say and do. Don't assume anything but humble yourself and ask God for divine direction. When you do that, His Spirit will bear witness with your spirit and you'll know what to do. If you don't seek direction and attend to His words then don't blame God when trouble happens. It is foolishness and ignorance to blame God for your mistakes especially when He was trying to help you all along. He was speaking but you were listening to something else. You need to start paying attention to the voice of God. Every day you have to choose what you're going to listen to. If you make the right choice it will help you whereas the wrong choice will hurt you.

Prov. 4:10 says, "Hear, my son, and receive my sayings, and the years of your life will be many." That in itself should motivate you to listen when God speaks. Living a good, long life is not automatic. The length and quality of your life is greatly affected by how well you pay attention to God and esteem His words. Do not disrespect God by being casual in the way you listen. It is possible to hear something but not have it register down in your heart. It is possible to hear and yet not hear (Matt. 13:13). You've got to attend to His words and pay attention to what He is saying. James 1:19 says, "Let every man be swift to hear, slow to speak, slow to wrath." Most people have this backwards. They're quick to get mad and upset, they're quick to talk, and they're slow to hear. Not everybody is a good listener. One of the most respectful things you can do for another human being is to genuinely listen to them and care about what they're saying. It is hard to do this if you're doing all the talking. This is why you have to talk less and listen more.

Prov. 10:19 says, "In the multitude of words sin is not lacking, but he who restrains his lips is wise." If you're always talking you're missing the mark somewhere, somehow. David said in Ps. 39:1, "I will guard my ways, lest I sin with my tongue; I will restrain my mouth with a muzzle while the wicked are before me." The heart of the Father is expressed in Ps. 81:13, "Oh, that My people would listen to Me, that Israel would walk in My ways!" God wants you to listen to Him but you can't do it if you're always talking. Put a muzzle over your mouth and get quiet. Be still and know He is God. He'll reveal Himself to you by speaking to you but you've got to be quiet and listen. Become a believer who pays attention and listens closely to the words God speaks to you. Prov. 1:5 says, "A wise man will hear and increase learning, and a man of understanding will attain wise counsel." Vs. 7 says, "The fear of the Lord is the beginning of knowledge, but fools despise wisdom and instruction." You fear God by giving Him respect and showing Him reverence. One way to do this is to take time and listen to what He says.

God wants you to listen to Him and do what He says because He wants to abundantly bless your life. This can't happen if you're not paying attention to what He is saying to you. He said in Ex. 15:26, "If you diligently heed the voice of the Lord your God and do what is right in His sight, give ear to His commandments and keep all His statutes, I will put none of the diseases on you which I have brought on the Egyptians. For I am the Lord who heals you." God has many blessings in store for you but first you've got to diligently heed the voice of the Lord and give ear to His commandments. In other words, you've got to listen to Him.

Luke 5:15 says, "Then the report went around concerning Him all the more; and great multitudes came together to hear, and to be healed by Him of their infirmities." First the people heard what Jesus said, then they received their blessing. You must grasp the fact that hearing God when He speaks is an indispensable part of receiving your blessing. The people didn't come to just receive their healing, they came to hear Him first.

The outcome of your life is based on the decisions you make. Many preachers have falsely taught that God is in control of everything and He's going to do what He wants regardless of what you say and do. That is not true for the decisions you make have everything to do with what happens in your life. God created you with a completely independent free will and you can choose to pay attention to Him or else you can ignore Him when He speaks. The choice is yours. Most people crave the blessings of God but don't want to be still long enough so they can hear from Him. They need to value the words of the Lord who said in John 6:63, "The words that I speak to you are spirit, and they are life." Decide today to rid your life of all those distractions that would hinder you from spending time alone with God. If you value Him and the words He speaks, you will do everything you can to hear His voice. The good news is that if you're willing to listen, you won't have any problems hearing from Him.

Be careful who and what you listen to. It is possible for you to expose yourself to serious harm if you listen to the wrong things. This is why Jesus said, "Take heed what you hear" (Mark 4:24). God's words are full of life and they have the power to set your life on an upward path. His words will heal your body and restore back to you that which was lost. Nothing He says is void of power and this is why the parable of the sower teaches you to keep His words in the midst of your heart. Don't be like those who never hear the Word or have a shallow reception of it if they do. No, have a heart that's made up of good ground that will hear and receive everything God says. This is to be a lifestyle for you and not something you do once a week or when a tragedy occurs. God said in Josh. 1:8, "This Book of the Law shall not depart from your mouth, but you shall meditate in it day and night, that you may observe to do according to all that is written in it. For then you will make your way prosperous, and then you will have good success."

You have a destiny to fulfill, a mountain to climb, and to reach the summit you must learn to listen to God. You need to learn that God has much in store for your life. He desires you to reach greater heights in life and to gain a new, life changing perspective that will empower you to live the exciting life you were created for. He wants you to soar above the clouds in your relationship with Him and in the thoughts you think about yourself. He wants you to soar in your ministry and in the lives of the ones you love. Above the clouds you see things differently. You see things the way God sees them. His thoughts are above the thoughts of the world and yours must be as well. Commit yourself to live the life God destined you to live. Your life is not an ordinary life and you must have an unusual willingness to mount up with a sense of energy and renewal as you rise high above the clouds and soar as eagles soar. This is your destiny. This is your calling in life. This is the reason God created you in the first place. Indeed, you were born for such a time as this.

Life is an adventure full of twists and turns, ups and downs, and everything in between. Still, you have a destiny to fulfill and God wants you to get to the place you're supposed to be. The journey to reach the top of your mountain takes commitment, perseverance, and a willingness to keep going forward no matter what. It will be a climb filled with challenge and struggle but in the end it will be worth whatever it takes to get there. God will direct your steps but you must take the time to listen to Him and hear His voice. Don't plan your time alone with God around your other activities. No, plan your calendar around your time with God. Put Him first in everything you do. People want God to speak to them but aren't willing to make time for Him in their busy schedule. The truth is, if you're too busy for God, you're too busy. You must clear out some space and give God room to speak. When you draw near to God, He will draw near to you (James 4:8). When He does speak, your life will never be the same.

When you train yourself to pay attention to God, He will give you opportunities to believe for things you've stopped believing for. The things you once thought were impossible for you to possess and achieve God says are now possible if you will only listen and believe. He will open doors for you that in times past you have closed. Get your hopes up once again and trust God. Don't put your dreams in a box. God is saying to open up that box and soar like an eagle. A doorway of opportunity is opening up for you but you must have the courage to walk through it. It takes courage to do that because on the other side of that door begins the climb to the top of your mountain. That door does not mark the end of your journey but the beginning. It marks the start of an exciting adventure where the only limits are the ones you put there yourself. But if you'll keep at it, if you'll never give up, there is no telling how far you can go and how much you can accomplish in the kingdom of God. It's what you've been born to do.

The choice is yours. Will you climb that mountain or won't you? You can't ask God to fix your marriage if you're not willing to take the climb to fix it. If you want God to do something for you then you will have to go on a journey with Him. It's a journey to the top of your mountain, a journey that will take you above the clouds. Most people don't believe for big dreams because the climb is too difficult for them. With big dreams come big trials and most people can't handle the scrapes and bruises of such a climb. They're not willing to pay the price that comes with every big dream. They prefer to camp at the base of the mountain where they think it's safe. Little do they realize that one day they will bow down before God and be asked why they didn't make the climb. God wants you to climb your mountain and there is a price to pay for not doing so. You can pay the price now or you can pay the price later. The choice is yours. Don't hesitate another moment. Put one foot in front of the other and trust God to lead you every step of the way.

As you get closer to the top of your mountain you'll have to limit the amount of talking you do. You must save your oxygen so don't talk to people you shouldn't be talking to. Don't get caught up in conversations with people who can't help you get to where you're going. Not only will you have to overcome the doubt in your life, you will have to overcome their doubt as well. Besides, you shouldn't be talking when you're supposed to be climbing. You won't reach the place God wants you to be if you're always stopping to talk to people you shouldn't be speaking with. There is a place you're supposed to be so don't let these people keep you from your miracle. Don't allow them to take you down the mountain when you're trying to go up the mountain. You need to stop talking and keep climbing. When you stop, the people behind you have to stop as well because you're blocking their way. Not only do you want to go higher in life, you want to help others go higher also.

The conversations you have will either help you go up the mountain or leave you stranded on the ledge. Be careful who you talk to on your climb. If there are questions in your mind, don't talk to people who don't have the answers. Talk to people who are well grounded in the Word and allow them to help you take one more step up that mountain. You are on a mission and you must make everything and everyone who is not helping you get out of your way. Remove the roadblocks and do it immediately. No loitering allowed! Talking not permitted! Also, don't be satisfied until you reach the top of your mountain. Don't allow yourself to feel satisfied because you've climbed halfway. Satisfaction may cause you to ponder going back down the mountain if you see that rocks and boulders are blocking your path. No, gird up your strength and climb over those big rocks that stand in your way. You've come too far to back up now.

It can be intimidating to face the challenge of a climb without knowing what lies ahead. This is why you have "to trust in the Lord with all your heart and lean not on your own understanding" (Prov. 3:5). Your climb is a journey of faith and this means you're not always going to have all the answers to your questions. God is telling you to trust Him anyway and keep climbing. He sees the end from the beginning and this is why in faith you can "know that all things work together for good to those who love God, to those who are called according to His purpose" (Rom. 8:28). The answers you seek are in front of you and this is why you must keep climbing. You don't wait for the answers to come to you, you go to the answers. If all you do is wait for the answers then you'll spend your entire life camped at the base of the mountain. You won't go anywhere and you'll do nothing significant with your life. To sit and do nothing is to forfeit the most important lesson you could ever be taught about the love and character of God, the lesson that He is a God who can be trusted.

The higher you climb, the more the character of God is revealed to you. God is moving behind the scenes and this is why you have to trust Him and keep climbing. Understand that faith and trust go hand in hand. Faith is what you're hoping for, trust is who you're hoping in. Faith says "God can," trust says "God is." The degree to which you genuinely know who God is determines the degree to which you can believe God can. Your job is to not talk yourself into a miracle but to wake up each morning and be so in tune with the Lord that you know His heart and who He is. That way when a trial comes your way and faith is needed you'll have something to work with. You've spent time alone with God and you know who He is as a person. You know His heart and the great love He has for you. Because of that, you trust Him and that is when faith comes alive. It's what gives you the perseverance to keep climbing and before long God will be doing things for you and, more important, through you. It is at this time that you've risen above the clouds.

In life there are many people who begin their climb up the mountain but very few who reach the top. They're great starters but poor finishers. Just because there is a plan in place to help you finish your climb does not mean the journey is always going to be smooth. Life's journey can be a struggle but God can use those hard times to bring good into your life. Jesus said in John 16:33, "These things I have spoken to you, that in Me you may have peace. In the world you will have tribulation; but be of good cheer, I have overcome the world." Life can be a struggle. Things don't happen as they should and other things may take longer to happen as you'd like. People are always in a hurry to get their prayers answered and to them God says, "Be still, and know that I am God" (Ps. 46:10). God will almost always tell you to wait but very rarely will He tell you to hurry up. He is more concerned with what He can do inside of you than what He can do for you on the outside. Where He's taking you is less important than what's He's doing in you.

You have dreams and, yes, reaching the top of the mountain is very important. God would not have told you to start climbing if He didn't want you to reach the top. You need to understand that the fulfillment of your destiny is only half the story. The other half, and probably the most important half, is who and what you become in the process. God is trying to mold and shape you into His image and this is what needs to be taking place on your journey. What good is reaching the top if your life is in shambles when you get there? This is what happens when you take the easy path up the mountain. God's attitude is "no pain, no gain" and this is why He will direct you to take the hardest route to the top. Struggle is a part of life because we live in a hopelessly broken world. To help make you strong God will take you on the long way up the mountain instead of the shortest and fastest way. You will need endurance and perseverance on this path and it only comes when you face head on the trials of life and not run away from them.

God is not the author of struggle but He can use it and turn it into your strength. He is more interested in the person you can become than in your comfort. Circumstances will come up and it takes longer for them to change than you'd like. Sometimes God will seem to be a million miles away. What's happening here? God is teaching you to trust Him even in the midst of your darkest hour. He wants you to believe and know that no matter how it may appear, you are never alone. He is a God who is with you every step of the way even though you may not sense His presence. When you realize you're not alone, that God is working in you and through you, you will have the courage and strength to keep going. James 1:2-4 (MSG) says, "Consider it a sheer gift, friends, when tests and challenges come at you from all sides. You know that under pressure, your faith-life is forced into the open and shows its true colors. So don't try to get out of anything prematurely. Let it do its work so you become mature and well-developed, not deficient in any way."

God has a gift for you. It's called hardship, struggle, not getting your own way. Trials and persecution can be a gift if you see them as God sees them. These are the things God uses to make you strong. Remember, no pain, no gain. He doesn't bring the struggle but as long as it's here He'll use it to help mold you into His image. You'll pray more, trust Him more, walk in faith more. You're becoming stronger and stronger on your way up the mountain and will come to realize that what you're becoming is more important than where you're going. It's the journey that makes you a strong, mature Christian. Nobody said this was fun and easy but it is worth it. After all, it's a gift from God. Look at your trial as God giving you the opportunity to become more like Him. See your struggle as a gift from God for it gives Him the opportunity to work His goodness in you. God is building something inside of you where you'll come out a better person, a better Christ follower, a more mature believer. That should be the primary reason you climb.

-18-

"SONS OF GOD"

One of the most important things you can do in life is learn how to hear from God. The world in its present condition is just too messed up to try to live here on your own. No, you need help from above and you need it right now. This is why it's so important to pay attention when God speaks to you. The words you hear Him say will give you divine direction for your life. David said that like a good shepherd the Lord will lead you beside the still waters and He'll lead you in paths of righteousness (Ps. 23;1-3). Miracles happen when you hear from God and do what He tells you to do. Jesus said in John 16:13, "However, when He, the Spirit of truth has come, He will guide you into all truth; for He will not speak on His own authority, but whatever He hears He will speak; and He will tell you things to come." The truth is what you need to know in every situation you're in and it's the truth that will set you free. When you train yourself to hear from God and be led by the Spirit, there is nothing the world can do to keep you from fulfilling your destiny.

Rom. 8:14 says, "For as many as are led by the Spirit of God, these are the sons of God." The Holy Spirit is a true gentleman in every sense of the word and He won't force

Himself on anybody. You must be willing to freely receive the guidance He wants to give you. The Amplified Bible says, "For all who are allowing themselves to be led by the Spirit of God are sons of God." The Holy Spirit knows everything about everything and He's your helper. If you will allow yourself to be led by Him then all the crooked places in your life will be made straight. Millions of believers, however, are not being led by the Spirit and aren't trying to be. Believers should be hearing from God all the time and it should bother them if they're not. You need to become more sensitive to those inward promptings and when you do hear from Him yield to what He tells you to do. When you yield to the small things He will soon talk to you about the big things. He who is faithful over a little will be made ruler over much (Matt. 25:23).

When you obey God in the little things you will be promoted and used by Him in the bigger things. It all comes down to how well you hear from Him and how quickly you yield to what He says. If God tells you to do something, do it as fast as you can. And, when you do obey, do it gladly and willingly. You never obey God with a frown on your face but with a smile that lights up the room. Get excited that God considered you worthy to talk to, a person He knows He can count on. Ps. 37:23 says, "The steps of a good man are ordered by the Lord." God will not show you the big picture at first but instead will lead you one step at a time. You need to prove your faithfulness to Him by willingly taking that first step and the one after that. As you do that, more and more direction will come and before long you'll see the big picture of what God has in store for your life. Many people are vagabonds going here and there because they didn't listen and obey when God first spoke to them. Don't let this happen to you.

God uses people who hear His voice and does what He tells them to do. What may appear to be small to you is a big thing to God because it's with the small things that you prove you're ready for the big things. When you take that first step things will start to get more significant and the things God will have you do will get bigger and bigger. He'll speak to you more and more and you'll receive greater direction for your life. Before long you'll be a Spirit led powerhouse in the kingdom of God. You'll be used by God in situations where He can't use other people. God will pour His blessings out on you more than others because you took that first step and they didn't. You obeyed God completely while they obeyed Him partially or not at all. Is. 1:19 says, "If you are willing and obedient, you shall eat the good of the land." There is nothing more dynamic in life than to hear from God and to be used to make a difference in the life of another person. This is what the fulfillment of your destiny is all about.

To be used by God you must follow Him fully and completely. The more you respond to Him and yield to what He says, the more aware of Him you will be. Your sensitivity will increase to the point where His whispers are crystal clear to you. There is nothing more precious than knowing the voice of God and hearing Him when He speaks. If you're going to hear from God then you must have a heart that is open to Him. You can't have a closed heart and mind that never takes the time to pay attention and listen. 1 Thess. 5:19 says, "Do not quench the Spirit." The Amplified Bible says, "Do not quench [subdue, or be unresponsive to the working and guidance of] the [Holy] Spirit." You quench the Spirit when you don't respond to His direction. People don't hear from God today because they weren't open to Him in the past. They've become dull of hearing and the voice of God they do not know. These people are only aware of what they want and are not aware of what God wants.

A person whose heart is open to God will put what He wants above anything else. Ps. 40:8 says, "I delight to do Your will, O my God, and Your law is within my heart." The Message Bible says, "And I'm coming to the party You're throwing for me. That's when God's Word entered my life, became part of my very being." A spiritual party takes place when you hear God speak and with a willing heart do what He tells you to do. A heavenly celebration happens because you followed in the footsteps of Jesus who said, "I always do those things that please Him" (John 8:29). Jesus always sought to please the Father. He knew that the secret to personal fulfillment is pleasing Him. This is why He said in Matt. 16:25, "For whoever desires to save his life will lose it, and whoever loses his life for My sake will find it." The more people try to please themselves, the more unhappy they will be. Being self centered always leads to disappointment and this is why millions of people in the world are miserable and lost.

To be led by the Spirit you've got to be open to what the Lord would have you do. You don't decide what your calling is, you discover it. Who you are and what you will become was decided by God in eternity past. It is your responsibility to be led by the Spirit to make sure His will and His plan is fulfilled in your life. Many believers are trying to do their own thing and fail miserably. The grace of God is not on them and they stumble and are unsuccessful in what they try to do. They blame God for their lack of success yet don't realize He is not obligated to approve and bless their plans. He can't help people who are outside His will. No, they must conform to His will and this is when the grace will flow. This is when they'll hear the voice of God and be led by the Spirit. God's Spirit will bear witness with their spirit and they'll know what to do. It is so important that you seek God's will and direction for even the smallest details of life. Everyday say, "Not my will but Your will be done."

You need to become more sensitive to the leading of the Holy Spirit. Most believers are not Spirit led and this is why there is a lack of peace in their heart. God will give you peace as proof that you have indeed heard from Him. Col. 3:15 (AMP) says, "Let the peace of Christ [the inner calm of one who walks daily with Him] be the controlling factor in your hearts [deciding and settling questions that arise]. To this peace indeed you were called as members in one body [of believers]. And be thankful [to God always]." You need to allow that inner peace to decide and settle with finality all questions that arise in your mind. Peace is a manifestation of the God of peace and, when you follow peace, you are following God. When a decision has to be made, let the peace of God rule in your heart. If you feel uncomfortable about something, stop what you're doing and seek direction from on high. When you've heard from God peace will be there and you'll know what to do.

Is. 55:12 says, "For you shall go out with joy, and be led out with peace." Peace is leading you so always follow after peace. Never make a decision until you have peace in your heart. Set your mind on the things of the Spirit because "to be spiritually minded is life and peace" (Rom. 8:6). When you walk in the Spirit you will set your mind on the right things. Is. 26:3 says, "You will keep him in perfect peace whose mind is stayed on You, because he trusts in you." If you want to make right decisions then keep your mind on the Lord at all times. Think about Him night and day. If you're confused and frustrated and don't know what to do, then your mind hasn't been on the Lord. You've been thinking about the wrong things and this means you've been carnally minded. This will rob you of your peace and joy and will stop you from being led by the Spirit of God. Stop thinking about those things that frustrate you and start thinking about God and all His goodness.

The sons of God are those who are led by the Spirit of God. The desire of their heart is found in Ps. 25:4,5, "Show me Your ways, O Lord; Teach me Your paths. Lead me in Your truth and teach me, for You are the God of my salvation; On You I wait all the day." Never make hasty decisions but be willing to take the time and wait until you've heard from the Lord. You will not be disappointed if you'll wait with expectation on Him for He will come through for you every time. Don't get in a hurry and don't get tired of waiting. Ps. 37:7 says, "Rest in the Lord, and wait patiently for Him." Slow down, don't panic, and realize that good things come to those who wait. Continue to live your life and keep doing what you know to do all the while in your heart you are waiting to hear from Him. You asked for divine direction and with confidence you know the answer will be forthcoming. Soon, and very soon, His Spirit will bear witness with your spirit and you'll know what to do.

Many people miss God by moving too fast. They're hasty in what they say and do and later regret that they didn't wait to hear from God. He knows everything and He knows when the time is right to do things. David knew this and wrote in Ps. 31:14,15, "But as for me, I trust in You, O Lord; I say, 'You are my God.' My times are in Your hand; Deliver me from the hand of my enemies, and from those who persecute me." He also wrote in Ps. 27:13,14, "I would have lost heart, unless I had believed that I would see the goodness of the Lord in the land of the living. Wait on the Lord; Be of good courage, and He shall strengthen your heart; Wait, I say, on the Lord!" God is "the God of patience and comfort" (Rom. 15:5) and He will never let you down if you will trust Him enough to wait on Him. The pressure to give up or act hastily will be strongest just moments before your answer arrives so hang in there just a while longer. The Lord rewards those who wait on Him and you'll have no regrets if you do.

God does not want you wandering around all the time not knowing what to do. No, He wants you to pay attention and be led by the Spirit so you'll know which direction to take in any given situation. His leadings are familiar and comforting, not strange and unknown. Jesus said, "My sheep hear My voice, and I know them, and they follow Me" (John 10:27). He also said in John 10:5, "Yet they will by no means follow a stranger, but will flee from him, for they do not know the voice of strangers." This is how you can tell if a certain thought or leading is right or wrong. If it's strange and unknown to you, don't entertain it and definitely don't follow it. The Holy Spirit is inside of you and you're familiar with His presence and His person. You know Him and when He speaks it will be familiar to you down in your heart. You'll have a witness, a confirmation, on the inside of you that will bear witness with your spirit. You will know that you know you've heard from Him.

There are many believers who are not led by the Spirit of God. They're led by reason and circumstances. They'll move out of town because they were offered a higher paying job when all along the Lord wanted them to stay and minister at the church they currently attend. They missed the will of God because of the hope of financial gain. These people are gullible and are willing to listen to others who say they heard from God concerning their life. Don't allow this to happen. Learn to hear from God for yourself. Even if a highly respected minister says they heard from God concerning your life, if it sounds strange and unknown to you, don't receive it as coming from God. You are born again and the sons of God are led by the Spirit of God. This is not to say that God can't use other people to minister direction to you. He can and He will. When this happens, what the other person says to you will bear witness with your spirit verifying that what was spoken indeed was inspired by the Lord.

Bad things happen when people don't hear from God. He is endeavoring every day to speak to His children but most of them aren't listening. This is why you need to be more sensitive to spiritual matters, to be more aware of God's presence and His direction. As a child of God you have a right to hear His voice and to be led by the Spirit. You're called to be saints, habitual sin has been dealt with, and now you need to pay attention and hear from God. Jesus said, "Blessed are the pure in heart, for they shall see God" (Matt. 5:8). The Amplified Bible says, "Blessed [anticipating God's presence spiritually mature] and the pure in heart [those with integrity, moral courage, and godly character], for they will see God." The Greek word for "see" in this verse means to 'perceive.' Jesus is saying that those who follow after holiness can know and perceive down in their heart the voice of God and the promptings of the Holy Spirit.

God has set you apart for His exclusive use and it is imperative that you hear from Him. If a certain thought comes to you and you're not sure if it came from God or your own imagination, check up on yourself and see if there is any unconfessed sin that needs to be dealt with. Light and darkness don't mix and a clear conscience is needed to hear from God. The Spirit that leads you is a holy Spirit and you must be holy to hear from Him. In life you will take on the qualities and characteristics of whichever spirit you yield to, whether it be the spirit of light or the spirit of darkness. The mad man of Gadara was possessed by an unclean spirit and became just like that spirit as he lived among the tombs and often cut himself with stones (Matt. 5:2-5). He was unclean until Jesus set him free. If you yield to a lying spirit you will become a liar but, if you yield to the Holy Spirit, you will take on His qualities and will be holy as He is holy.

Do you want to be used by God to make a positive difference in the lives of other people? Then be holy as He is holy. You serve a holy God and you can live a holy life. You can hear from God and you can be led by the Holy Spirit. An example of this is found in 2 Peter 1:21, "For prophecy never came by the will of man, but holy men of God spoke as they were moved by the Holy Spirit." These men would not have been used by God had they been unclean with lives stained by sin. No, they were holy men who served a holy God and were moved by a holy Spirit. The same thing can happen with you if you'll maintain a clear conscience and pay attention to the moving of the Spirit. Cleanse yourself of those things that defile and bring condemnation. Don't keep company with those who mock God and sin willfully. If you don't separate yourself from these things you'll lose your sensitivity to hear from God. Surround yourself with God fearing people who want to serve God like you do. Keep company with like minded believers and then get ready to hear from God.

Set a goal for yourself to hear from God daily with a willingness to respond to what He says. If you'll do that, He'll show you what to do and what not to do. What was once bitter and sour can become sweet and loving if you'll allow the Lord to direct your steps. If you'll be sensitive to His leading you'll avoid accidents and pitfalls you may have had otherwise. You'll always be at the right place at the right time and you'll prosper and succeed in all you do. For this to happen you must be steadfast and stable in all your ways. You can't be up one minute and down the next. James 1:7,8 says, "For let not that man suppose that he will receive anything from the Lord; he is a double-minded man, unstable in all his ways." It is a tormenting life to always be wavering and plagued with indecision. One day you heard from God and the next day you're not so sure it was Him. You're "like a wave of the sea driven and tossed by the wind" (vs. 6). You don't know if you're coming or going. This is not how life is supposed to be for the person who is Spirit led.

Abraham was a man who did not waver. Rom. 4:20,21 says, "He did not waver at the promise of God through unbelief, but was strengthened in faith, giving glory to God, and being fully convinced that what He had promised He was also able to perform." Never question God once you've heard from Him. Be like Abraham who was so persuaded that he heard from God that he acted on what He said. He was stable and he wavered not. You must be the same way. Don't be moved by doubt and indecision. Don't act like hearing from God is a difficult thing to do. It's not. Paul said in 2 Cor. 11:3, "But I fear, lest somehow, as the serpent deceived Eve by his craftiness, so your minds may be corrupted from the simplicity that is in Christ." Hearing from God is a simple thing but people waver when they consider things they shouldn't be considering. Abraham considered not his own body and the deadness of Sarah's womb (Rom. 4:19). When God tells you something, do not consider anything else.

Jesus was led by the Spirit every day of His earthly life and you have inside of you the same Holy Spirit He had. This means you can be just as led as He was. When decisions have to be made, make sure you've heard from God first. This is so important because decisions determine direction, and direction determines destiny. Prov. 14:12 says, "There is a way which seems right to a man, but its end is the way of death." Always seek God's counsel because if you do you'll never make a bad decision and will always arrive at the right destination. God has promised to guide you and direct your steps if you will pay attention to what He says. Ps. 32:8 says, "I will instruct you and teach you in the way you should go; I will guide you with My eye." Use your faith and believe that you can hear from God. Believe that He'll lead you and guide you and make your paths straight. You are responsible for your own life so never want or expect others to make decisions for you. This is a responsibility that is yours and yours alone.

Micah 7:5 says, "Do not trust in a friend; Do not put confidence in a companion." Jesus referred to this in Matt. 15:14 when He said, "And if the blind leads the blind, both will fall into a ditch." What should you do? Micah 7:7 says, "Therefore I will look to the Lord; I will wait for the God of my salvation; My God will hear me." Always look to God for divine direction. He'll speak to you down in your heart so always keep it pure and clean. The condition of your heart determines how well you hear from Him. Many don't hear from God because their heart is not right. It's cluttered with too many ungodly things. These are not the people you want to go to when you need advice and direction. There is nothing worthwhile in their heart for them to tell you. Always get God's counsel. Prov. 19:21 says, "There are many plans in a man's heart, nevertheless, the Lord's counsel - that will stand." He knows what's best so always pay attention to Him.

Heb. 2:1 says, "Therefore we must give the more earnest heed to the things we have heard, lest we drift away." The Lord is not going anywhere. He'll never leave you or forsake you yet millions of believers have left Him. They didn't pay attention to Him and as a result they drifted away. God is not hiding anything from you and the things He wants to say are not hard to understand. It's just that you've got to have a willingness to get alone with Him and take the time to listen to what He has to say. This is a dark, oppressive world and there are forces out there who are trying to hinder you from hearing God when He speaks to you. This is why extra effort is needed so slow down and take time to listen. Also, when He does speak, have the respect to write it down so you don't forget it. If you don't, in as little as fifteen minutes you may forget what was told you. On purpose the enemy will bring thoughts to you in an effort to get your mind off what God said. Don't allow this to happen. Write down what God tells you.

To hear from God you need to develop and perfect powers of concentration. You can't allow yourself to be distracted by your feelings and those things you see and hear that are contrary to the Word of God. There are many things going on around you but nothing is as important as hearing from God. Attend to His words and pay attention. Don't allow yourself to be distracted. Turn off the radio and television and put away your telephone. Take the children to grandma's house and go home and spend time alone with God. Do whatever it takes to put yourself in a position where you can hear from Him. The enemy can rule over and dominate those who walk in darkness. These people have hardened their hearts and don't pay attention because they don't think it's important enough. These people are deceived and are in for a world of hurt. In a very short while a dilemma will arise in their life and they won't know what to do about it.

Hearing from God should be the top priority in your life. What He says about everything should take the preeminence over what you or anybody else says. If Jesus is your Lord, then what He says should be first place in your life. This is not true in the lives of millions of believers. Hosea 4:6 says, "My people are destroyed for lack of knowledge. Because you have rejected knowledge, I also will reject you from being priests for Me." People hear the Word but openly reject it because they want to do something else. They don't want to love their enemies or forgive those who did them wrong. This is when darkness enters in causing them to no longer see the light. Prov. 1:7 says, "The fear of the Lord is the beginning of knowledge, but fools despise wisdom and instruction." Fools don't pay attention to God because they despise what He has to say. His words and His direction have no value to them and for Him there is no respect. This is why their lives are in the mess it's in. Nothing good will ever happen to them until they highly esteem the Lord and value those things which He says.

Prov. 9:9 says, "Give instruction to a wise man, and he will be still wiser; Teach a just man, and he will increase in learning." A person who is wise and just wants to hear what God has to say. They know that when they respect and reverence God more, they'll immediately begin to experience His presence in a more powerful way. If you will honor God, He will honor you by allowing you to feel His presence. There is nothing more wonderful than that, nothing more honorable. God is a rewarder of those who diligently seek Him (Heb. 11:6) and if you'll reach out to Him, He'll reach out to you. Something good will happen to you every day of your life. He is a good God and He goes where He feels welcome. When you invite Him into your life, when you honor Him and pay attention to what He says, good things will begin to happen to you. You are a child of God and you're led by the Spirit of God. He is directing each and every step you take. You are living a good life and, most important of all, your destiny is being fulfilled. All this is happening because you honor God and pay attention to what He says.

Randall J. Brewer

-19-

"WILLING AND OBEDIENT"

Rom. 8:14 says, "For as many as are led by the Spirit of God, these are the sons of God." There is a reason that God speaks to His children, a divine purpose that He would allow you to hear His voice. It is the will of God for it to be on earth as it is in heaven and, for that to happen in your life, He is willing to direct your steps each and every day. Your responsibility is to take the time to hear from Him and then do what He tells you to do. Hearing from God won't do you much good unless corresponding actions come as a result of your willingness to take the steps He gives you to take. The biggest problem in the earth today is rebellion. People know what to do but they just won't do it. The Lord said in Is. 1:2,3, "I have nourished and brought up children, and they have rebelled against Me; The ox knows its owner and the donkey its masters crib; But Israel does not know, My people do not consider." It is a sad day when an ox and donkey have more sense than a born again believer.

The Lord then said in Is. 1:19,20, "If you are willing and obedient, you shall eat the good of the land; But if you refuse and rebel, you shall be devoured by the sword." The Message Bible says, "If you'll willingly obey, you'll feast like kings. But if you're willful and stubborn, you'll die like dogs." Rebellion is the nature of the devil himself and the word "obey" is not popular in today's society. There should be little wonder as to why the world is in the condition it's currently in. Darkness prevails because people are rebellious and don't walk in the light they've been given. This is why people need to walk in the footsteps of Jesus who said in Matt. 11:29, "Take My yoke upon you and learn from Me, for I am gentle and lowly in heart, and you will find rest for your souls." The way of the sinner is hard and there is no rest for the defiant and rebellious and disobedient. This is not how it is with those who are willing and obedient for Jesus said in vs. 30, "For My yoke is easy and My burden is light."

Heb. 5:8 (NLT) says, "Even though Jesus was God's Son, He learned obedience from the things He suffered." Jesus did whatever it took to obey and please the Heavenly Father. If He had to suffer to do so, then suffer He did. He wouldn't let anything stand in His way from doing what the Father told Him to do. He was willing and obedient every day of His life, and so should you be. Take His yoke upon you and obey the Father with a clear conscience and a willing heart. If you will do that then all your problems will be over. If you're not eating the good of the land then get serious about it and find out why. Check up on yourself and see if you've missed the mark somewhere. Spend time alone with God and He will show you what adjustments need to be made in your walk with Him and your daily behavior. Miracles happen and needs get met when you hear from God and do what He tells you to do. You obey Him because you trust Him in your heart even if there are things you don't understand in your mind.

If you don't obey God, you won't be on the path you're supposed to be on and you won't encounter the things He's prepared for you. If you're on the wrong path you'll have problems you shouldn't be having because you won't be where God wants you to be. You must trust God enough that you'll follow Him unconditionally and this is how and when you'll eat the good of the land. The more you willingly obey Him, the more of His blessings you'll partake of. It's not complicated. When God tells you to do something, do what He tells you to do. Refusing to do this is not innocent ignorance, it's rebellion that opens the door for the devil to come in and wreak havoc in your life. The devil doesn't play fair and he'll destroy your life if you'll give him the opportunity to do so. This is what happens when you sin willfully and rebel against God's divine direction for your life. What's even more deceiving is that those who do rebel will try to justify what they're doing. They'll admit anything except the fact that they did wrong.

Along with the spirit of disobedience is the spirit of deception. People do wrong and will try to justify what they did. If you'll listen to yourself long enough, you'll convince yourself that you're justified in not doing what you were instructed by God to do. Reasons and excuses will abound but that doesn't change the fact that you openly rebelled against God. Adam blamed Eve for his sin and Eve blamed the serpent. This didn't alter the fact that they both sinned and were cast out of the garden and all the blessings that were there. In your own life you must learn to identify the spirit of rebellion, those things that would cause you to harden your heart against God and the direction He gives you to take. Rebellion is devilish and it will ruin your life. Obedience should be one of the first principles anybody should ever be taught. Paul wrote in Eph. 6:1 (NLT), "Children, obey your parents because you belong to the Lord." Vs. 3 says, "If you will honor your father and mother, things will go well for you, and you will have a long life on the earth."

If people don't learn to be obedient at an early age, things will not go well with them and they may not live a long life. If they don't learn to show respect and obey at home, they won't obey at school, at work, at church, or anywhere else. The laws of the land will mean nothing to them and their life will be destroyed. They'll live by the sword and they'll die by the sword. Rebellion is the scourge of humanity, the blight of the earth, and the more people rebel, the more like the devil they'll become. You need to despise rebellion and all it stands for. The prophet Samuel said, "Behold, to obey is better than sacrifice, and to heed than the fat of rams. For rebellion is as the sin of witchcraft, and stubbornness is as iniquity and idolatry" (1 Sam. 15:22,23). The devil is called "the god of this world" (2 Cor. 4:4) and he is influencing most of the planet. This is why there is defiance everywhere you look. People have an attitude of rebellion and do not value humility, submission, and obedience.

Jesus said in John 6:38, "For I have come down from heaven, not to do My own will, but the will of Him who sent Me." Jesus completely submitted to the will of the Father in everything He said and did. He was willing and obedient and you need to learn to be this way also, the sooner the better. If you don't, then you'll put yourself in a place where God can't help you. Yes, you can repent and turn back to God, but why wait until you're divorced, unemployed, or in a jail cell to do this? Learn to identify this defiant spirit right now and make sure you don't succumb to its power to control your life. If you will do that, you will qualify to eat the good of the land. God will direct your life in such a way that all will go well with you. God will prepare the way for you and all that you do will prosper and succeed. You'll experience favor with God and man. You'll have all you need to live a good life and to fulfill your destiny. The proud get resisted but the humble get the grace that will help you achieve all you set out to do.

Ps. 68:6 (AMP) says, "God makes a home for the lonely; He leads the prisoners into prosperity; Only the stubborn and rebellious dwell in a parched land." Always be willing to submit your will to the will of God. It may not always be easy but do it anyway. People who say submission is easy for them don't know what true submission really is. Submission is not easy for anybody. It wasn't easy for Jesus, and it won't be easy for you. Submission is when something is not your will but you do it anyway. If you want to do what you're being asked to do, then there is no submission involved. It takes faith to submit to what you don't want to do, a willingness to trust God and overcome fear. If you're proud and rebellious, you'll harden your heart and resist what God told you to do. But if you'll humble yourself, you'll repent and ask God for help. When you have a willing heart, God will give you the strength to submit and do what's being asked of you.

Rebellion is defiance, a refusal to obey. God told the children of Israel to cross over into the promised land but they wouldn't do it. God called it a land of milk and honey but the people called it a land of giants. They refused to cross over even though Caleb assured them they were well able to take the land. The result of their defiance was that they wandered around in a dry and parched land for forty years and all who rebelled died in the wilderness. They learned the hard way that it's better to obey God than rebel against Him. They didn't learn soon enough that rebellion is offensive to God yet man and angels alike have rebelled against Him since the dawn of time. God hates rebellion and defiance not only because of its impact on Him but mainly what it does to the people who are rebelling. The outcome of unchecked and unrepented of rebellion is destruction. This is why God is continually looking for a people who will submit themselves to Him willingly, a people who will obey Him because they want to.

Rebellion is a manifestation of pride and James 4:6 says, "God resists the proud, but gives grace to the humble."

People rebel because of pride and selfishness but submission comes when they have a humble heart. The humble get the grace and humility comes when you submit yourself to God. Vs. 7 says, "Therefore submit to God. Resist the devil and he will flee from you." You can't resist the devil until you first submit to God. The Young's Literal says, "Be subject then to God. Stand up against the devil and he will flee from you." Paint a picture in your mind of you yielding to God and standing up to the devil. It will remind you of young David standing up to Goliath and chopping his head off. Understand that you can't stand up to the devil if you're resisting God. Submission to God comes first. Carnal believers who sin habitually can resist the devil all day long and it won't do them any good. If you're resisting God you are in reality yielding to the enemy. The devil don't flee from those who are on his side.

People get defiant when they proclaim that nobody is going to tell them what to do. This is a spirit of rebellion, a spirit of error which Eph. 2:2 says "now works in the sons of disobedience." The entire planet is infused with the spirit of rebellion for there is defiance everywhere you look. People have an attitude problem and believe their way is the right way no matter what anybody else may say, including God. These people need to submit to God and subject themselves to those God has placed in authority over them. The word "subject" is a military term and means 'to rank or arrange under' and "submit" means 'to yield to or surrender to.' To submit to someone means you acknowledge they have a place of authority over you and you yield to their will. This is contrary to what your flesh wants but you can't let your flesh dominate you. You must submit to God at all costs. This means you submit to His Word, His Spirit, and those people He places in authority over you.

Rom. 13:1,2 (WNT) says, "Let every individual be obedient to those who rule over him; for no one is a ruler except by

God's permission, and our present rulers have had their rank and power assigned to them by Him. Therefore the man who rebels against his ruler is resisting God's will; and those who thus resist will bring punishment upon themselves." Those in authority are people and they make mistakes just like you. You may not agree with everything they say and do but you must honor and respect the position they hold. If you disrespect them, you disrespect God because He was the one who put them there. Those who resist and rebel bring destruction on themselves and the enemy knows this. This is where faith comes in. You must submit to those over you trusting God to make sure everything turns out right. Don't rebel against your pastor or your husband or your boss at work. Do those things they ask you to do that are not sinful and put your faith in God believing that He will bless you for doing so.

1 Peter 5:8 says, "Be sober, be vigilant; because your adversary the devil walks about like a roaring lion, seeking whom he may devour." Most Christians know this verse but are unaware of the context in which it was written. Vs. 5 says, "Likewise, you younger people, submit yourselves to your elders. Yes, all of you be submissive to one another, and be clothed with humility, for 'God resists the proud, but gives grace to the humble.'" Peter is saying that the devil will destroy those who are rebellious and don't submit to those God has placed in authority over them. The devil knows that if he can get you to rebel like he did, then you will be destroyed just like him. This is why you have to humble yourself before God and cast all your care on Him. Look out for the enemy for he is searching for those who resist God and by doing so are yielding to him. Through defiance and rebellion the devil can destroy your life. This is why the temptation to disobey is ever present in the lives of every believer. These are the wiles of the enemy and you must be aware of them.

Samuel said rebellion was as the sin of witchcraft yet many are proud of how stubborn and defiant they can be. They think being hard headed is honorable but Paul said in 1 Tim. 3:6 that those who are puffed up with pride will fall into the same condemnation as the devil. Every sin that has ever been committed happened because of rebellion. Every death and every pain is the result of the defiant act of rebellion and one day God will separate those who are rebellious from those who are submissive and obedient. Judgment comes to those who rebel and this is why the devil tempts you to be that way. He is seeking access to your life because he wants you to be judged just like he was judged. He wants you to be resisted and he wants you to fall from grace. Prov. 17:11 says, "An evil man seeks only rebellion; Therefore a cruel messenger will be sent against him." If you rebel, you will be devoured but Prov. 28:13 says, "He who covers his sins will not prosper, but whoever confesses and forsakes them will have mercy."

The new birth involves confessing that Jesus is your Lord. If He is your Lord, then that means you're not your own lord and neither is anybody else. This should be obvious to all yet millions of believers call Jesus their Savior but not their Lord. If Jesus is your Lord then you submit your life to Him and your will to His will. You do what He tells you to do, not what you tell yourself to do. You want to be more than a believer, you want to be a disciple as well. A disciple is a person who follows Jesus at all costs, a person who makes Jesus their Savior and their Lord. A disciple is willing and obedient and always eats the good of the land. They'll live in the best houses, have the highest paying jobs, and drive the nicest cars. Their spouses are happy, their children are disciplined, and their neighbors speak well of them. Nothing will be too hard for those who are willing and obedient. Be like Jesus who was meek and lowly in heart and obedient to the Father every day of His earthly life.

You can't fix a stubborn heart. You must make a choice to be willing and obedient. You must humble yourself and repent of your rebellion. When you do that, you will find mercy and grace to help in time of need. You'll "escape the snare of the devil, having been taken captive to do his will" (2 Tim. 2:26). Breakthrough comes when you repent and believe the truth of God's Word. Repentance is not a bad thing as long as you're genuine when you do it. Be sincere when you confess your wrong and don't be ashamed to shed a few tears or to put your nose in the carpet. This is a display of the humility that is in your heart and soon you'll stand up cleansed and pure. You'll break free from the bondage of the enemy and there will be no more condemnation. You won't be judged but rather will go on to fulfill your destiny. God is on your side and you are now walking in the light. You're willing and obedient and nothing can stop you from achieving all your God-given dreams and goals.

Faith is a choice and if you trust God you will do what He tells you to do. If you trust God, you will submit to those He puts over you because you believe He will take care of you even if those in authority miss the mark a time or two. To not trust God is rebellion and this the Lord condemns. Mark 16:14 says, "Afterward He appeared to the eleven as they sat at the table; and He rebuked their unbelief and hardness of heart, because they did not believe those who had seen Him after He had risen." God hates rebellion and the spirit of disobedience. This is why you have to make up your mind once and for all to not be conformed to this ungodly world. Do not allow yourself to be stubborn and rebellious. Jesus said to Paul on the road to Damascus, "I am Jesus, whom you are persecuting. It is hard for you to kick against the pricks" (Acts 9:5). A prick was a pointed stick that was used to goad an ox. A submissive ox would move but a rebellious ox would stand there and get poked and kicked. Jesus is saying you don't want to be like a rebellious ox or a hard-headed donkey.

Submission and obedience have not been respected and desired as they should be. In today's world to be told what to do is the last thing anybody wants to hear. Also, people think meekness is weakness so they run away from it. They become proud and boisterous and these are the very people God resists. God hasn't changed and His will always has been and always will be that you be willing and obedient and do those things He tells you to do. Wise people submit and want to be like Jesus. They know that if they'll put their flesh under they'll reap great rewards and eat the good of the land. These people are blessed because they learned a long time ago to be quiet and do what they're told. That is a revelation all believers need to learn. There is too much talking and too much rebellion in the Christian church today and this is why many are not reaping the benefits of a rich, prosperous life. The blessings in the land of promise were for those who obeyed and entered in, not for those who rebelled and stayed out.

You have a free will and the choices you make determine what happens in your life. Nobody can make you rebel just like nobody can make you be willing and obedient. Choose today to submit your will to the will of God. Be like Jesus who said, "Nevertheless, not My will but Your will be done" (Luke 22:42). God has given you your one and only life so don't waste it doing those things that you want to do. Seek the will of God and do what He tells you to do. Be assured that He will show you what His will is in any given situation you're in. You are a child of God and it is His character to show you what His will is. He has a specific plan and purpose for your life and He's more than willing to show you what that plan is if you truly want to know. God wants to be involved in every decision you make because what you decide to do reveals what's in your heart. If Jesus is in your heart then your decisions will be based on God's perfect plan for your life.

God will reveal His will to you because it is consistent with who He is. How can He expect you to do His perfect will if He doesn't tell you what His will is? Ps. 16:11 says, "You will show me the path of life; In Your presence is fullness of joy; At Your right hand are pleasures forevermore." Ps. 32:8 also says, "I will instruct you and teach you in the way you should go; I will guide you with My eye." Paul prayed "that you may be filled with the knowledge of His will in all wisdom and spiritual understanding" (Col. 1:9). If necessary, God will go to the extreme and move heaven and earth to show you His will if hearing from Him is the deepest desire of your heart. The will of God begins with the Word of God so read your Bible every day. Believe that God will lead you to the scriptures you most need to hear. You then need to spend time in prayer. If you want to know what God's will is, you need to ask Him. Ask Him what decisions you should make today and then be still and listen for an answer.

1 John 5:14,15 says, "Now this is the confidence that we have in Him, that if we ask anything according to His will, He hears us. And if we know that He hears us, whatever we ask, we know that we have the petitions that we have asked of Him." If you're listening, God will show you what His will is. If, for some reason, you're not hearing from Him then stop and check your heart and see if there is any defiance there. Say to Him, "Search me, O God, and know my heart; Try me, and know my anxieties; And see if there is any wicked way in me, and lead me in the way everlasting" (Ps. 139:23,24). The problem with a lot of believers is that they're not still long enough to hear from God. If they don't hear from Him in a minute or two they stand up and go about their business. This is not right for God is worth waiting for. He is not holding out on you but you've got to be still as long as necessary for you to get in position spiritually so He can tell you what you need to hear. How long you wait depends on how willing you are to listen.

What motivates you to respond the way you do when important decisions have to be made in your life? Decisions in life should be faced with confidence, not intimidation. Decisions have to be made every day and you need to understand that consequences always follow each and every decision you make. This is why you need to seek God and always make your decisions based on what He told you to do. Many people don't know how to make a godly decision and to them David writes in Ps. 25:12, "Who is the man who fears the Lord? Him shall He teach in the way he chooses." The GWT says, "He is the one whom the Lord will teach which path to choose." God is willing to give you direction concerning those critical issues in your life but you must be ready and in a position to hear from Him. God created you with His plan and purpose in mind and He wants you to make those decisions that will cause your destiny to be fulfilled. He will speak to you clearly and reveal Himself to you if He knows your heart is right and you are willing to obey Him at all costs.

David said God will instruct the person who fears the Lord. You need to reverence God and stand in awe before Him. You need to acknowledge who He is and His right to tell you what to do. Ps. 111:10 says, "The fear of the Lord is the beginning of wisdom; A good understanding have all those who do His commandments. His praise endures forever." A person who sins habitually will not hear from God nor will they receive clear direction for their lives. God wants you to hear from Him so you won't wander through life like a vagabond not knowing if you're coming or going. This is why you have to purge your heart of any known sin. A holy God will not speak to an evil heart. Sin is to your mind what fog is to the road you're driving on. It blocks your vision and prevents you from seeing what's ahead of you. If God did speak to the willful sinner then He'd be condoning their wrong behavior and this He will not do. God will give you direction with no doubt that it came from Him and it all starts when you have a pure heart and a clear conscience.

It pays to have a pure heart and to obey God for obedience always brings with it a blessing into your life. Ps. 24:3-5 confirms this vital truth, "Who may ascend into the hill of the Lord? Or who may stand in His holy place? He who has clean hands and a pure heart, who has not lifted up his soul to an idol, nor sworn deceitfully. He shall receive blessing from the Lord, and righteousness from the God of his salvation." A blessing is an expression of God's goodness and love toward you and it happens when you do what God tells you to do. Noah obeyed God and he and his family were saved from the flood. Abraham obeyed God and became the father of many nations. The Bible is full of stories about people who obeyed God and got blessed because of it. God always honors obedience and this is how you live a good life. When you obey God you will be blessed beyond what you could ask or think. This will happen without exception. You'll have peace, joy, and overwhelming contentment and satisfaction. Better yet, you'll draw closer to God and have an improved relationship with Him.

An intimate relationship with God is the most valuable blessing you will ever possess. This blessing has no equal and is better than the false glamour of fortune and fame. Everything you'll ever have or receive comes from the relationship you have with Him and how well you walk in obedience. Walking in His will is a step by step continual act of obedience. You obey God because you trust Him, and the more you trust Him, the more your faith will grow. With faith and obedience comes a greater awareness of God's presence in your life and there is no greater blessing than that. Every act of obedience does not go unseen by God and He is forever ready to bless you because of it. God is God and He has made you the apple of His eye. He wants to bless you, He wants you to be happy. All He needs from you is faith and obedience. If you'll willingly obey Him you'll have a pure heart and a clear conscience. This will allow you to hear from God and when you do what He tells you to do, the blessings will flow. This is the life those called to be saints is all about.

-20-
"NO PRICE TOO HIGH"

Freedom. People have fought for it and millions have died for it. The desire for freedom is the top craving of every human heart and nations have gone to war for the sole purpose of giving its citizens the right to be called free. People cry out "give me liberty or give me death" for the taste of freedom is sweet and worth dying for. Those who have tasted the redemptive blessings of being free would rather their life end than to never again bask in the glories of true, unadulterated freedom. It was for freedom that the Heavenly Father sent his only begotten Son to the earth to save all people from the shackles of a bondage so oppressive that no man, woman, or child could be loosed from it on their own. Setting people free from the bondage of sin and death was the purpose for which Jesus lived and died. He said in John 8:36, "Therefore if the Son makes you free, you shall be free indeed." This freedom is not free nor is it cheap. It cost Jesus His life to give it and will cost you your life to obtain it.

Matt.16:24-26 says, "Then Jesus said to His disciples, "If anyone desires to come after Me, let him deny himself, and take up his cross, and follow Me. For whoever desires to save his life will lose it, and whoever loses his life for My sake will find it. For what is a man profited if he gains the whole world, and loses his own soul? Or what will a man give in exchange for his soul?" The Message Bible says, "Anyone who intends to come with me has to let me lead. You're not in the driver's seat; I am. Don't run from suffering; embrace it. Follow me and I'll show you how. Self-help is no help at all. Self-sacrifice is the way, my way, to finding yourself, your true self. What kind of deal is it to get everything you want but lose yourself? What could you ever trade your soul for?" There is no price too high to pay for this freedom although most people have chosen to drink the bitter waters of death, hell, and the grave.

Paul spoke of a man named Demas who "has forsaken me, having loved this present world, and has departed for Thessalonica." (2 Tim. 4:10). Even Jesus said, "Enter by the narrow gate; for wide is the gate and broad is the way that leads to destruction, and there are many who go in by it. Because narrow is the gate and difficult is the way which leads to life, and there are few who find it" (Matt. 7:13,14). The Message Bible says, "Don't look for shortcuts to God. The market is flooded with surefire, easygoing formulas for a successful life that can be practiced in your spare time. Don't fall for that stuff, even though crowds of people do. The way to life - to God! - is vigorous and requires total attention." Difficult is the way that leads to a good life in Christ Jesus but most people choose to travel the road of least resistance. They spend most of their time looking for shortcuts around the path of hardship instead of pressing on and learning to fight like the soldiers they're called to be. They don't realize that if something is not worth fighting for, then it's not worth living for.

Paul said in 2 Tim. 2:6, "The hard-working farmer must be first to partake of the crop." It's the diligent farmer who gets the produce but too many believers are living lazy, sloppy, and fleshly lives. To avoid fighting for what rightfully belongs to them they instead quote scripture out of context thinking they've found the shortcut to an easy life. This leads to a life of deception for people will think they're more spiritual than they actually are. They'll have no defense against the wiles of the devil and this deception opens the door for the enemy to come in and wreak havoc in their lives. Jesus did not promise you an easy life. He did say if you would put on your armor and fight you could have a victorious life, a good life of freedom that nobody can take from you. Our society has produced a generation of people who want things handed to them without any work or effort on their part and this "want something for nothing" attitude has crept into the local church.

To obtain freedom without fighting for it born-again believers often quote John 8:32 which says, "And you shall know the truth, and the truth shall make you free." They confess this verse over and over again because they think it's a shortcut to freedom. Little do they know that not all believers will know the truth and be set free. This verse is almost always quoted out of context and to get the full meaning of what Jesus is saying one needs to back up and read vs. 31 first. "Then Jesus said to those Jews who believed Him, 'If you abide in My word, you are My disciples indeed. And you shall know the truth, and the truth shall make you free.'" This verse is speaking to disciples. Being a believer doesn't automatically make you a disciple. In vs. 31 Jesus was talking to people who were already believers. He then said "if" and that is a conditional word. The Message Bible says, "If you stick with this, living out what I tell you, you are my disciples for sure." The Amplified Bible states, "If you abide in My word and hold fast to My teachings and live in accordance with them, you are truly My disciples."

Believers are those who believe in Jesus but disciples are those who continue in His Word and become followers at any cost. Just like the student trains to become like his teacher, the true disciple of Jesus trains to become just like his Master. He seeks to become more and more like Him every day. In Greek the word "disciple" means 'learner' and 'follower' and is the same as being an intern and an apprentice. A disciple is not only a pupil but is an imitator of the teacher much like an oriental martial arts student who copies and mimics the ways and moves of his master. This is more than a scholastic study where you sit in a chair and take notes. You don't learn everything from a book but like in the eastern culture you imitate what you've been taught. This is not a small, trivial matter. It will cost you to become a disciple of Jesus like nothing has ever cost you before. Becoming a disciple requires a greater level of submission than a believer, a greater level of commitment.

Jesus told some fishermen that from now on they'd be fishing for men and women and "they forsook all and followed Him" (Luke 5:10,11). This describes the beginning of becoming a disciple of Jesus. Luke 5:27,28 says, "After these things He went out and saw a tax collector named Levi, sitting at the tax office. And He said to him, 'Follow Me.' And he left all, rose up, and followed Him." This is not the same as saying "believe in Me" because only believing in Him will not change your lifestyle. If your life and priorities don't completely change, then you didn't become a disciple, you just became a believer. Becoming a disciple will require great discipline on your part. You will have to live like a highly trained athlete and the Holy Spirit will be your personal trainer. He'll lead you and train you in the ways of the Master. Luke 6:40 says, "A disciple is not above his teacher, but everyone who is perfectly trained will be like his teacher."

After Pentecost the disciples were operating just like Jesus. They told a crippled man "rise up and walk" and he did (Acts 3:6). They forsook all but soon realized that there is no price too high to become like Jesus and do the same things He did. Paul said in 1 Cor. 9:24, "Do you not know that those who run in a race all run, but one receives the prize? Run in such a way that you may obtain it." This verse describes being a disciple and Paul compares it to having the lifestyle of a top athlete. Every athlete in training submits to strict discipline. He says in vs. 27, "But I discipline my body and bring it into subjection, lest, when I have preached to others, I myself should become disqualified." The NIV says, "No, I strike a blow to my body and make it my slave." Other translations say, "I harden my body with blows" and "I beat my body black and blue." Paul is talking about training spiritually so that you can become a disciple of Jesus.

You must train and maintain your spirituality at the level of an Olympic athlete who begins training when they're children. They train year after year and endure injuries and soreness and they follow a strict diet. You must discipline yourself and become like Paul who said, "I bring my body under total control." Millions of believers have no concept of this at all and we now live in a generation of weaklings and whining babies. When Paul was stoned to death he got up and went back to the same town he came from and preached the gospel. He was a highly disciplined disciple of the Lord and wrote in 2 Tim. 2:3, "You therefore must endure hardness as a good soldier of Jesus Christ." Olympic athletes and soldiers are all disciplined and don't get distracted and entangled with other things. To become a disciple you must commit yourself to the Lord and do what He tells you to do when he tells you to do it. It doesn't matter how you feel. The Lord needs you when He needs you, not when it's convenient for you.

It is a good thing to become a disciple of Jesus and is worth any sacrifice you'll have to make. In Luke 14:26,27 Jesus told a great multitude of people that becoming a disciple will cost them everything for it requires a great commitment. "If anyone comes to Me and does not hate his father and mother, wife and children, brothers and sisters, yes, and his own life also, he cannot be My disciple. And whoever does not bear his cross and come after Me cannot be My disciple." Jesus is not saying to literally hate your family but to love them less than you love Him. He said in Matt. 10:37, "He who loves father or mother more than Me is not worthy of Me." Many believers are not disciples because daily they demonstrate that they love somebody else more than Him. It may appear to be a noble thing to say that your family is your top priority in life but if family comes first then God is not first and you cannot be His disciple.

To obey the Lord's command to "follow Me" will change your life and your priorities dramatically but there is nothing better in existence than a life committed to Jesus. He's training you to rule and reign with Him for all eternity in His glorious kingdom. The price to become a disciple cannot be compared to the glory that is to be revealed. Jesus taught about the true cost of discipleship in Luke 9:57-62, "Now it happened as they journeyed on the road, that someone said to Him, 'Lord, I will follow You wherever You go.' And Jesus said to him, 'Foxes have holes and birds of the air have nests, but the Son of Man has nowhere to lay His head.' Then He said to another, 'Follow Me.' But he said, 'Lord, let me first go and bury my father.' Jesus said to him, 'Let the dead bury their own dead, but you go and preach the kingdom of God.' And another also said, 'Lord, I will follow You but let me first go and bid them farewell who are at my house.' But Jesus said to him, 'No one, having put his hand to the plow, and looking back, is fit for the kingdom of God.'"

No man can serve two masters (Luke 16:13) and there is a place for only one person at the top of your priority list. Family does not come first, nor does your job or education or anything else. There is one Master, one Lord, and He is to be first. Many people miss the plan of God because of procrastination for family's sake. They wait until their elderly parents die or until their children finish school or until their business becomes successful. Months turn into years, years turn into decades and, before they know it, their life is over. If you choose a person over God, that person will not love you for it or be thankful for you for doing it. If you miss the plan of God because of your spouse or children it will not endear you to them. Even if you do what they ask they will not respect you for it because they'll see you as being weak even though they won't admit it. Down in their heart they know you're being disobedient to God and there are millions of people in this situation right now.

If you want the perfect will of God for your life then you must do the perfect will of God in accordance to His plan. The best favor you can do for somebody you love is obey God. Go with Him whether they go with you or not.

Many believers say they want to be a disciple of the Lord but do they really know what they're saying? People move and speak too quickly and make commitments based on what feels good at the time without counting the cost. Jesus said, "For which of you, intending to build a tower, does not sit down first and count the cost, whether he has enough to finish it - lest, after he has laid the foundation, and is not able to finish it, all who see it begin to mock him" (Luke 14:28,29). Consider the cost before you start. People set goals all the time but aren't honest with themselves that it's going to cost them something and whether or not they're willing to pay the price for what they want. It will cost you to buy that new house and to lose that thirty pounds. How much do you want to become a disciple of the Lord? Be honest with yourself. Do you want it enough to pay the price?

After telling the multitude to count the cost Jesus said, "So, likewise, whoever of you does not forsake all that he has cannot be My disciple" (vs.33). Some things are worth paying the price for. Do whatever it takes to become like Jesus. You are not your own for you were bought with a price. You have a Master and you are in training to be just like Him. You can pray like Jesus prayed and you can help people like Jesus helped people. There will be hardness and tough trials to endure but you must gird up your loins and press forward. Marathon runners experience great pain but they keep going anyhow. They set their face like flint and they've got their eyes on the finish line. They push themselves past all comfort levels and bypass past performance levels. They push through the pain for they consider it worth the price for what they will accomplish. There is a cost involved in becoming a disciple of Jesus but too many people think of this in a negative sense. People get quiet and uncomfortable when you talk about sacrifice and submission.

We live in a no-sacrifice generation and people don't like to be asked to give up anything, but Jesus said to become His disciple you must give up everything. Many boldly proclaim that they'll die for the Lord but won't clean toilets at church or stand in the heat and cold to help park cars at the church service. They won't go to church if they were up late the night before or if the weather is too bad even though bad weather won't keep them from going to work on Monday morning. They'll die for Jesus but won't live for Him, won't lose sleep for Him, and won't miss a meal for the gospel's sake. Becoming a disciple requires a greater commitment than what many believers are willing to give. A disciple is to be like a highly-disciplined athlete and a well-trained soldier who push themselves and endure strict training. An athlete may not feel like running ten miles every day but he does it anyway. You learn by doing for it's the doer who gets results. Paul told Timothy, "So, my son, throw yourself into the work for Christ" (2 Tim. 2:1 MSG).

When you're strong you don't talk about how you feel. You lay your feelings aside and do what you're supposed to do. Strong Christians have feelings but are not ruled by them. Your training will teach you that when the Master tells you to do something you lay aside your feelings and do what He says. Soldiers have a sense of duty and when they're given orders they pick up their gear and go no matter how hot or cold it is or how dangerous the situation appears to be. You've got to be willing to step out in faith and stay with it even if in the natural you see no immediate results and it looks like you made the wrong decision. If you're His disciple and He's leading you in a certain direction then you go where He tells you to go and stay where He tells you to stay. There are millions of believers who are content just being saved and they don't even try to become like Jesus.

Most churches are filled with believers and non-believers and maybe three disciples and they do all the work. These same three people volunteer for everything. They have other things to do but don't have more important things going on so that they would neglect the work of the ministry. You make time for what's important to you and if you're bothered about making sacrifices for Jesus then you're not worthy to be His disciple. Paul said, "Yes, all the things I once thought were so important are gone from my life. Compared to the high privilege of knowing Christ as my Master firsthand, everything I once thought I had going for me is insignificant - dog dung. I've dumped it all in the trash so that I could embrace Christ and be embraced by Him" (Phil. 3:7-9 MSG). This life will be over with real soon and there will be no reward in heaven for how high you climbed the corporate ladder or how much money you saved and how early you were able to retire.

In the Parable of the Great Supper (Luke 14:15-29) the Master said "Come" but all the people made excuses for they had other things to do. Many are called to become disciples but few accept the invitation, few make the commitment. The Master got angry at all their excuses and even today there are millions of believers all over the world who won't show up. There is no good enough reason not to accept the invitation to "come." God uses people who are available, people who will come, people who will show up, people who have made a greater commitment to follow Him and do what He says to do. Is all this possible? Yes!! It's what you're made for. You are predestined to become like Jesus. It's your destiny, your future. It's why you exist. You're not here to punch a time-clock, mow the grass, and wash a pile of dirty clothes. You're here to become just like Jesus.

To become a disciple of Jesus you must train yourself like an Olympic athlete and discipline yourself like a good soldier. Keep your mind and your mouth and your desires under control. Every day you're becoming more and more like the Master. Philip said, "Show us the Father" and Jesus responded, "If you've seen Me, you've seen the Father" (John 14:8,9). Our goal is exactly the same thing. If people see us, they've seen Jesus. If they've seen Jesus, they've seen the Father. People who believe they can get the same results as Jesus but not live like He lived believe they are above the Master. If Jesus sought the Father's will and only did those things that pleased Him, then you must do the same thing. You must become like Jesus. Luke 6:40 (AMP) says, "A pupil is not superior to his teacher but everyone, when he's completely trained, readjusted, restored, set to rights and perfected, will be like his teacher." The purpose of becoming a disciple is to be just like Jesus.

Called To Be Saints

Millions of people all over the world are believers but that's all they are. They believe Jesus died for their sins and they confess Him as their Savior and that's all they do. They go to church sometimes and read a Bible verse here and there and they pray when they get into trouble. These believers are oblivious to anything beyond confessing Jesus as their Savior. Another group believes they can become like Jesus but are unwilling to do what it takes and are not willing to change their life enough to become like Him. And then there are the few, the faithful, the disciples. They believe they can become like Jesus and that there is no price too high to become His disciple here and now in this life. 1 John 4:17 says, "As He is, so are we in this world." That's what you're called to do, become like Jesus here and now in this world, to be conformed to His likeness and His image. The objective is to be so radically changed that when people see you they see Jesus. Even people who don't know Jesus will hear Him when they hear you talk and see Him when they see you act.

I John 3:2 says, "Beloved, now are we children of God." When? Now! You can be more like Jesus today than you were yesterday and more tomorrow than you are today. You should strive to be like Jesus every day from the moment your eyes open in the morning to the time you lay down to sleep at night. Be willing to make radical changes in your life and make up your mind to be one of the chosen few. Jesus said in Matt. 9:37, "The harvest truly is plentiful, but the laborers are few" and Matt. 20:16 states, "So the last will be first, and the first last. For many are called, but few chosen." People call themselves "Christian" yet there are many believers who are nothing like Jesus. People who say "I'm only human" are saying don't be surprised if they sin and don't become like Jesus. Isaiah 59:19 says, "When the enemy comes in, like a flood the Spirit of the Lord will lift up a standard against him." A disciple has a standard and His Name is Jesus. A Christian is "one like the Christ" for He is their standard.

In Biblical times before the people were called "Christians" they were first called "disciples." It was the disciples whose standard had not been dropped and lowered who were called "Christians." A "standard" is a banner or emblem much like a country's flag represents what the people believe and what they hold precious and valuable and important. It is "a degree or level of requirement, excellence, or attainment that is widely recognized or employed as a model of authority or excellence." Discipline yourself daily to stand strong and hold fast to the standard Jesus set. Hold up the standard and live by it. Stop watching bad television shows and speak the truth in love. Don't lie and watch porno movies and commit adultery. We have one standard and it's the Master. Eph. 4:13 (AMP) says, "that you may arrive at really mature manhood, completeness of personality which is nothing less than the standard height of Christ's own perfection." This is what you are called to. The New Living Bible says, "Measuring up to the full and complete standard of Christ."

How do you measure up? You need to change and don't be conformed to this world (Rom. 12:2). The world is telling you that homosexual marriage is an acceptable behavior and that it's okay to kill babies before they're born. The enemy is the inventor of low standards and the more you tolerate what is wrong the lower you'll go. Tolerance is the first step toward conformity and today the world has no standard and has fallen into a bottomless pit of sin and deception. Jesus is the standard by which every person will be judged. No longer is He called "the only begotten Son of God." Now He is called "the firstborn among many brethren" (Rom. 8:29), people just like Him. He's the King of kings and Lord of lords. Disciples are in training to be kings and lords. They're the kings He's King of, kings just like Him. He'll show you the light and then you raise your standard and walk in it. There is no price too high to fulfill your destiny to become like Jesus.

The more like Him you become, the better your life will be, the more you'll live the good life.

-21-
"SEEKING THE KINGDOM"

From the beginning of recorded history all people have been searching for the same thing. They search for purpose and meaning and for everything to be perfect in their lives. Everybody wants to live in a perfect world, to have a life that is ideal. All knowledge that has ever been gained and all inventions that have ever been created happened because of man's desire to live in a better world. All progress is built on the search for a world that is flawless and supreme. Man is trying to find a world he can't explain so he keeps coming up with ideas that will give him hope that one day he will find what he's looking for. Man is not seeking for a religion but for a better life. The problem is he keeps failing and thus keeps searching. When he can't find what he's looking for he moves to a different city or country, he goes from job to job, and some even divorce their spouse and go look for another one. The search is in everybody's heart and many have gotten desperate enough to turn to religion to fill that void.

Most people don't go to God because they want a relationship with Him. They go to Him because He promised to give them a better life. He promised to give them eternal life, to pay all their bills, and to heal their diseases. Going to heaven is attractive to these people because they hate the world they are in. Suicide bombers are manipulated into becoming a murdering martyr because they are told they'll go to a better place. No person is looking for the do's and don't's of religion. They're searching for a perfect civil society, a world of equality and fairness, and a community of love and security. These people don't know where to find these things and, if the truth be told, they don't even know why they're searching in the first place. The spirit of man cannot search for what it's never had. You don't search for a lost shoe unless you had the shoe in the first place. Search implies previous possession and you can never miss what you never had. Somewhere in the heart of every human is the desire to go to a place where the spirit of man used to be.

Seven billion people are searching for something they cannot define that they lost. People get married hoping it's in the marriage. They join cults and street gangs hoping it is there. Something is telling them that somewhere there's got to be a place that's perfect. This search motivates all human behavior. Everything people do is an attempt to find something they lost. Unknown to them is the fact that their spirit is searching for the close relationship it had with God in the Garden of Eden before the fall of man. In other words, it is searching for the kingdom of God. Their spirit knows that everything they need is found in God's kingdom. Everything they're searching for is found in one place and, when they find the kingdom, they stop searching. People today have forgotten the world man used to live in but deep in their spirit is the memory of a perfect world. Jesus knows what you're looking for and this is why He said in John 14:14 (NLT), "But those who drink the water I give will never be thirsty again. It becomes a fresh, bubbling spring within them, giving them eternal life."

The deepest passion in the heart of man is to recreate the lost world. To make that happen the Father sent Jesus to the earth to return to man that which was lost. The search for a perfect world is found in the person of Jesus. The angel Gabriel announced, "He will be great, and will be called the Son of the Highest; and the Lord God will give Him the throne of His father David. And He will reign over the house of Jacob forever, and of His kingdom there will be no end" (Luke 1:32,33). Jesus will manifest Himself and the kingdom of heaven in whatever heart He is in. When you ask Jesus into your heart, He brings the kingdom with Him. You partake of the kingdom when you say, "Create in me a clean heart, O God, and renew a steadfast spirit within me" (Ps. 51:10). And then, as you grow in Him, God will give you an assignment to fulfill that will help bring the kingdom of God into the lives of other people. This will fill the void in their lives just as the void in your life was also filled. No longer do you live for yourself but now you labor for God's will to be done on earth as it is in heaven.

God has a specific plan and purpose for your life. He wants you to be abundantly blessed and He wants you to fulfill your destiny. He even tells you how to make these things happen. Jesus said in Matt. 6:33, "But seek first the kingdom of God and His righteousness, and all these things will be added to you." Most people get excited over the second half of this verse but don't realize these blessings won't happen until they first seek the kingdom of God. These people are waiting for God to move when in reality it is God who is waiting for them to move. God is waiting for people to seek His kingdom and in the same chapter Jesus tells you what and where His kingdom is. In what is known as the Lord's Prayer Jesus said to pray, "Your kingdom come. You will be done on earth as it is in heaven" (Matt. 6:10). The kingdom is where the King has dominion, therefore, God's kingdom is where His will is done. The YLT says, "Thy reign come: Thy will come to pass, as in heaven also on earth." To seek God's kingdom means to seek for His will to be done in your life.

A lot of people seek to make a good living but don't realize there is another way to live. You are to live by faith and this means you don't spend all your time and effort seeking for your needs to be met and your desires fulfilled. No, you need to seek the advancement of what God reigns over and, as you're doing that, He will add everything you need to live a good life. Jesus is telling you not to seek what the world is seeking after but to seek God's will to be done on the earth as it is in heaven, especially in your own life. God's dominion in your life is not automatic but only happens to the degree that you are yielding to Him. He's not going to make you do anything. You are to submit your life to God and help advance His kingdom instead of being like those who are selfishly asking God to build their kingdom. They're not interested in what God wants as long as they have a nice car in the garage and a big boat on the lake. They're seeking their own dreams instead of the specific plan God has for their life.

God's top priority is the advancement of His kingdom and this needs to be your top priority as well. The greatest challenge in life is the daily demand to choose what your priorities will be in the limited time you have on any given day. The scheme of the devil is to bring alternate priorities into your life that will distract you from your top priority. There will be a constant demand placed on you competing for your time and attention and you must learn to discern what things are important and what things are not. A truth you must always remember is that life was designed by God to be simple, not complicated. Some people spend way too much time deciding what clothes to wear each day. They don't understand that they're making life more difficult than what it's supposed to be. The key to living a simple life is to prioritize everything you do. You need to determine the order of dealing with things according to their relative importance.

Each day you have to organize your priorities and then you must discipline yourself to keep each one of them in order. The word "discipline" means 'self imposed restrictions' and is needed so you can achieve a desired goal. Self-discipline is how you govern your life according to the priorities you set for yourself. Life is too important not to have priorities and the key to a successful, fulfilled life is to identify the correct and right priorities. Don't spend five minutes with God and then take an hour deciding what shoes to wear. David said in Ps. 63:1, "O God, You are my God; Early will I seek You; My soul thirsts for You; My flesh longs for you in a dry and thirsty land where there is no water." Some people wake up and the first thing they want to do is eat. They have the wrong priorities. Jesus said to seek first the kingdom of God and His righteousness. Everything else is second place. In everything you do, seek the influence of God in that area first. If you'll do that, Jesus said all of life's blessings would come seeking for you.

Keep life simple. Don't worry about food and clothes and a college education but rather seek first the kingdom of God. Too many people are working themselves to death and growing old too fast and when their life is over they have nothing to show for it. Other people will be spending the money they made and living in the houses they built. The legacy you should leave is that you spent your life seeking God's kingdom and leading other people to Christ. By doing this God said He would add everything else to your life. You don't have to work yourself into an early grave because when you take care of God's business, He will take care of your business. Prov. 19:22 says, "The blessing of the Lord makes one rich, and He adds no sorrow with it." The kingdom of God is God's number one priority and you must commit your life to the study, pursuit, and the understanding of His kingdom. You must do everything in your power to obey whatever makes it possible for you to be in right standing with Him.

Jesus said in Matt. 5:6, "Blessed are those who hunger and thirst for righteousness, for they shall be filled." You need to be thirsty for right positioning with God. Thirst is a natural experience and does not have to be created inside your body. Thirst is automatic and Jesus is saying this should happen to you spiritually. If you're thirsty for God you don't approach Him casually. No, you draw near to Him with a passion that is so strong that it takes over your whole life like a thirst that needs to be quenched. A casual desire does not get God's attention. He knows everything and He knows if you're serious or not. You can't say you love God on Sunday and live like the devil the rest of the week. Instead, like a desperate child you must crave to be in the arms of your loving Heavenly Father. You must hunger and thirst to be in His presence and in right standing with Him. Be willing to do anything to have a place in His kingdom. Desire to be used by Him to make a positive difference in the life of someone else. Desire for His will to be done in your life just as it is in heaven.

How desperately do you want to please God? Jesus said in John 8:29, "And He who sent Me is with Me. The Father has not left Me alone, for I always do those things that please Him." If you will do the same thing then Ps. 84:11 was written to you, "For the Lord God is a sun and shield; The Lord will give grace and glory; No good thing will He withhold from those who walk uprightly." Some people all they think about is food but Jesus said, "My food is to do the will of Him who sent Me, and to finish His work" (John 4:34). The priorities of Jesus were in the proper order and, if yours are also, God will supply all your needs. Jesus was not concerned about food and drink, He was concerned about pleasing the Father. To be like Jesus you can't tread in the shallow waters of the kingdom. God wants you to launch out into the deep and make His kingdom your top priority. Forget about where your next meal will come from. Seek first the kingdom of God and all these things will be added to you. God will then use you to mesmerize the earth because of all the good He will do in your life. How wonderful is that?

Luke 16:16 says, "The law and the prophets were until John. Since that time the kingdom of God has been preached, and everyone is pressing into it." Seven billion people are trying to force their way into the kingdom and they're using a form of religion to do it. Religion doesn't work and that's why it's depressing for most people, including born again believers. People use religion thinking it will get them a new house and a new car. Their motivation is wrong and God knows it. They don't go to church to advance God's kingdom but rather that He would help them pay all their bills. Yes, if you'll seek first the kingdom, God will supply all your needs but you don't go to church because of those needs. You go to church to draw close to Him. Christianity is not a religion, it's a relationship between God and people who make His kingdom their top priority. People who are religious are spiritually poor and hungry. They're searching for something and can't find it because they're looking in all the wrong places with the wrong motivation. The only solution to spiritual poverty is the kingdom of God, a kingdom that must be sought after in order to be found.

The Bible is not a book about religion, it's a book about a King and His kingdom. It's a book about His royal family and His desire to fill the earth with His presence. The King is a wonderful Father who has a plan for His children and His kingdom. This plan was revealed in Gen. 1:26 when God said, "Let Us make man in Our image, according to Our likeness; let them have dominion over the fish of the sea, over the birds of the air, and over the cattle, over all the earth and over every creeping thing that creeps on the earth." Kingdoms are meant to expand but this won't happen if the only thing God's children want is fortune and fame. This is why Jesus said to seek first the expansion of God's kingdom. This is God's ultimate plan for all humanity. This is why you are here. You are to surrender your will to His will and by doing so you will be used to help manifest His kingdom and His will on earth as it is in heaven. This is what should be on your mind as soon as you wake up in the morning. You are called to be saints and were born for such a time as this.

The first words Jesus spoke when He began His earthly ministry are recorded in Matt. 4:17, "Repent, for the kingdom of heaven is at hand." The word "repent" is the first word Jesus spoke and it refers to mental transformation. To repent means to change the way you've been conditioned to think, to change everything you've been taught by your culture and educational system. It means to turn around in your thinking for your thoughts determine what your life will be like. Prov. 23:7 says, "For as he thinks, so is he." To change your life, you've got to change your thought patterns. You've got to change the way you've been programmed to think. Why does Jesus want you to do this? Because the kingdom of heaven has arrived and you are part of that kingdom. This is why you can no longer think as the world thinks. God's thoughts must now become your thoughts. To your mind say, "Open up, ancient gates! Open up, ancient doors, and let the King of glory enter" (Ps. 24:9 NLT).

Kingdoms are to expand because the glory of a king is based on how much territory they rule over. Ps. 24:1 (NLT) says, "The earth is the Lord's, and everything in it. The world and all its people belong to Him." The more territory a king controls, the greater his glory. God not only wants to rule over the unseen world but that which is seen as well. He created the physical universe so that His kingdom could expand beyond the gates of heaven. Is. 45:18 (AMP) says God "formed the earth and made it; He established it and did not create it to be a wasteland, but formed it to be inhabited." The NLT says, "He made the world to be lived in, not to be a place of empty chaos." God wants the glory of heaven to impact the earth with His nature and His glory. He wants the planet to be a colony of heaven, a place where He could expand His kingdom to a foreign territory. A colony is an extended territory of a kingdom that is filled with its culture. When a king colonizes you, he takes away your past history and replaces it with his history.

2 Cor. 5:17 says, "Therefore, if anyone is in Christ, he is a new creation; old things have passed away; behold, all things have become new." A person who has been born again has been colonized. When Jesus becomes the Lord of your life, when He becomes your King, He takes away your past and gives you heaven's future. God's will becomes your will, His plan becomes your plan. You must learn the language of the King so you can understand Him and then be educated and transformed into His culture so you'll think like Him. Colonization is when the people in a foreign territory begin to act and think like the people in the kingdom. This is what Jesus was saying when He told you to pray for God's will to be done on earth as it is in heaven. He wants earth to become just like heaven. Religion always talks about people going to heaven but Jesus talked about bringing heaven to the earth in the lives of those who make Him their King. This is why He told His disciples in Matt. 10:7, "And as you go, preach, saying, 'The kingdom of heaven is at hand.'"

When you become a kingdom citizen, God will literally teach you how to operate under the country of heaven even though you live in a foreign territory called earth. For this to happen Jesus says you must put forth much effort to study, pursue, and learn about God's way of doing things. Make this your top priority each and every day of your life. Jesus said that you are also to seek after His righteousness. This is a legal term and means to align yourself with the government which you live under. You are to seek first to get into the kingdom and then seek to maintain right standing in God's government. Jesus said if you would do these two things everything else would be added to your life. If you want to receive the benefits of the kingdom of God you must first get in the kingdom and stay aligned with its authority. This is why your righteousness is so important. You shall be filled with all of God's goodness when you hunger and thirst after righteousness.

When you come into the kingdom of God you have the responsibility to follow the laws of the kingdom. The Bible is the constitution of the kingdom of heaven and in it are the laws of God which you must be willing to obey at all times. When Adam disobeyed God he lost his place in the kingdom of God and became a shell of the person he once was. He became poor in spirit and so did every person born after him. The good news is that Jesus said in Matt. 5:3, "Blessed are the poor in spirit, for theirs is the kingdom of heaven." The void in the human spirit cannot be filled with religion, power, or money but only with the kingdom of heaven. Adam lost the kingdom but Jesus came to bring it back to man. He came to bring heaven back to earth. This is why He told you not to pray that you could leave and go to heaven but rather to pray that heaven could come to the planet. Jesus prayed to the Father in John 17:15, "I do not pray that You should take them out of the world, but that You should keep them from the evil one."

The original plan and motivation of God was to extend His heavenly kingdom on earth. He wanted to establish a kingdom in the seen world and, to make that happen, He created in His own image a family who would be just like Him. Adam and Eve were created to be His representatives on the earth and were to establish His kingdom here just as it was in heaven. It was never the plan of God to establish a religion. Religion is for people who are lost and before man fell there was no need for religion. Religion is man-made and comes from the root word that means 'to search.' It is man's attempt to find something they believe they lost. It was created by man to satisfy his hunger to find God. What is amazing is that God solved this problem for him. Instead of allowing man to spend his entire life trying to find Him, God made the decision to come to earth and discover man. Religious people haven't found what they're looking for and never will. What they need is a personal relationship with the One they walked away from, the One they abandoned.

God is searching for sons and daughters who will be citizens in His kingdom and ambassadors for Him. Paul said in Phil. 3:20, "For our citizenship is in heaven" and 2 Cor. 5:20 says, "Therefore we are ambassadors for Christ, as though God were pleading through us." To be a son you must represent your Father, to be a citizen you must represent your country, and to be an ambassador you must represent your government. It was God's original intent to rule the seen world from the unseen realm of heaven through the unseen inner man of a person living in a seen body. The territory owned and controlled by a ruler is called his domain. A king together with his domain is called a kingdom. God's domain includes the seen and the unseen realm and His kingdom is the heart of what the Bible is all about. If you are born again you are in God's domain and were created to have dominion in a territory called earth. The reason you're here is to dominate this planet. Inside of you is a dominion spirit and a dominion mandate. You have been commissioned by God to rule and reign on this planet.

God created man in His image to have dominion over all the earth yet many are controlled by a plant that grows in the ground called a tobacco leaf. It is a sad day when a believer is controlled by a plant. Things that grow out of the ground are used to make illegal drugs and alcohol and many have succumbed to their addictive powers. Do not allow your life to be controlled by a cocoa plant or grape juice. Have more dignity than that. Do not be dominated by the thing you were created to dominate. You're not supposed to work for money, money is supposed to work for you. Poor people work for money and this is why they will always be poor. If you chase after money it will flee from you but if you'll send it out it will come looking for you. Take dominion over your life. God gave you this authority and you are to be a ruler in His kingdom. The earth is still the Lord's but He leased it to man when Adam was created. One day you will give an account to Him of what you did with it. Did you rule over it or did it rule over you? God takes this serious and so should you.

Ps. 115:16 says, "The heaven, even the heavens, are the Lord's; But the earth He has given to the children of men." You were born to rule this planet. People get high blood pressure and become ill when things on the earth control their lives. This is not how God planned it so their body is rebelling against what is taking place. When people get sick they then want to leave this planet and go to heaven but God doesn't want them there. Heaven is His territory and the earth is your territory. God wants you to stay here and rule and reign until your destiny is fulfilled. Never desire to go to heaven early. There will be plenty of time to enjoy the glories of heaven in the eternal future but for now you need to be where God wants you to be. This planet God has given to you and it is your responsibility to govern it. What happens here is your responsibility. God doesn't move until you move. This is why Jesus said in Matt. 18:18, "Assuredly, I say to you, whatever you bind on earth will be bound in heaven, and whatever you loose on earth will be loosed in heaven."

You can't bind and loose anything in heaven because that's not your territory. Jesus is saying that He can't do anything on earth without the permission and access through those God gave the authority to. Things that are wrong on the earth are happening because people are allowing them to happen. If you don't understand this then you won't understand what prayer is all about. Prayer is when you give God permission to move on the earth. You are the one who has the authority here and He needs your permission to interfere with what's happening on this planet. God wants to move in your life and this is why Luke 18:1 says "that men always ought to pray and not lose heart." You're not supposed to go to a prayer meeting, you're supposed to be one. You're supposed to pray at all times wherever you are at. You are to pray morning, noon, and night. God is saying that you better keep praying if you want Him to keep moving in your life. If you don't like what's happening in your life, then make arrangements with God to change things and this happens through prayer.

Prayer is when you do business with a government from which you are an ambassador. Prayer gives God access through your faith to come into the planet and change things for the better. You and God can do anything and you can change your life by understanding prayer and the kingdom principles of God. Dominion is a family affair and God created man because He wanted children who would share in His dominion. His plan is for Him to dominate heaven and for man to dominate earth. God is the King of kings (Rev. 19:16) and is the One who sets the standard for everything. The word "king" means 'to set a measure' and God created you to maintain His standard on earth. This is why you're here, to make sure everything on this planet is being maintained according to the standard of God. That's what being a king is all about. The responsibility of man is to make the earth look just like heaven. As a king on earth you have the same power and authority as the King in heaven, so much so that Jesus said you could do greater works than He did on the earth (John 14:12).

As a citizen of heaven you are to rise up and take your rightful place in the kingdom of God. Eph. 2:6 (AMP) says, "And He raised us up together with Him [when we believed], and seated us with Him in the heavenly places, [because we are] in Christ Jesus." Religion puts you beneath Jesus but the Bible says you are seated with Him. The same Spirit that raised Christ from the dead dwells in you (Rom. 8:11) and this means you have the same power and authority to rule on this planet just like God rules in heaven. You are who God says you are, not what some false religion says you should be. Remember this, you attract people who are just like you. If you want to know what type of person you are, check out the people who come around you. People will treat you the way you treat yourself and this is why you have to believe and act like you're the head and not the tail, above and not beneath (Deut. 28:13). In other words, rise up and be the king God created you to be.

-22-
"KINGDOM AUTHORITY"

Six thousand years ago God made man in His image for the purpose of giving him dominion on the earth over all that He had created. Ps. 8:6 says, "You have made him to have dominion over the works of Your hand; You have put all things under his feet." The NLT says, "You gave them charge of everything You made, putting all things under their authority." God created you and He cares about you. You are the reason there is a planet, a sun, and a moon. You were created to have dominion and the devil does not want you to know that. Thousands of years of deception and defeat have reduced millions of Christians to spiritual weaklings and babes. They believe they'll rule and reign once they get to heaven but not down here in this life. People who believe this way do not understand the rightful position they've been given in the kingdom of God. Rom. 5:17 says, "For if by one man's offense death reigned through the one, much more those who receive abundance of grace and of the gift of righteousness will reign in life through the One, Jesus Christ."

If a believer is not reigning in life, it is because he does not understand grace and his ability to stand before God knowing that he has the same nature God has. God wants you to reign and that is why He sent His beloved Son to die on the cross for your sins. 2 Cor. 5:21 says, "For He made Him who knew no sin to be sin for us, that we might become the righteousness of God in Him." When you asked Jesus into your heart, God made you righteous so that you could reign in His kingdom. The devil never dreamed God could be that good for now you have the authority to put the devil under your feet. You need a continual consciousness of your right standing with God for this is what allows you to reign in life and have dominion in God's kingdom. When you reign, the devil does not reign and neither does sin and death, sickness and disease, poverty and lack. Fear and doubt no longer have a grip on your life because the grace of God and His favor have been poured out on you. And it is His grace and favor that allows you to reign in life.

God made you for one purpose and one purpose only. He made you to have dominion. Everything else falls after that. If you don't have dominion, you won't fulfill your destiny, you won't have a godly family, and you won't live a long life. God has lots of planets but this one is yours. God gave it to you to rule over and it is your responsibility to not let the devil rule it for you. What happens in your life and on this planet is in your hands and in your control. God created you to rule and to reign. He made you to have dominion over everything on this planet. When God raised Jesus from the dead, He raised you also. When He seated Jesus at His right hand, He placed you there with Him. This means you have the same power and authority as Jesus which, in turn, allows you to resist temptation and control your flesh. As time grows closer to the Lord's return, demon activity will become more rampant on the earth. Understand that you have dominion over the devil and have the authority to either let him into your life or keep him out of it.

Satan knows the end is near and his time is running out. This is why millions of demons with their satanic power abound around the earth and are continually seeking whom they may devour. They are here because believers don't rise up and use the authority they've been given. It is time for the instigators of all this evil activity to be cast down. To make this happen, God has created a family of purified believers who have been ordered to rule and reign over the devil in this life. Eph. 3:10,11 says, "To the intent that now the manifold wisdom of God might be made known by the church to the principalities and powers in the heavenly places, according to the eternal purpose which He accomplished in Christ Jesus our Lord." God wants you to make known to the devil and his cohorts the manifold wisdom of God. He wants you to take authority on the earth over these evil spirits. God wants you to be His instrument in declaring to these rebellious powers that they no longer have authority in the lives of those who are citizens in the kingdom of heaven.

In times past, God had a wonderful plan where He would prepare a people who would come forth, people who were called, chosen, and faithful, and He would place them in heavenly seats to rule through the ages to come, even right now in this present age. This is, and always has been, the eternal purpose of God. It is God's plan that in you the purpose of the ages may be fulfilled. You bring glory to God when you take this kingdom authority and exercise dominion on this planet. Draw a line in the sand and forbid the enemy to cross over it. When you walk in the Spirit you live in the heavenly realm and daily you need to take your seat with Christ at the right hand of the Heavenly Father. Give thanks to God for all that this seat of power implies. You have been seated far above all the powers of the air and they are in subjection to you. As you grow in faith in this area you will find the forces of darkness yielding to you in ways they didn't do before. As you increasingly exercise this authority that fearlessly binds the forces of darkness, you will notice the power of the enemy backing out of your life.

Authority protects you when you submit to its power and, if you understand the authority you've been given, it will change the way you live your life. Every morning brings with it the opportunity for you to change. God is calling you to have an even greater experience with Him. Each day you are given the opportunity to redefine your purpose in life and what your priorities will be. A lot of people deal with things that are urgent but that does not mean they are important. A new day gives you the opportunity to bury the past and a chance to move into the future. Rom. 13:11 says, "And do this, knowing the time, that now it is high time to awake out of sleep; for now our salvation is nearer than when we first believed." The Message Bible says, "But make sure that you don't get so absorbed and exhausted in taking care of all your day-to-day obligations that you lose track of the time and dose off, oblivious to God. The night is about over, dawn is about to break. Be up and awake to what God is doing! God is putting the finishing touches on the salvation work He began when we first believed."

Wake up and be aware of what's happening in your life and then rise up and do something about it. A lot of people wake up but they never get up. Eph. 5:14 says, "Awake, you who sleep, arise from the dead, and Christ will give you light." The Lord will not shine in your life until you wake up and get up. You must initiate your own awareness of what's going on in your life and then you must act to bring forth what you want to achieve. Putting action to your faith is when God will shine His light on you so you can see what you're supposed to do. God moves but you must wake up and move first. Paul then says in vs. 15,16, "See then that you walk circumspectly, not as fools but as wise, redeeming the time, because the days are evil." Are you using your time properly? The word "redeem" means 'to own; to repossess something you once had.' It means to own something twice, to take control of it again. To redeem your time means to control your time again. Don't let other people control your time but awake and repossess the management of your own life.

Time is the most valuable thing you have for time is life and life is time. This is why you need to spend your life and time doing what God told you to do. You are a king in God's kingdom and you are to rule and reign on this planet. God sent you here to be His representative in a foreign land and you are to dominate the earth until it looks just like heaven. Wherever you go, the culture of heaven goes with you. Every miracle is a sign that the culture of heaven has arrived. Sickness and disease tremble when you walk into a room for divine healings are normal when the kingdom of heaven arrives. There was no sickness and poverty in the Garden of Eden and there should be none now. God walked with Adam and He walks with you today. This is why Ps. 91:7 says, "A thousand may fall at your side, and ten thousand at your right hand; But it shall not come near you." You are protected because you are doing what the King told you to do. Obedience is the most important force in a kingdom because when you obey, you are protected. It is obedience that positions you for success and this is why people need to argue less and obey more.

Authority requires obedience because the words of a king are law. Eccl. 8:4 says, "Where the word of a king is, there is power." This is why being in the presence of a king is the most powerful position you can have. When he speaks to you, it becomes a law that can never be changed. The centurion understood this and in Matt. 8:8 he said to Jesus, "Lord, I am not worthy that You should come under my roof. But only speak a word, and my servant will be healed." If you will spend enough time with the King, one day He will look at you and say, "What do you want?" Your answer He will make into a law. When God speaks, nobody can stop you from having what He said you could have or doing what He said you could do. Submission to the words of God is the key to success because a king speaks to those who are submitted. The words of a king are law and the King of kings says He has given you authority here on the earth. This is a law and when you discover the authority you've been given, you will discover the key to true freedom.

The most powerful position on earth is to be under God's authority because your authority comes when you are under His authority. The centurion said, "For I also am a man under authority, having soldiers under me" (Matt. 8:9). His authority came as a result of him being submitted to those in authority over him. Stress comes when you try to operate under your own authority but when you submit to God's authority, He becomes responsible to carry out what you want done. Submission to authority destroys stress and this is why Jesus told you not to worry about what you should eat or wear. When you seek first the kingdom of God it becomes His responsibility to supply these things for you. The devil wants you to rebel against authority because he knows if he can get you to do your own thing then you will have no power over him. The problem in the church today is that there are many leaders who are not under authority to anybody.

You never exercise authority unless it's been given to you. Matt. 10:1 says, "And when He had called His twelve disciples to Him, He gave them power over unclean spirits, to cast them out, and to heal all kinds of sickness and all kinds of disease." The disciples had this authority because the Lord gave it to them and they received it. They had authority because they were submitted to God's authority. This is the key to ruling and reigning in life. To be given authority is to be promoted. It creates opportunities for people to be released and gives them permission to function. If you are not under authority then your life is out of order and this is why you need to find authority and get under it. Everything in life submits to something. Fish submit to water, birds submit to the air, and plants submit to soil. God made nothing that doesn't need to submit to authority. Authority brings order, productivity, protection, preservation, promotion, and freedom. When you are under authority your life will be in order. It puts you in a position to be given authority which will allow you to have dominion on this planet.

Jesus was also under authority. Matt. 3:13 says, "Then Jesus came from Galilee to John at the Jordan to be baptized by him." Jesus was thirty years old when this happened yet at age twelve He knew He had to be about His Father's business (Luke 2:49). He knew that He was called and anointed and that He was the Son of God. He knew what He was called to do but for thirty years He lived in submission to His earthly parents. In Biblical times, thirty years is the age a young man had to be in order to become a rabbi. Jesus knew He had to be under the authority of His parents until then otherwise He would not qualify to be heard by the people. He grew up and at age thirty He was ready to fulfill what He was called to do. The power of God was inside of Him but He also knew that power was not the same thing as authority. This is why the first thing Jesus did was He left home and went looking for John to be baptized by him. He didn't leave to begin His ministry, He left to find someone who had some God-given authority. His first act was to find someone He could submit to.

The ministry of John the Baptist was foretold in Mal. 3:1, "Behold, I send My messenger, and he will prepare the way before Me." John had been given the authority to prepare the way for the coming Messiah. God's authority on the earth at that time was John the Baptist yet he said to Jesus in Matt. 3:14, "I have need to be baptized by You, and You are coming to me?" John was wrong when he said this. Jesus had the power but John had the authority. Jesus then said to John, "Permit it to be so now, for thus it is fitting for us to fulfill all righteousness" (vs. 15). The word 'righteous" is not a religious word but is a legal term that means 'right positioning with authority.' To be righteous means to be in right alignment with authority. Jesus knew He couldn't exercise His power until He first received the authority to do so. For that to happen He had to submit to John's authority and this is what gave Him permission to use the power. John baptized Jesus and immediately "the heavens were opened up to Him and He saw the Spirit of God descending like a dove and alighting upon Him" (vs. 16).

Nobody knew who Jesus was except John but then something amazing happened. Matt. 3:17 says, "And suddenly a voice came from heaven, saying, 'This is My beloved Son, in whom I am well pleased.'" The heavens opened and a voice spoke but it wasn't speaking to Jesus, it was speaking to the crowd of people who were there with Him. When you submit to authority, God will tell the people who don't know you who you are. When you are in submission you don't need to promote yourself, God will promote you Himself. Before His baptism Jesus had no ministry and no followers but He submitted to the man who had both of them. He did this because He knew that you become greater than the person you are submitted to. John knew this would happen for he said in Matt. 3:11, "I indeed baptize you with water unto repentance, but He who is coming after me is mightier than I, whose sandals I am not worthy to carry. He will baptize you with the Holy Spirit and fire." He later said in John 3:30,31, "He must increase, but I must decrease. He who comes from above is above all; he who is of the earth is earthly and speaks of the earth. He who comes from heaven is above all."

John turned his entire ministry over to the One who had submitted to him. God never gives power to someone who is not submitted. Elisha submitted to Elijah and had twice as many miracles happen in his life. Likewise, Jesus submitted to John and had a greater ministry than him. When you submit to Jesus you will be seated in heavenly places and the Lord Himself said, "Most assuredly, I say to you, he who believes in Me, the works that I do he will do also; and greater works than these he will do, because I go to My Father" (John 14:12). When you submit to Jesus and walk in the authority you've been given, you will do greater works than Jesus. He will use you to influence the entire earth. Your work for Him will multiply and will surpass everything you've ever done in the past. The authority of the kingdom of heaven is upon you. You are a king and you have dominion on this planet. The divine purpose and plan of God is to use people who are submitted to Him to influence the earth with the culture of heaven. This is why you are here. This is why you are a king.

A king has power, he has influence, and he has authority. A king wears a crown and this is a symbol of power. In his hand is a sensor that burns incense and this represents influence in his domain. When God says He wants to fill the earth with His glory, He's talking about the influence of the culture of heaven coming to the earth. In the king's other hand is a scepter, an ornamental staff carried by rulers as a symbol of authority. This is the most important of the three because a king can have no power or influence without authority. Gen. 49:10 (NIV) says, "The scepter will not depart from Judah, nor the ruler's staff from between his feet." Power and influence is not mentioned here because once you have the authority, you have everything else. Don't be influenced by people with power because they may not be authorized to use it. Matt. 7:22,23 tells how some people prophesied and cast out demons in His name but Jesus said, "I never knew you; depart from me." These people had the power but they didn't have the authority.

A person under authority is more dangerous than a person with power. A person with authority says "Go," and someone goes. He says "Come" and he comes. He says "Do this" and he does it (Matt. 8:9). Ps. 45:6 says, "Your throne, O God, is forever and ever; A scepter of righteousness is the scepter of your kingdom." The NIV calls it a "scepter of justice" and the psalmist is saying that God's power is in His authority. Ps. 110:2 (NIV) says, "The Lord will extend your mighty scepter from Zion, saying, 'Rule in the midst of your enemies!'" You don't defeat the enemy with power because the devil is not afraid of your power. You defeat the devil with authority. Jesus said in Luke 22:29, "And I bestow upon you a kingdom, just as My Father bestowed one upon Me." The Message Bible says in vs. 29,30, "Now I confer on you the royal authority My Father conferred on Me so you can eat and drink at My table in My kingdom and be strengthened as you take up responsibilities among the congregations of God's people."

God has conferred on you a kingdom and the word "confer" means to literally 'extend authority; to delegate the authority of a country on a person.' There are two types of authority. There is personal authority that you exercise as your gift and then there is divine authority that you submit to in order to operate your gift. You were born with personal authority but you must pursue divine authority that comes from above. You have a gift from God, a talent and ability with which you can use to bless the body of Christ, but you must be under divine authority in order for it to function properly. Natural talent will only take you so far and not being under divine authority opens the door for the devil to enter your life. Don't try to be like somebody else. Be the person God called you to be and submit to His authority so you can rule and reign in His kingdom. The key to success in this life is submission to authority. The word means 'author; authority; authorization; authenticity.' When the Author gives you authority, you get the authorization to be authentic.

God has a kingdom and there is a place in it for you. He created you in His image and that means you are everything He is. You will never know your true identity by listening to what other people say about you. You have to go to your Bible and discover all the wonderful things God created you to be. You must put forth the effort and study your Bible every day. God wants you to draw near to Him and remain close to Him for this is how you become like Him. The very fact that you are alive today means that you still have a purpose to fulfill. You have great potential and God has given you everything you need to fulfill your destiny. Your greatest enemy is yourself because you are the only person who can limit your potential. God is on your side and your potential is as high as you perceive it to be. Open your entire life up to the Lord and allow His will to be done in your life as it is in heaven. In His work of redemption everything He did was for you. There is no limit as to how high you can go in life for you are a king in the kingdom of God. And if God be for you, who can be against you (Rom. 8:31)?

You were not born by mistake. You were sent here on purpose to do something valuable. God has a specific job that only you can do and for that to happen your birth became a necessity. God creates only those things that will fulfill His purpose and this is why He created you. Most people will only achieve in their life a fraction of what they're capable of. The greatest tragedy in life is not death, it is a life without purpose, a life where dreams do not get fulfilled. There is nothing worse than being alive and not knowing why you're here. Without purpose life has no meaning and many die not knowing what their destiny was supposed to be. You need to understand that success and failure are both predictable. You can plan to succeed or you can plan to fail. Life is designed by God for your success. He is more committed to your success than you are because it is important to Him. God needs you to succeed and this is why He placed inside of you everything you need to be successful. He even gave you an instruction manual called the Bible and if you will do what it says you will not fail.

The Bible is a book of promises and laws. You plan for success by doing what the Bible tells you to do. People plan for failure by disregarding what the Bible says. These people want to do things their own way and not God's way. This is why they fail and never do anything significant with their lives. Obedience, on the other hand, brings with it a promise from God that you will be successful in life. God gives you this promise because if you tell people you're born again, it is His reputation that is on the line. Your success is necessary to protect the reputation of the God you serve. The worst thing that could ever happen is for God's creation to fail. His reputation and His influence on the earth can be destroyed if His children are not successful. Your success shows people how good God is. If you tell people you're born again then it's a certainty that they'll be watching you to see what happens in your life. If you succeed, then you serve a good God but, if you fail, in their eyes God is not so good and not worth giving their life to. What happens in your life does have an affect on those around you whether you know it or not.

When God created you the first thing He put on you was His image. When people see you, they see a product that was manufactured by God. They see an image of God Himself and this is why your failure destroys His reputation. To prevent this from happening, God has to make sure the vision He gave you succeeds because His reputation is on the line. The children of Israel rebelled against God and He was ready to pour out His fury on them but He didn't do it. Instead, He said in Ezek. 20:9, "But I acted for My name's sake, that it should not be profaned before the Gentiles among whom they were, in whose sight I had made Myself known to them, to bring them out of Egypt." No matter what you're going through, you can have the confidence that God will bring you out of it, not for your sake but for His name's sake. God will back you up and this means you have the ability to do whatever He told you to do. Why? For His name's sake! Don't ask God to make you a success for your sake, ask Him to make you a success for His name's sake. You don't become successful so you can feel good, you do it so God can feel good.

You've got to succeed in order to protect God's reputation. This is why you cannot fail. Whatever God's plan is for your life has to come to pass. This is why you are told in Hab. 2:2 to "Write the vision and make it plain on tablets, that he may run who reads it." When you announce to the public what God told you then it puts pressure on Him to bring about your success. Talk about your vision and tell everybody about it. Tell them what God said He would do with your life. When you do that, God will act because He has to protect His reputation. This is not your dream, it's His dream and He gave it to you. This is why you can be bold and have the confidence that your destiny will be fulfilled. God cannot fail and this means you cannot fail. The things people laughed at when you told them about it will soon come to pass. You're fulfilling your destiny and they aren't fulfilling theirs. You're planning for success while they're planning for failure. You know God is a good God and they don't but they soon will when they witness how good God is being to you.

God built success into everything He created. A bird was created to fly, a fish was created to swim, a seed was created to grow, and you were created to succeed. If none of these things happen then God's reputation is in trouble. God takes His reputation very seriously and this is why He built into everything laws that would guarantee its success. God told Joshua, "This Book of the Law shall not depart from your mouth, but you shall meditate in it day and night, that you may observe to do according to all that is written in it. For then you will make your way prosperous, and then you will have good success" (Josh. 1:8). Laws were given to guarantee success. They were not given to be explained, they were given to be followed. Don't ask God to explain everything He tells you to do. Just do it and you will be successful. Jesus told the disciples to cast their nets on the right side of the boat. They obeyed and a great multitude of fish was caught. Likewise, your success will be the result of you making the decision to do what He tells you to do.

Whatever you decide to do is what determines your destiny. Everyone becomes what they decide to become so make the choice today to be successful by fulfilling your destiny. Decide today to follow the laws of God that will guarantee your success. Don't smoke because it will destroy your lungs, don't drink alcohol because it will destroy your liver, and don't have sex before marriage because it will give you a baby you can't pay for. Your vision determines how disciplined in life you will be. If you don't know where you're going, you'll do many wrong things in your life but purpose will give you the discipline you need. Stay away from people who don't help you fulfill what you're called to do. They'll distract you and rob you of much valuable time that is needed to fulfill your dream. That person is your enemy and not your friend. Stay away from people like this for your success is not on their mind. Draw close to God instead and allow Him to become your best friend because, in His eyes, your success is His success.

-23-

"DIVINE PURPOSE"

God created you for a purpose and this means you can't take life casually. Life is a gift from God and to be here is a divine privilege. There is no future for the unfaithful and those who don't take life seriously. God put you here to be an influence in the lives of other people, to change the course of events on planet earth, and to protect and maintain His purpose for all mankind. This is why you are here. God gave you life, He gave you a purpose for your life, and He then committed Himself to fulfill that purpose for you. Ps. 138:8 (ESV) says, "The Lord will fulfill His purpose for me; Your steadfast love, O Lord, endures forever. Do not forsake the work of Your hands." God will never abandon you and you must never abandon the work God gave you to do. God doesn't want you to miss out on what He's already guaranteed you'll succeed in. Eph. 1:11 (NIV) says, "In Him we were also chosen, having been predestined according to the plan of Him who works out everything in conformity with the purpose of His will." Your success is guaranteed as long as you don't walk away from your divine purpose.

You are here because God predestined something for you to do. He even promised to have all things conform to His purpose for your life. If you make a mistake, God will correct that mistake and turn it into a testimony so that your purpose can keep going forward. If you fail, God will conform it to keep you on the path He set for your life. Your mistakes are not more powerful than your purpose and no failure can stop God's destiny for your life. Is. 46:10 (NIV) says, "I make known the end from the beginning, from ancient times, what is still to come. I say, 'My purpose will stand, and I will do all that I please.'" The NLT says, "Everything I plan will come to pass, for I do whatever I wish." God always begins with the end before He starts. When God begins something, that is proof that it is finished. God does not allow anything to start that is not already ended. God ends it first and then He begins it. Remember this because if you forget that your end is already finished, you'll get discouraged on your way to the fulfillment of your destiny.

Your divine purpose is established and finished and your life is a journey to that end. God is not worried about your future for you were born to reach and fulfill the predetermined end of your destiny. The very fact that you are alive is proof that there is something already ended that you were born to start. Right now you are at the beginning of your end and you have to stay on the path God set for you. God is committed to your destiny and so must you be also. There is a choice you have to make. You have to choose your chosen destiny.

Just because God predestined you to become great does not mean you will become great. You have to choose to be great, you have to choose what God chose. Your destiny is established but is not guaranteed until you choose to pursue it. Because man possesses the power of free will, you have to choose the direction your life will take. There is nothing more powerful than a God-influenced decision. Your destiny is determined by the decisions you make so stay on the course that leads to the fulfillment of your divine purpose.

Your ending determines the route you choose to get there. Your destiny decides your course in life and your choices determine if you will stay on that course. Once you know where you're supposed to go in life, once you know what your destiny is, this is what determines what your daily habits and activities will be. You've got to make decisions to get on the course that is in keeping with your destiny in God, a course that will take you to your dream. Be committed to do more with your life this year than you did last year. Make plans to do something that will leave an eternal mark on this generation. Prov. 16:9 says, "A man's heart plans his way, but the Lord directs his steps." If you have no plans, then God has nothing to direct. This means you can't sit back and expect God to do all the work for you. No, you must be an active participant in the fulfillment of your destiny. Don't expect God to guide you if you don't know where you want to go. You've got to have a plan and each new day gives you the opportunity to review and, if necessary, revise your course.

Step over into a new life. Change your course and become a better person, a person who will do great things in the kingdom of God. Make plans that will take you where you want to go. Airplanes are not allowed to leave an airport until a flight plan is filed. The pilot must know where he is going before the plane is allowed to leave the ground. Once in flight the pilot is then in constant communication with the control tower. God is the tower in your life and He is continually directing your steps. Like those working in the control tower, God sees the complete picture and this is why by faith you have to trust Him and do those things He tells you to do. Daily you must follow His instructions because He knows what's going on around you even if you don't. When you put your trust in Him you will get to where you want to go. This gives you a reason to live, a reason to get up each morning. You should never desire to die and go to heaven until you complete what you were born to start. Death never attracts a person who has discovered their purpose. What does attract you is the chance to please your Heavenly Father by doing what He called you to do.

People with purpose have great potential. Do not allow the educational system to determine how far you can go in life. They say if you fail their college exams then you won't succeed in life yet many of the greatest people in the world today never finished school. Do not allow an exam you failed twenty years ago determine whether or not you fulfill your destiny. Do not be like most people who only use a fraction of their power and ability. What they're settling for disappoints God and, what they're proud of, God is ashamed of. God made you the head and not the tail and it matters not to Him what your test scores are. Your success in life is based on your obedience to God and following the flight plan He filed for your life. Never believe the bad things other people say about you. Rom. 3:4 says, "Indeed, let God be true and every man a liar." Lift your head up high knowing God has a plan and purpose for your life. Your destiny will be wonderful and spectacular if you will but yield to Him and make Him your passion in life.

Everyone becomes what they decide to be. Success in life is the result of the right decisions you make. Don't make your decisions based on what other people say about you, base them on what God says about you. You don't have to try to win in life anymore, in Christ you've already won. You are more than a conqueror in Christ Jesus. More than that, you have divine purpose. Purpose is what you live for. It's the finish before the start, the destination before the journey. God created you with a destiny and purpose in mind. You were not created just to make a living and until you discover your divine purpose you will never be fulfilled. You'll spend your life being tired and frustrated, going to jobs where you work to make other people rich. The greatest tragedy in life is not death, it's life without purpose. It is a tragedy to be alive and not know why you are here. Many people die not knowing why they were born and for that reason they wasted their life. The cemetery is filled with books that were never written, music that was never prayed, visions that were never fulfilled, and dreams that never came to pass.

It is God's plan for you to die empty. Everything you have, everything that is inside of you, is to be poured out into the world in which you now live. God will satisfy you with a long life (Ps. 91:16) and when there is nothing more for you to give, you can be like Jesus who said "It is finished" and then go home to the eternal glories of heaven. But first you must do something special with your life. You must fulfill your divine purpose. Don't go to your grave when you still have something to give. Pour out everything that is in you. Don't be like those who were called to be leaders but died followers. You were born to leave a deposit on this planet and in the lives of other people. This is what your destiny is all about so don't die old, die empty. Inside of you are gifts and blessings that belong to other people and you are to spend your life making sure they receive what you have to give them. The last thing you want to do is die when you've still got something to give. If you do then you've missed your purpose.

Inside of you is untapped strength and hidden ability that is waiting to be released. People are waiting for the real you to be revealed, they are waiting to receive what you have to give them. They are crying out for you to leave your gift to them, to give them what they so desperately need. Do not allow yourself to rob people of those things God sent you to give them. This is why you were born. Procrastination is a thief and most of the things you've done so far is small in comparison to what you're supposed to be doing. You are full of things to give and God wants you to procrastinate no more. Don't get so caught up in your petty little problems that you forget there is an entire generation out there crying out for you to give them what God said was the solution to their problem. God is all powerful and He wants to channel that power through you into the lives of other people. He is saying to you the same thing He said to Abraham in Gen. 12:2 (NLT), "I will make you into a great nation. I will bless you and make you famous, and you will be a blessing to others."

You are valuable to the world. Inside of you is a destiny and a future that will be glorious. The devil is fearful of the potential of born again believers and this is why every day he tempts unwed mothers to get an abortion. Not only does he want to destroy a life, he wants to destroy a destiny. Your future is trapped inside of you and this is what makes you a threat to the devil. If he can't get you aborted, he'll try to destroy your life with drugs and alcohol and sex. If that don't work, he'll try to destroy your marriage or cause your children to run away from home. The devil isn't after you, he's after your destiny. He's afraid of who you really are on the inside. He's afraid of the damage you will do to his kingdom. He wants your divorce to derail you so you'll never be sane again. Inside of you are seeds of greatness, seeds that are designed to grow and multiply. The devil knows that the death of a seed is the death of a forest. The devil comes to kill, steal, and destroy (John 10:10). If he can kill a seed, he'll destroy a destiny and steal from an entire generation.

The devil is a thief and he comes to destroy your destiny. The good news is that God loves you and He'll never forget the greatness He put inside of you. He loves you so much that He sent Jesus to die for you, not just for you as an individual but because of the seeds of greatness He deposited on the inside of you. Paul said in 2 Cor. 4:7, "But we have this treasure in earthen vessels, that the excellence of the power may be of God and not of us." God hid in you something the world needs and this is why Christ paid the ultimate price to get it back from the hands of the enemy. People look at you from the outside but God looks at you on the inside. He sees greatness there, a purpose and a destiny. People see a seed, God sees a forest. Only God can look at an old man named Abraham and see the father of many nations. Only God can look at a dirty shepherd boy named David and see a king, a murderer named Moses and see a deliverer of over a million people. Only God could look at a serial killer named Saul and see a man who would write most of the New Testament. Because of what God sees, there is hope for you.

When God looks at you He doesn't see what your parents see or what your neighbors see. He sees what's inside of you, a destiny and a purpose, and this is why you're alive today. You don't draw close to Him because of some religious ritual, you draw close so you can find out what He knows about you. Seek what's in His heart, not what's in His hand. God has a purpose for your life and this is the reason for your birth and the meaning for your existence. He will make known to you that which is to come. Your future is not ahead of you, it's inside of you. Your future is your destiny and God put it inside of you before you were even born. Your end was established before your beginning which means God put inside of you the person you really are. It is your responsibility to become that person, to be who you were called to be and to do what you were called to do. God will not allow you to see what doesn't already exist. You were not born to make a living, you were born to change the world. You were born to fulfill your divine purpose, to fulfill your destiny.

Whatever you were born to do is inside of you, and the success of your life depends on you becoming all that is trapped in you. Success in the kingdom of God is the completion and fulfillment of the original intent and purpose for your existence. Success is not measured in how you compare to other people but rather how you compare with what you're capable of doing yourself. Success is to finish what you begin and this is why Jesus said in Matt. 24;13, "But he who endures to the end shall be saved." You were born with a purpose to fulfill and God wants you to be a bright light in the galaxy of life. To make that happen, He has placed inside of you everything you need to become all you were born to be. Eph. 3:20 says, "Now to Him who is able to do exceedingly abundantly above all that we ask of think, according to the power that works in us." The power to succeed is inside of you and you were born because there is something God wanted done that only you can do. Job 36:5 (NIV) says, "God is mighty, but despises no one; He is mighty, and firm in His purpose." The word "despise" means 'ignore' and this means God will not ignore the purpose He placed in you.

Prov. 19:21 (NLT) says, "You can make many plans, but the Lord's purpose will prevail." You were born to do something critical and before you make any plans for your life you need to consult God concerning His purpose for you. Never make plans without spending time with Him. You need to begin each day in His presence for God knew your future long before you were created. His purpose will be revealed to you for God knows it will be a tragedy if you become successful in the wrong thing. You were born to accomplish something specifically and success is making it to the end of your purpose. This is why you have to discipline your life and walk away from those things that will stop you from fulfilling your divine purpose. Eccl. 3:1 says, "To everything there is a season, a time for every purpose under heaven." You were born to do something great but you don't have forever to do it. You are in a race to fulfill your destiny before you leave this planet. Death should be a great motivator to you. When you think about it you should work even more hard to fulfill your call.

Eccl. 3:10,11 says, "I have seen the God-given task with which the sons of men are to be occupied. He has made everything beautiful in its time." The word "beautiful" means 'mature' and this verse is saying God will give you time to fulfill and mature everything you were created to do. You need to find your purpose and maximize your time to the glory of God. You are not important because of how long you live, you are important because of how effective you live and the donation you make to the world around you. You are here to influence those who cross your path and this is why you need to surrender your plans to the plans and purpose of God. Success is guaranteed when you do this for Is. 14:24 says, "The Lord of hosts has sworn, saying, 'Surely, as I have thought, so it shall come to pass, and as I have purposed, so it shall stand." The Message Bible says, "Exactly as I planned, it will happen. Following My blueprints, it will take shape." With you or without you, God's purpose will stand and it's up to you to decide if you want to be a part of His purpose or not.

Jesus said in Matt. 5:18 (NLT), "I tell you the truth, until heaven and earth disappear, not even the smallest detail of God's law will disappear until its purpose is achieved." God is going to get His way and this is why you don't argue with Him, you obey Him. You pray for His influence to be on the earth as it is in heaven. You surrender your purpose to His purpose and then you go out and change the world. You are not here so you can one day go to heaven, you are here to bring heaven to earth. You are here to help transform this planet into the culture of heaven. Stop wasting time doing those things that hinder you from doing what you were called to do. Choose friends who will help you reach your goal, read books that will take you to your destiny, and eat the proper foods that will keep you in shape as you go about your Father's business. Success will come but don't stop there for there will be other mountains to climb. The greatest enemy to forward progress is your last success if you stop and meditate on it for too long. There's more work to be done so don't stop doing what you know to do.

God will take you from glory to glory, from success to success (2 Cor. 3:18). If you want to face the future with confidence you've got to be convicted in your heart that your life is in line with God's plan. You've got to believe that God already decided who and what you would become before He placed you in your mother's womb. Ps. 139:15,16 (NLT) says, "You watched me as I was being formed in utter seclusion, as I was woven together in the dark of the womb. You saw me before I was born. Every day of my life was recorded in Your book. Every moment was laid out before a single day had passed." The Message Bible says, "The days of my life all prepared before I'd even lived one day." Your future was planned before your birth. In a big city a skyscraper is never built until all the blueprints are drawn up and completed. The builders will not start building until they first know what the tower is going to look like. This is how it is with you and your divine purpose. God knows the end from the beginning and He knows what you would be like before He created you.

Your future is far better than what you're doing right now. Job 42:12 says, "Now the Lord blessed the latter days of Job more than his beginning." The book God wrote about your life is already finished and each year of your life is a chapter in that book. God is the "author and finisher" (Heb. 12:2) and you need to contact Him and find out what is supposed to happen in the chapter you are currently in. It is your divine purpose to accomplish some specific things that God has already planned for your life. Your future is inside of you and you need to possess it today, not tomorrow. You can rest knowing that God is committed to your future and this allows you to face the future with fearless confidence. Don't worry about the provision needed to turn your dream into a reality. God is your source and the provision will be there waiting for you when you need it. Paul said in Phil. 1:6 (NLT), "And I am certain that God, who began the good work within you, will continue His work until it is finally finished on the day when Christ Jesus returns."

Ps. 57:2 (AMP) says, "I will cry to God Most High, Who accomplishes all things on my behalf [for He completes my purpose in His plan]." When God's purpose becomes your purpose, He will fulfill it for you. God will give you those things you think you have to work hard for. On the other hand, faith without works is dead (James 2:26) meaning that there will be some things you think God will give you that He says you have to work for. Either way, God will get to you what you need. This means you never have to worry about failure because you cannot fail if God is working out His purpose for your life. He said in Jer. 15:11 (NIV), "Surely I will deliver you for a good purpose; surely I will make your enemies plead with you in times of disaster and times of distress." Don't be surprised if God uses your enemies to finance your future. Prov. 16:7 says, "When a man's ways please the Lord, He makes even his enemies to be at peace with him." Trust God and He will make a way where there seems to be no way. Take your limits off God and watch Him move in your life.

Your destiny is chosen by God but its fulfillment is decided by you. Your future is certain but whether you arrive there is up to you. God's future for your life is a good future but because of hard times many people run away and create a different future for their lives. They don't understand that trials and difficulties are good for you because they literally force you to grow up and mature. You never grow in good times because pressure is the incubator for progress. Your problems can only grow so big but in Christ there is no limit how high you can grow. What appears to be a big problem today can become a small problem tomorrow. Your faith can grow bigger than any mountain that stands in your path. No matter what problems may come, always remember that your future is already set. Your future is unreleased destiny, it is purpose that has not yet manifested. Your future is God's past because He has already been where He wants to take you. This is why you can have peace and confidence when hard times come. The trials are there but they can't stop you from fulfilling your divine purpose.

God places the future of everything in itself. Inside of an apple are little seeds that can be planted to make more apple trees that produce more apples. The future of that apple is inside itself in the form of the seeds that are there. And so it is with you. Your future is not ahead of you, it's inside of you and you need to possess it now. The fact that you began to fulfill your destiny is evidence that there is something finished that you were born to start. God does not allow anything to start unless it is already finished. This is why you should never panic when trials come your way. You don't fret or worry when your future is finished and your destiny is fulfilled. You only worry when you're not sure what the outcome will be but, if the outcome is already completed, then there is no need to worry. You can have confidence knowing God's work in you is already finished. On your journey He'll give you wisdom and insight that will help take you to where you need to go. And if and when one door closes in your life, rest assured, God will open another.

You need to be so sure that your future is secure that you can't wait to get there. Everything you need to fulfill your destiny already exists and, when you need it, it will come to you. Eph. 1:3 says God has already "blessed us with every spiritual blessing in the heavenly places in Christ." Before God chose you, He put on reserve every provision you will need to do what He has called you to do. This is why fear and worry should have no place in your life. The Message Bible says in vs. 4, "Long before He laid down earth's foundations, He had us in mind, had settled on us as the focus of His love, to be made whole and holy by His love." Everything you need is history to God. It already exists and it will come to you when it is needed, not before. Most people who struggle receiving God's provision do so because they want it before they need it. God is never late but neither is He early. People get discouraged because they're trying so hard to get God to move when all they have to do is believe they'll receive what they need when the time is right for them to get it.

Paul is saying here in Eph. 1:3,4 that God first blessed you, then He chose you. God made the blessing first and then made you so you could be blessed. When you obey God, when His purpose becomes your purpose, Deut. 28:2 says, "And all these blessings shall come upon you and overtake you, because you obey the voice of the Lord your God." The blessings of God will overtake you when you seek first the kingdom of God and His righteousness. God told the children of Israel in Josh. 24:13, "I have given you a land for which you did not labor, and cities which you did not build, and you dwell in them; you eat of the vineyards and olive groves which you did not plant." All these cities and vineyards were prepared for the people before they crossed over into the promised land. When the people did obey and crossed over, the blessings were there waiting for them. And so it will be with you when you fulfill your divine purpose. What was Joshua's response to this great blessing? He said in vs. 14, "Now therefore, fear the Lord, serve Him in sincerity and truth," In other words, fulfill your destiny.

Randall J. Brewer

-24-
"YOUR FULL POTENTIAL"

Where are you going with your life? Where will you be ten and twenty years from now? What do you want to do with yourself for the next forty years? What do you see as your future destiny? Most people do not have an answer to these questions. They spend the majority of their life waiting for their next paycheck so they can pay the latest bill that came in the mail. This they do for fifty years and then they retire and die without doing anything significant with their lives. Know that nothing can bury you faster than a career you are trapped in. God, on the other hand, wants you to know that you are not just here as a passing fantasy but because there is something you need to do that is still undone. You were created to live life with meaning and purpose and until you discover why you are here you will never be fulfilled. You were born to do something important in this world. You were created for a purpose, equipped with potential, and designed for a destiny. You were born to do something the world needs and until you discover your purpose you can never maximize your full potential.

Your purpose is the most important thing you can discover in life because, when you find it, you automatically find your potential. No human opinion can stop you when you find your purpose in life. You'll be unstoppable when you maximize the potential that is inside of you. With reckless abandon you'll actively pursue the fulfillment of the dream God put inside of you and one day you will hear the Lord say to you, "Well done, good and faithful servant" (Matt. 25:21). Life is not measured by how old you are, it's measured by how much is left inside of you. Jesus was a young man when He died but He had nothing left to give. This is why His final words on the cross were "It is finished" (John 19:30). In Greek the word "finished" means 'to finish, fulfill.' Jesus was saying, "Mission accomplished! Everything that had to be done has been done! It is finished!" This was not the gasp of a worn-out life but the deliberate utterance of a man who knew that His work was finished and all of God's purpose accomplished.

The grave yard is filled with people who never reached their full potential. Inside of them was dormant ability and untapped power. They had potential that is defined as hidden strength and reserved energy. It is unused success and unleashed talent. Whatever you have done in your past is no longer your potential. Potential is always what you haven't done yet but one day will do. Your potential is the "you" nobody has seen yet. Your future greatness is trapped inside of you and your potential is all that you haven't achieved yet. God is not concerned about the past because once you've done something, it's over. He is always motivated by your potential because He knows what He put inside of you. Where you're at today is not the end of your journey. There is much more work to do and much to be accomplished. Don't become so attracted to the success you've had that it stops you from going forward and maximizing your full potential. The greatest enemy of progress is your last success. Potential demands that you never settle for what you've already accomplished.

Potential is always asking the question, "God, what's next?" He did something great in your life yesterday but He isn't there anymore. Don't get caught staying where God used to be. Some of your testimonies are so old that even God is tired of hearing about them. He is too creative to repeat Himself and this is why He says in Is. 43:18,19, "Do not remember the former things, nor consider the things of old. Behold, I will do a new thing, now it shall spring forth, shall you not know it? I will even make a road in the wilderness and rivers in the desert." The Message Bible says, "Forget about what's happened; don't keep going over old history. Be alert, be present. I'm about to do something brand new. It's bursting out! Don't you see it?" God is calling you out from the old and into the new. He is calling you to come out of the ordinary and rise to new heights with Him. The Bible declares that God has carved a road to lead you and positioned rivers of provision to refresh you. Don't be discouraged by the bumps in the road but taste and see what God will do in your life and be amazed by it all.

Not one time did God ever duplicate a miracle in the Bible. He was always doing a new thing. God didn't create you to live an average, ordinary life. He created you to use your potential and do something new and extraordinary with the purpose you've been given. The next time you see the stars shining in the night sky, remember that the God who created those stars is doing a new thing in your life. He is all powerful and the great things He's done in times past is only a glimpse of what's to come. God is still creating new things and you have to use your potential to draw out and manifest those things in your life. God is able to do more than He has already done, and so can you. Believe it and receive it today. God called Abraham when he was an old man to be the father of many nations. God knew what his limitations were but He called him anyway. He said to Abraham, "I am Almighty God; walk before Me and be blameless" (Gen. 17:1). He was saying, "Abraham, you're weak but I am powerful. I can do anything I say you should do."

God will not tell you to do anything that is not already done. Rev. 22:13 says, "I am the Alpha and the Omega, the Beginning and the End, the First and the Last." God wants you to start something new in your life that is already finished. He said in Is. 14:24 (MSG), "Exactly as I planned, it will happen. Following My blueprints, it will take shape." He is saying to you, "I am Almighty God. Let's you and Me go do something great together." He is all powerful and He has full potential and He is working in your life. Everything God created has potential and there is nothing the two of you can't do. Purpose is the reason something exists and potential is its ability to perform the task at hand. When God creates something for a purpose, He puts in it its own potential. This means that potential is a byproduct of purpose. When God tells you to do something then you can have the confidence that you are well able to do it. Success is guaranteed for God said in Is. 14:27 (AMP), "For the Lord of hosts has decided and planned, and who can annul it? His hand is stretched out, and who can turn it back?"

When God tells you to do something there are no legitimate excuses as to why you can't do it. He put inside of you the potential to do what He told you to do so stop making excuses. In the Bible the first place God introduced potential is found in Gen. 1:11 where He said, "Let the earth bring forth grass, and herb that yields seed, and the fruit tree that yields fruit according to its kind, whose seed is in itself, on the earth." The phrase "whose seed is in itself" is talking about potential. God made the trees and the plants and hid in them their own seed. A tree has inside itself the potential to become a forest and an apple has the potential to become an orchard. God placed the seed of everything inside itself, therefore, you have inside of you the potential to become and do all that God has called you to do. Knowing this is the key to greatness. God finishes everything first and then He puts it in His creation in the form of a seed. That little acorn inside of you is growing into a huge forest of giant oak trees.

The work inside of you is already finished and this is why there is no need to fear and panic when hard times come. That trial you are now facing is only a little bump in the road that you'll soon pass over. You have potential and there is nothing that can stop you from fulfilling your destiny. The seed of your ending is growing inside of you and you are becoming more powerful with each passing day. You know that God never starts something until He finishes it first and this is what gives you the confidence to keep going forward no matter what obstacles may cross your path. Inside of you is the knowing that you were created to do something important. Even before those seeds of greatness break through the top soil of your life God will give you a vision of the mighty forest those seeds will become. You'll see the end from the beginning and this is what propels you forward. A child dreams and to them there is no limit to what they can do. You must become the same way.

One of the greatest gifts God ever gave to man is vision, the ability to look into the future and see the work God has already finished. Sight is the function of your eyes but vision is the function of the heart. Sight shows you what is, vision shows you what can be. The greatest enemy of vision is sight and this is why the Bible says in 2 Cor. 5:7, "For we walk by faith and not by sight." Vision allows you to see what's already finished. Once you've seen what's finished, you will know that what you see today is temporary. Joseph saw himself sitting on a throne and when he was thrown in prison he knew it was only temporary. He had a vision that would not be denied. Vision will take you to the higher realm of glory so take comfort knowing that a year from now you won't be where you're at today. There is a seed inside of you that is growing and growing every day. Inside of every acorn is a giant oak tree waiting to be manifested and inside of you is a dream waiting to be fulfilled.

Seeds grow and they multiply. In the Garden of Eden God planted one man on the earth and the first thing God said to him and his wife was "Be fruitful and multiply" (Gen. 1:28). Inside of that one man and his wife was the potential to populate the entire planet many times over. Through that one man there are now seven billion people on the earth today. Imagine what you can do with the seed that's planted inside of you. When God looks down on you He doesn't see your past, He looks at the seed He planted in your heart and all the great things you have the potential to do and become. Inside of you is an awesome treasure. You are who God says you are and you can do what He says you can do. You have vision and you have potential. Your destiny is already finished and each day you're marching toward its fulfillment. Dream big and never again focus on your retirement. The word "retirement" is not in the Bible for you never retire from the work of the Lord. When you fulfill your destiny you don't retire, you go home to be with Jesus forevermore. You empty yourself and then you leave.

You are as big as your dream so believe what God told you. See yourself doing the things He said you could do and going to the places He said you could go. The sky is the limit for inside of every seed is a forest waiting to spring forth and cover the earth. Don't be distracted by what you're going through today but look ahead and see what's coming. Heb. 12:1,2 says, "Let us run with endurance the race that is set before us, looking unto Jesus, the author and finisher of our faith, who for the joy that was set before Him endured the cross, despising the shame, and has sat down at the right hand of the throne of God." Jesus did not look at what He was going through, He looked at where He was going to. He never lost sight of where He was headed and neither should you. For the joy of what's coming you're able to endure whatever the devil throws your way. 2 Thess. 3:3 says, "But the Lord is faithful, who will establish you and guard you from the evil one." You've seen the end of your journey so you know what's happening today is only temporary.

Believe in your vision and never let anybody talk you out of what you see. In the book of Numbers twelve spies were sent by Moses to spy out the promised land. While there Caleb saw a mountain that he wanted as his own. This became his dream and he was consumed with possessing this mountain. The others could have the flat land but he wanted his mountain. When the other spies returned to Moses and gave him a negative report you can imagine the intensity of Caleb's desire as he pleaded, "Let us go up at once and take possession for we are well able to overcome it" (Num. 13:13). Caleb was a man with a lot of faith and potential and he never gave up and neither did he lose hope. Dreams are given to give your life direction. You know what to do today because of where you want to be tomorrow. Dreams are like magnets that pull you in the direction of its fulfillment. The children of Israel wandered around in the wilderness for forty years but not one day went by that Caleb did not dream about his mountain.

The Bible says in Hab. 2:3, "For the vision is yet for an appointed time; But at the end it will speak, and it will not lie. Though it tarries, wait for it; Because it will surely come. It will not tarry." It is interesting to note that Habakkuk is an unusual Hebrew name derived from the verb "habaq" which means 'embrace.' His name means "one who embraces or clings." At the end of his book this name becomes appropriate because Habakkuk chooses to cling firmly to

God regardless of what happens to his nation (Hab. 3:16-19). Your biggest enemy is discouragement but this can be defeated if you'll only keep dreaming. Discouragement only comes when you begin to think your dreams won't become a reality. Was Caleb discouraged? Not one bit! He embraced his dream and kept it ever before him. And then, forty years later, he rose up and said to Joshua, "Give me this mountain" (Josh. 14:12). And guess what? He got it! He had his dream, he embraced it, and forty years he did what you should do every day of your life. He kept dreaming!

Without dreams there is no desire and without desire there is no hope. Without hope there is no faith and without faith it is impossible to please God. Dreams are faith imaginations and they come alive when you use your heart and mind to imagine God's purpose for your life becoming a reality. Since faith and dreams are so closely related you can see why it is so important for you to keep dreaming for as long as there is breath inside of you. When you stop dreaming you no longer have a reason to live. There is a story in the Bible where Jesus confronted a man who had stopped dreaming (John 5:1-9). The crippled man at the Pool of Bethesda had been there for 38 years and had lost hope that he would ever be thrown into the pool when the water stirred. When he was approached by Jesus he was asked a very unusual question. Jesus asked, "What do you want?" This man had a bigger need than the need to be healed. This man had stopped dreaming and this was the problem Jesus confronted.

By asking the question "What do you want?" Jesus was trying to bring to the forefront what the real problem truly was. This man had no dreams, no desire, no hope, and no faith. He had given up and lost hope of ever getting healed. All he had was excuses. Jesus came to show this man that it is in your dreams and faith imaginations that you meet God and experience His divine power. Your dreams is like the

Holy of Holies in the Old Testament. It's where you come face to face with God. It's the meeting place with the King of kings and Lord of lords. When you stop dreaming all hope is lost for God has chosen to meet you in your dreams. When you dream you are in fact saying, "God, I put my hope and trust in You." The crippled man at the Pool of Bethesda began to dream again and shortly thereafter he picked up his bed and walked away a happy and fulfilled man. The lesson to be learned from this story is that when you dream you meet God and with Him all things are possible.

God has placed a dream inside of you and gave you the potential to fulfill it. You and God together can do the impossible for this is the realm in which God lives. He is a miracle-working God and He lives in the realm of the impossible. So should you. God wants to be involved in everything you do and if what you were called to do was possible with natural gifts and abilities then He wouldn't be needed. So what does He do? He gives you big dreams and calls you to do the impossible. That way you will always be seeking Him out for His divine help, guidance, and intervention. If you by yourself can fulfill your vision then your vision is too small. It's not from God for He always deals with the impossible. Facing the impossible keeps you trusting God for without faith it is impossible to please Him. Therefore, don't get discouraged every time you run into a brick wall. That roadblock is just another opportunity for you to call out to the God of the impossible. After all, that's what He's there for.

Prov. 16:9 says, "A man's heart plans his way, but the Lord directs his steps." This verse is saying that you and God are partners together in the fulfillment of your divine purpose. There is a part you play and there is a part He plays. God demands your involvement in everything He has called you to do. More times than not God will not move and do His part until you first step forward and do your part. When you receive from Him the call on your life you should get goals for its fulfillment. You need to start making plans for things you can do and actions you can take. It's when you step out of the boat and put action to your faith that God will step in and direct your steps. A parked car gets you nowhere but once you take off God will give you direction on where He wants you to go. Abraham left his family to go to a land he knew not where but as he went God gave him direction. He trusted God enough to take that first step and this is why he is called in Rom. 4:16 the father of all who believe.

Dreams are given to be fulfilled and in the parable of the prodigal son (Luke 15:11-32) a story is recorded about the fulfillment of one man's dream and the things he did before and after his dream became a reality. The story begins about how the son of a rich man went to his father and demanded his portion of the inheritance that was due him. The father gave his youngest son what rightfully belonged to him and soon after the young man went off and journeyed to a far country. There he wasted his fortune on wild and prodigal living. Eventually a severe famine arose in the land and the young prodigal went to work for a farmer who sent him out into the fields to feed a herd of swine. He was hungry because nobody gave him anything to eat and he would have gladly filled his stomach with the same food the pigs were eating. But one day the young man came to himself and decided to go home and fall on the mercy of his father. Thus began the fulfillment on one man's dream.

Since his young son rebelliously went away all the father could think or pray about was the return of his much loved son. He set his sights on the joyful reunion between his wayward son and the rest of his household. The first step in the fulfillment of a dream is to aim high. Always expect the best and go for the top. A mountain climber will always aim high and set his sights on the top of the rock or mountain that is before him. As the saddened father anxiously waited for his son's return he knew that one day his lost son would come home. This is what he prayed for and this is what he expected. Nothing else would do. Always aim high! A long road led to the home and ranch of the rich father and daily he focused his attention on this trail over which his dream would become a reality. He knew one day his son would come walking down that road. The second step in the fulfillment of a dream is to keep watch. Faith always expects. Expect your dream to become a reality. Look for it to come to pass.

Many times great opportunities will pass you by because you're looking in another direction. Don't take your focus off the dream God gave you. Your level of focus reveals the level of hope and desire you have for your dream. Your faith feeds off of your desire and what you hope for is what the power of your faith will bring to pass. With confident expectancy look for your dream to become a reality. Keep watch! The father never lost hope in the dream of his heart. One day he looked down that dusty road and saw a great way off a lone figure coming toward him. Knowing this could be none other but his long lost son he immediately began to run toward him. Likewise, you should run after the fulfillment of your dream. The proof of desire is pursuit so don't sit around and wait for your dream's fulfillment to come to you. Set goals for whatever needs to be done. Make plans and apply works to your faith. The fulfillment of your dream is out there waiting for you to come possess it. Take action. Pursue your dream. Run to it.

When the running father reached his returning son he fell on his neck and kissed him. He held his son close to his chest and together they shed tears of joy. What once was lost has now been found. Nothing could have stopped his father from clinging to his son. They were insupportable. They could not and would not be pulled apart. As the father did to his son you also do to your dream. Don't let it go. That dream belongs to you and don't allow the devil or anybody else to pull it away from you. Hold on to what God has given you. Don't let go of your dream. Cling to it! The dream that was in the father's heart and soul had now become a reality. Immediately the father called for a great celebration to be held in honor of the fulfillment of his dream which was the safe return of his son. The best robe was placed on his son along with a ring on his finger and sandals on his feet. Dreams are given to meet the needs of others and the first thing the father did was meet the physical needs of his son.

A fatted calf was then brought in and the father called for everybody to eat and be merry. Celebrate your dream! "Rejoice in the Lord always. Again I say, rejoice!" (Phil. 4:4). The motive for everything you do should be to bring glory to the Heavenly Father. There is joy in blessing others and there is joy in getting blessed. What results is a continuous cycle of giving thanks with uplifted hands and singing praises to your God for He is great and worthy to be praised. So rejoice in the fulfillment of your dream. Eat and be merry. Have a celebration! All dreams and spiritual gifts are for the benefit of others. 1 Peter 4:10 says, "As each one has received a gift, minister it to one another as good stewards of the manifold gift of God." Somebody, somewhere, at this time is going before the Father with a special prayer request. At the same time the Father will know that because of the call on your life and the gift you possess that you, and only you, can be used by Him to help answer that prayer better than anybody else.

Could it be that when it comes to meeting the needs of another person that you were born for such a time as this? Are you willing to be obedient and used by God? The greatest work on earth will be done by ordinary people who have extraordinary potential. God has given you unlimited potential and unless you make demands on it you will spend your life not doing anything great in the kingdom of God. Potential must be exercised in order for it to be fulfilled. Unless you believe you can do things you've never done before, you can never experience the full potential that is inside of you. This is not potential based on your skill level or your educational background or anything your own humanity may produce. There is inside of you a divine purpose and with it a divine potential put there by the hand of a divine God. He wants to release you into this world to participate in and be a part of His purpose and plan for His kingdom on the earth. The potential is there. God would not have called you if it wasn't and it's up to you to choose to develop that potential and use it.

God said to Jeremiah, "Before I formed you in the womb, I knew you; Before you were born I sanctified you; And I ordained you a prophet to the nations" (Jer. 1:5). God longs for you to understand that in His creative mind's eye He looked and saw you before He began the process of forming you in your mother's womb. God knew you before you took your first breath and He made you according to what He saw. His making of you was with purpose and intention and you must embrace the reason for which you were born. When you do that your potential gets released. Paul said in Eph. 2:10, "For we are His workmanship, created in Christ Jesus for good works, which God prepared beforehand that we should walk in them." God is involved in your existence. He formed you and purpose is revealed by His design. Never regret being the person God made you to be and, by all means, never wish you were somebody else. That is an insult to God. That is telling Him that He didn't know what He was doing when He made you. Besides, the person you wish you were cannot do the purpose for which God created you to fulfill.

With purpose comes satisfaction and fulfillment. There is nothing more fulfilling than knowing you are doing what God called you to do. This is why you must focus your passion and have a strong desire to fulfill your destiny. Do not settle for anything less than the intention for which God made you. Focus your passion because whatever you're passionate about is what you will pursue. Passion will push you to go the extra mile, to keep you going forward when others give up and quit. People make excuses for things they don't want to do but become creative to find a way to do the things they want to do. Phil. 3:12 says, "Not that I have already attained, or am already perfected, but I press on, that I may lay hold of that for which Christ Jesus has also laid hold of me." God set you apart for a specific purpose and He will not allow you to be completely satisfied doing anything else. He then ordained you and this word means 'to enable, to empower, to authorize.' God called you and He then empowered you to fulfill your destiny. This is godly potential and it was put there by the hand of God.

You were given potential so you can live out your God-given dream. Each day is a day of new beginnings and with it comes the opportunity to do what you were born to do. God wants to use you to open the storehouses of His grace and bring blessing and salvation to multitudes. Before you can live the dream you've got to first dream the dream. Take time every day to meditate on all the things God says you can and will do, on those things that are uppermost in your heart and soul. Learn to listen to Him for when He speaks to you it will cause your faith to come alive. This will help you to keep pressing on when the going gets rough. When you spend quality time with Him you will be shown the end from the beginning. You will see the outcome of all your hard work and effort and this will give you the assurance that what you're doing is not in vain. The victor's crown is for those who press through the barriers and stay the course and end up fulfilling their destiny. You dream the dream, you live the dream, and then you fulfill the dream. Is there a more exciting reason to live? Certainly not!

Called To Be Saints

Randall J. Brewer

Called To Be Saints